MW00834539

THE OLD-TIME MAORI

BY

MAKERETI

SOMETIME CHIEFTAINESS OF THE ARAWA TRIBE,
KNOWN IN NEW ZEALAND AS
MAGGIE PAPAKURA

Copyright © 2013 Read Books Ltd.
This book is copyright and may not be
reproduced or copied in any way without
the express permission of the publisher in writing

British Library Cataloguing-in-Publication Data
A catalogue record for this book is available from the
British Library

CONTENTS

Makereti Papakura

Margaret Pattison Thom, better known as Makereti Papakura, was born on 20 October 1873, at Matata, a town located on the North Island of New Zealand. Her father was an Englishman, William Arthur Thom, a storekeeper who also worked in the Resident Magistrate's Court at Rotorua, and her mother was a high-born Te Arawa woman, Pia Ngarotu Te Rihi.

Papakura spent her early childhood in the care of her mother's paternal aunt and uncle, learning the genealogies, history and customs of her tribe, the Te Arawa. She did not speak English until her father took over her education at the age of ten, sending her to schools in Rotorua and Tauranga, as well as receiving tuition from an English governess. With an unusual ability to move between the Pakeha (a Maori term for New Zealanders of European descent) and Maori worlds, Papakura became a highly sought after local guide. She married Francis Joseph Dennan, a local surveyor in 1891, with whom she had one child. However, the marriage only lasted a short time, and Papakura filed for divorce in 1900. In 1901 she was chosen to welcome the Duke and Duchess of Cornwall and York on a visit to Rotorua, after which she

1

achieved international recognition and even greater demand as a guide.

The rights of her peoples remained a constant concern throughout Papakura's life and she was a strong advocate for the right of the Maori to self-determination. She undertook a massive tour of England in 1911, as part of the *Festival of Empire* celebrations, in order to promote Maori culture – the highlight of which was the launching of a 45-foot canoe at the Henley Royal Regatta. Despite the tour's financial difficulties, it was during this time that Papakura became acquainted with Richard Charles Staples-Browne, a wealthy landowner from Oxford, whom she married in 1912. She decided to stay in the UK, and on the outbreak of war in 1914, opened her home to New Zealand troops as a gesture of support. Unfortunately, Papakura's second marriage ended in divorce in 1924, but she decided to remain in England, lecturing on Maori history from her home in Oxford. She enrolled at the *University of Oxford* at the age of 53 to study anthropology. In preparation for her thesis, Papakura collected her lifetime's worth of notes, journals and diaries but tragically died on 16 April, 1930 - just two weeks before her thesis was due for examination. She is buried at Oddington cemetery in Oxfordshire, in accordance with her wishes. Papakura's thesis was posthumously published in 1938, and provides a fascinating account of the cultural traditions, daily life and role of women in Maori society. The book was the first anthropological work to be written by a Maori scholar, and reflects the great self-awareness of an author who possessed the utmost respect for her people.

TO
MAIHI TE KAKAU PARAOA
AND
MARARA
AND TO ALL MY OTHER OLD PEOPLE

MAKERETI

MAKERETI, SOMETIME CHIEFTAINESS of the Arawa
Tribe of the Maori of New Zealand, is better known to the
world as Maggie Papakura, the famous hostess and guide to
the hot springs and geysers of the Rotorua district. It was under
this name that she was presented to the late King George and to
Queen Mary when they visited Whakarewarewa as Duke and
Duchess of York in 1901, and again during the Coronation
year in 1911. She came by the name in a curious fashion.
Europeans who saw her as a child naturally shortened her
name to Maggie, and an unusually inquisitive visitor tried to
find out whether she had another Maori name. She had not,
of course, but was willing to oblige them, and as she happened
to be standing near a well-known geyser called Papakura, she
promptly said "Papakura", and the name stuck to her family.
Among others who have borne the name with distinction are
Bella, famous for her knowledge of the genealogy and lore of
her people, and Tiki, one of the greatest of Rugby full-backs,
known in England and New Zealand as Dick Papakura.

This brief introduction is in no sense a biography, for her
biography is her book, the life-story of her old people, to
whom it is dedicated. The tale of the village in which she was
born is the story of her own early life, for a Maori considers
himself one with his people, and the life of one is the life of

all. To Makereti, the *kainga*, or village, was home, and she uses the word as home throughout her book. The genealogy of the village is her own genealogy, the record of marriages and births and the chanting of the Tohi rite over the children, the collection and cultivation of food, all represent the life of her own relatives as observed in her childhood and later years. The house was her own house, built for her by her people, the objects which she described were her own. So intimately bound up with her people was she, that she could not write their history without unconsciously writing her own.

She was born on October the 20th, 1872, at Whakarewarewa, and died on April the 16th, 1930, in Oxford. Two factors at her birth had a powerful influence on her life. The first was that she was *te aho ariki*, the first-born of the eldest line of noble and sacred ancestors. In her came together the lines of all the chiefs and learned and sacred tohunga (priestly experts) who first arrived in New Zealand in the Arawa Canoe round about 1350, and through them, she was descended from the gods, and from Te Po, the chaos out of which the gods came. Moreover, she was related to seven of the eight canoes from which all of the Maori tribes in New Zealand are descended, and seven ribbons were used in the unveiling of her memorial at Whakarewarewa, one for each of the canoes. Her family was *whare ngaro*, a house of the lost, for children had died at birth in it, and as her life was very important to the Arawa Tribe, she was taken from her mother soon after she was born, and brought up by her great uncle and great aunt (her mother's father's brother and sister), Maihi te Kakau Paraoa and Marara Marotaua, and it was from them for the first nine years of her life that she learned the genealogy and history of her people, and all the duties that she would be called upon to perform in life. The reader can best learn from her own chapter on children how continuous and thorough, and yet how gentle and kindly, was the instruction, both in the round of daily work, and on the long walks from Parekarangi to Whaka, and during the long winter evenings by the embers in the *whare* when she listened to the genealogy and lore of her old people, and repeated them from memory, a memory taken for granted by the Maori, who had no writing or printed books, but a memory at which those who have had only a European training never cease to marvel.

During the most impressionable years of her life, then, her education was entirely that of a Maori. The second most powerful factor in shaping her life was her English father, Mr. W. A. Thom, who was responsible for the English part of her education from the age of nine onward, and thus indirectly responsible for the part she played in European society. She married twice, her first marriage in 1891 being to Mr. W. F. Dennan, by whom she had one son, sometime living in England, but regarded by the Arawa as Te Aonui, *te aho ariki* of the tribe. In 1911, she brought the village of Whakarewarewa with its carved houses to the White City for the Festival of

Empire in the Coronation year, and it was during this festival that she became engaged to Mr. R. C. Staples-Browne, whom she had known since 1907. Up to 1911, she had lived nearly the whole of her life at Whaka, but after her marriage to Mr. Staples-Browne at Bampton, she lived in or near Oxford, except for a six months' visit to New Zealand in 1925 and 1926.

Her English schooling lasted from the age of nine to the age of fourteen, one year at a college for English girls at Tauranga, one with a governess, and three at Hukarere College, Bishop Williams's school, at Napier. For this last school she always felt considerable affection. The authorities recognized the strength and beauty of her character, and wisely allowed her to develop in her own way. Thus in the space of a few years she made the transition from a Neolithic Age to all the complexities of modern European society, and took her place in both environments with conspicuous success. To a European who marvelled at the serene unselfconsciousness and authority of her bearing in both societies, the Maori reply would be, "And why should she not, seeing who she was?" Great and lovable characters are great and lovable regardless of time or place. Such virtues and manner as Maihi and Marara taught her were not peculiar to Maori or to European, or to any race, but are the stuff that is best in human nature. "Seeing who she was", they taught her with a love and care for which she was grateful to the end of her life, and it was this knowledge of her position and responsibility which for ever dominated her character. Though she enjoyed an international repute, and counted many famous people as her friends, her chief pride and joy were always in her mother's people, and it is no exaggeration to say that her whole life was directed to the end of preserving and keeping vigorous all that was best in the old Maori life.

When she removed to England, she brought with her all her possessions, including the carved house with all its furnishings and the ancient carved *pataka*, both described in this book, greenstone and other weapons and ornaments, feather and flaxen cloaks, and everything that could possibly explain the life of the old Maori in all its aspects. These it was her delight to show to her friends and to explain, and those of us who knew her can never forget the slight turn of her body which set the *piupiu* skirt curling and uncurling, or the graceful and intricate movement of the *poi* balls in the Canoe Song composed by her sister Bella, or the thrill of the motion of a weapon which she took from our awkward hands and held as it should be held. When she wore Maori dress, she became not only her former self, but all her people, and it was not only the chieftainess who stood before us, but the *tangata whenua*, the lords of the land. No people ever had a better ambassador and interpreter than the Maori had in her.

It was in 1926 that she became a member of the University of Oxford, at the suggestion of Professor Henry Balfour, Dr.

R. R. Marett, and Miss Grace Hadow, Principal of the Oxford Society of Home-Students, and began to arrange a life-time's accumulation of notes for what she planned as a series of books on every feature of the life of the Maori as he was, and in 1928 she was advised to present a part of the material for the B.Sc. degree. While she was a member of the School of Anthropology, she gave several informal lectures, and one public lecture before the Anthropological Society, in which she brought the greater part of her collection to the Museum, and showed a film of Maori life which had been made under her constant supervision, a unique and valuable film, because, like her book, it shows Maori life as it appears to a Maori, rather than to an outsider.

My own part in this book has been a modest one. For the last two years of Makereti's life I spent a morning or an afternoon three or four times a week at the house in North Oxford which she had taken in order to be free from all social engagements while she was writing. We began by going over the genealogies, the framework of her history, and every name had memories. These memories were sorted out into the various chapter-headings of this book. I asked her what order the notes should take, took them home, and typed them out. She then took the manuscript and re-wrote it entirely, often several times, until she was satisfied that the chapter was a true presentation of the facts and of the spirit. She wrote regularly to her people at home to make certain that they were willing to allow the publication of various facts, or that the facts were exactly right. The night before she died, she sent for me and asked me to remove two of the *karakia* (incantations) from the chapter on food, and I have done so. In fact, the reason why the publication of her work has been so long delayed is for reasons of this sort. I promised her that I would do my best to make certain that nothing would be published against the sanction of her old people, and I have sent the manuscript to New Zealand so as to avoid the possibility of publishing any name, fact, or karakia which is forbidden, and to be sure that everything is rightly put down. If there is any error, I beg the Arawa people to believe that it is entirely my fault in working with unfinished manuscript, and not in the least the fault of Makereti. She observed the laws of tapu carefully, and never allowed the genealogies to be consulted in a room where food was kept, and I have faithfully observed the rules since her death.

The book is dedicated to Maihi te Kakau Paraoa and Marara, and to all other her old people, in the hope that the younger generations of the Arawa people may read and learn how fine a heritage they have, and try to keep what is best in it, for it was her belief that a people is a great and living people only so long as it is mindful of its heritage. The secret of her own greatness of soul lay in knowing who she was.

She was always grateful to Dr. Marett, Professor Balfour, and Commander Walker for regular help and encouragement, and to Mr. Elsdon Best and Mr. W. B. Te Kuiti for their inspired and faithful accounts of Maori life. She died so suddenly that there was no time to learn all that should be done and of many whom she would have mentioned, for no one was ever more careful than she in the acknowledgement of help, or more grateful for kindness.

The first of the four photographs of Makereti shows her at the age of twenty-one or two, wearing the royal huia feather in her hair, and the kiwi cloak which is the privilege of chiefs. Round her neck is the *tiki* of greenstone whose name is Te Uoro. It is over five hundred years old, and has been buried five times with ancestors, and dug up after thirty years have elapsed. The second, taken about 1908, shows the chiffon head-dress which she made popular throughout the world, and a cloak of white pigeon and red and green parrot feathers, sometime the property of her mother, Pia te Ngarotu. She is standing beside the centre post of her house at Whakarewarewa, *pou-toko-manawa*, the post which supports the heart. The third shows her at about the age of fifty, in the wool and kiwi cloak she wore in the Coronation year, holding a greenstone *patu pounamu*, and wearing Te Uoro and greenstone ear-pendants. In the fourth, she is dressed in a *korowai* cloak, woven of flax with *kiekie* streamers, and round her head is a fillet of *taniko* work, an ornament worn on chiefs' cloaks only. She is weaving a *korowai* cloak which she brought unfinished from New Zealand. Her unfinished cloaks are now in the Pitt-Rivers

Museum at Oxford, a remarkable and unusual possession, because the old Maori believed it extremely unlucky to take away an unfinished cloak from the maker or place of origin.

Her mother's cloak and many other ancestral cloaks and greenstones covered her bier during the funeral at Oddington Church, where she had recently placed a memorial for the Maori contingents who fell in the Great War. A year after her death, her people in New Zealand erected a memorial to her at Whakarewarewa.

"Turn once again your face to the shadowy land from which we came, to the homes of our ancestors far away, to great Hawaiki, to long Hawaiki, to Hawaiki-of-great-distance, to the Hono-i-wairua, the place of spirits, the land where man was formed from the earth by great Tane-of-the-sky and had life first breathed into him."

Ranginui married Tahatiti, Rangiroa, Hinerangi; Rangipouri, Mokonui; Rangipotango, Akanui; Rangiwhetuma, Rahui; Rangihekere, Aotakare; Aonui, Pikirama; Aoroa, Te Korupe; Aowheneke, Te Tipiotawhiti; Aowheta, Hikitia; Te Unuhanga, Tuia; Te Hoehoenga, Ariari; Taaneitekapua, Puhiawe; Rangi, Hineari; Ao, Tupawhaitiri Puhaorangi, Te Kuraimonoa; Ohomairangi, Muri te Kakara; Muturangi, Te Rakautororire; Taaunga, Hape; Tuamatua, Karika; Houmaitawhiti, Hine-i-kukutirangi; *Tamatekapua, chief and captain of the Arawa Canoe, married Whakaotirangi;* Kahumatamomoe, Hine-i-tapaturangi; Tawake Moetahanga, Puparewhaitaita; Uenuku

Mai Rarotonga, Te Aokapuarangi; Rangitihi, Papawharanui; Tuhourangi, Rakeitahaenui; Uenukukopako, Te Aotaramarae; Hinemaru, Umukaria; Wahiao, Hinekete; Tukiterangi, Pareheru; Tuohonoa, Kaireka; Ngaepa, Te Anatapu; Parerauawa, Te Awa-i-Manukau; Te Aonui, Te Naho; Maata, Marotaua; Ihaia, Makereta; their daughter was Piaterihi or Pia te Ngarotu; and her daughter was *Makereti*, nineteen generations from the Canoe.

She was also of the line of Hei, a chief in the Arawa Canoe, of Waitaka, Papawhero, Tu Ahuriri, Tu Araitaua, Manaia, Hou, Papawharanui, Tuhourangi, Maruahangaroa, Murimanu, Rangimaikuku, Ahiahiotahu, Rangimamao, Tawari, Te Amo, Te Rangikotua, Te Awa-i-Manukau, Te Aonui, Maata, Ihaia, and Pia te Ngarotu, Makereti being twenty-three generations from the Canoe.

She was also of the line of Ika, a chief in the Arawa Canoe, of Marupunganui, Tua Rotorua, Tangaroa Mihi, Tukonohi, Whaki, Te Huinga, Te Rua, Te Ipu, Waiata, Te Pahau, Makereta, and Pia te Ngarotu, Makereti being fourteen generations from the Canoe.

She was also of the very sacred line of Ngatoroirangi, the learned and very tapu Tohunga whose wisdom and incantations brought the Arawa Canoe across the Ocean of Kiwa, of Tangihia, Tangimoana, Kahukura, Tuhoto Ariki, Rangitauira, Tukahua, Tumaihi, Tumakoha, Tarawhai, Te Rangitakaroro, Kahurangi, Tu Tangata, Takirirangi, Awhituri,

Waiata, Te Pahau, Makereta, and Pia te Ngarotu, Makereti being twenty generations from the Canoe.

Thus she could know her old people as many could not, and seeing who she was, they were willing that she should write.

T. K. PENNIMAN

THE OLD-TIME MAORI

I

SOCIAL ORGANIZATION AND RELATIONSHIP TERMS[1]

Iwi, the tribe

A MAORI TRIBE IS made up of all the descendants of the ancestors who arrived in Aotearoa (New Zealand) in a particular canoe. Take for instance Te Arawa tribe, whose ancestors came in the canoe Te Arawa in the great migration about 1350. The chief in charge was Tama te Kapua, son of Hou-maitawhiti who remained in Hawaiki. I should say here that Hawaiki means "the distant home", and refers to any place from which the Maori came in their ancient wanderings. The Tohunga, the learned and tapu chief, was Ngatoroirangi. Chiefs who came over with them were Hei, Tia, Ika, Maka, Tauninihi, Rongokako, and others, with their families. Te Arawa people saw land first in the Bay of Plenty, and they sailed along the coast till they came to a point of land jutting into the sea. When Tama te Kapua saw this land, he said, "Ko te Kurae tanga o taku ihu te Kumore o Maketu," The prominent part of my nose is the headland of Maketu. In olden days when a chief bespoke a piece of land, he likened it to a part of his body. The people of Te Arawa canoe landed here, and the place was called Maketu, a place-name brought from Hawaiki. This place they claimed, and settled in the surrounding country. Some of the chiefs made their way inland, and settled as far away as Taupo in the centre of the North Island. Many of them settled on the coast. In all they covered a great area extending about a hundred miles from where they landed in one direction, and about fifty miles or more across. In the course of a few years they had covered this area, the families as they increased settling a few miles apart from each other.

The whanau, family group

These families began as a man with his wife and children. When their children married and had children, they would call themselves a whanau, or family group. If the head man was called Te Rangi, they would be termed Te whanau a Te Rangi, the family group of Te Rangi.

The hapu

As these families increased to a great extent, say about one hundred and fifty to two hundred or more, they formed themselves into a hapu, taking the name of a famous ancestor as a name. As they increased again, some of the members of these families again branched off, and settled not far from the original hapu, so that there were hapu all over the area claimed by the Arawa ancestors who settled within a few miles of each other, ten, twenty, thirty, and fifty or more miles away from where the canoe landed.

The family groups formed the hapu, and the different hapu made up the Iwi (tribe), who would all be descended from the common ancestor Tama te Kapua, or one of the other chiefs of Te Arawa canoe. The big name for all these people would be Te Arawa tribe, or just Te Arawa. Sometimes the descendants of one of these descendants of Tama te Kapua might be so numerous, and live so near each other, that one might refer to them as a tribe, as well as a hapu. For example, I belong to the hapu of Ngati Wahiao (the descendants of Wahiao), and also to the *hapu or tribe* of Tuhourangi, the great great grandfather of Wahiao, and to the tribe of Te Arawa. I might speak of myself as belonging to the tribe of Tuhourangi of Te Arawa.

Numbers

A whanau may number fifty to one hundred or more people, a hapu may contain one to three hundred or more, and an Iwi may contain anywhere from three hundred to a thousand or more people.

The kainga

The word kainga means literally village, but to the Maori it means home, and that is the English word that best translates it for me. I have described the life of the kainga elsewhere.

Here I shall only speak of the families living in a typical kainga, at Whakarewarewa, about 1880. They belonged to Ngati Wahiao, and I will give them as far as I can remember. The first genealogy shows the three sons of Wahiao who remained with him, and the others show the families descended from them, who made up the kainga of Whakarewarewa at the time I mentioned. As hereafter in the genealogies in the book, men will be printed in capital letters, and women in small letters.

Sons of Wahiao

TAMA TE KAPUA
|
TAWAKE MOE TAHANGA
|
UENUKU MAI RAROTONGA
|
RANGITIHI
|
TUHOURANGI
|
TAKETATE HIKUROA
|
TUTEA
|
UMUKARIA
|
WAHIAO

1. *TE ANUMATAO*	2. *TUKITERANGI*	3. *TAUPOPOKI*

Pages 40–1, 45, and 56–7, show the whole village, and the relationships of the families in it to each other. The wives and husbands are all from related hapu, and a discussion of this appears in the following chapter on marriage. Families which are repeated elsewhere in the genealogy are placed in brackets. A study of the village and the relationships of the families together with a knowledge of the communal life of the Maori

should help to explain the relationship terms discussed later in this chapter.

Relationship of hapu

Wahiao had twelve children by his three wives, but all these children did not remain with Wahiao when they grew up, some marrying into other hapu or tribes, and going to live with the husband's or wife's relations, as the case might be, and the children and descendants taking the name of another ancestor and settling elsewhere, perhaps a few miles away, perhaps further. Some of course, such as Ta Angaanga-wearo, son of Wahiao, married and settled in Waikato, and from this line came Tawhaio, King of the Waikato, termed the Maori King.

The hapu also spread through intermarriage with the descendants of other canoes, who settled in other parts of Aotearoa, and the descendants of such marriages can claim relationship to Wahiao, and to his ancestors up to Tama te Kapua, through the lines of their father's or their mother's genealogy.

Importance of genealogy

Every Maori, especially if he came of a good family, knew his or her genealogy and exact relationship to every relative. This was most important to a Maori. If he went to a strange place, he would only need to repeat his genealogy to make himself known to any relatives whom he might have there. Though these relatives lived under the clan name of another ancestor, he and they would claim relationship through the genealogy.

Names of hapu

We have been speaking of the hapu of Ngati Wahiao. Wahiao's sister Hinemoa married Tutanekai, the son of Chief Whakaue who lived on Mokoia Island. Their children and descendants who settled there and on the shores of Lake Rotorua at Ohinemutu called themselves Ngati Whakaue, and Ngati Uenuku Kopako. Some other hapu were those of Ngati Rangiwewehi, who lived on Te Awahou side of Lake Rotorua, Ngati Pikiao, who lived at Lake Rotoiti adjoining Lake Rotorua, Ngati Rangitihi at Te-Awa-e-te-Atua in the Bay of Plenty (Rangitihi was the father of Tuhourangi), Ngati Kahungunu in Hawke's Bay, Ngati Porou in Poverty Bay, and Ngati Tu-wharetoa in Taupo.

There are many other hapu and sub-hapu from the various ancestors who came over in Te Arawa canoe, and all these people are akin to each other. I myself claim relationship to all the descendants of Tama te Kapua, Ngatoroirangi, Hei, and Ika, of Te Arawa canoe, and to other tribes through intermarriage, and the line of genealogy on page 49 shows this.

General character of social order

Various phases of the social organization of the Maori are treated in the different chapters under the appropriate headings. Here it will suffice to give a very general idea of some of the chief characteristics of Maori life.

It was communal, and every member of the community, no matter what his rank, joined in the work which was to be done. There were no lazy ones. The Maori were extremely hospitable, and I have never seen their equal in hospitality in the many countries I have visited. They had plenty of courage in their dangerous and adventurous undertakings, and showed these qualities in their long ocean voyages and endurance of hardship.

The Maori did not think of himself, or do anything for his own gain. He thought only of his people, and was absorbed in his whanau, just as the whanau was absorbed in the hapu, and the hapu in the Iwi.

In each kainga or pa (fortified village), there were several families, each forming a self-controlled unit, but all under one hapu name. Each family had its own piece of ground on which a whare or whares were built, with a wharau or kauta (cooking shed). The families attended to all the matters which concerned them, except in matters of great importance which affected the hapu. The chiefs of the various whanau took part in the discussions of the hapu. In the work of the kainga, as I have shown, everyone took part regardless of rank. The main division of labour was that between men and women. This subject is treated elsewhere, and it will suffice here to mention the facts briefly. Women did the household work, cooking, collecting of firewood, preparing of the hangi (ovens), the making of baskets and plates, cloaks, and floormats, the collecting of shellfish, tawa berries, and the gathering of food and material generally. They cleaned the marae, and used the tumu, or grubbing stick, and did weeding in the plantations. Men used the ko (digging stick) in agriculture, felled trees and built houses and canoes, made paddles and weapons, nets, eel-baskets, etc., and did the hunting, fishing, and snaring.

So important was the whanau or hapu to a Maori that even if he were at enmity with another whanau, and anyone from another hapu or tribe said anything against any of his people, or tried to harm them in any way, he would at once set aside all personal feeling, and help his own people. This he did throughout his whole life. Again I must emphasize how carefully the Maori learned all his lines of genealogy.

Close organization of hapu and tribe

A Maori tribe always kept to itself, and did not let other tribes come in or interfere with it. All outsiders were barred, except as guests, and then they would be entertained in a most hospitable and ceremonious manner. No one from outside could ever become a member of the tribe or hapu. Even if a man married into a tribe, he never became a member of it. If he had children, they became members of the hapu or tribe through their mother. Nor did a woman become a member of a tribe through marriage, but her children would be members because of their father. A man who married into another hapu or tribe never took advantage of his position, but his wife's hapu would treat him with the greatest respect and affection. In great gatherings he would be asked to make speeches, if he were gifted with oratory, and he could join with his wife's people in all that they did, on account of his children. But he never became one of the tribe, or inherited any of their land, though his children could inherit.

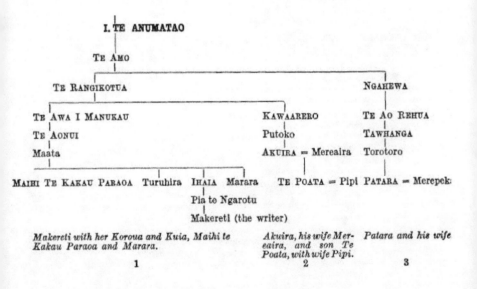

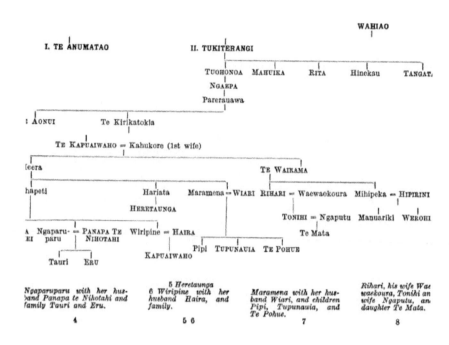

WAHIAO

I. TE ANUMATAO II. TUKITERANGI

TUOHONOA MAHUIKA RITA Hinekau TANGAT,
NGAEPA
Parerauawa

: AONUI Te Kirikatokia

TE KAPUAIWAHO = Kahukore (1st wife)

Teera TE WAIRAMA

hapeti Hariata Maramena = WIARI RIHARI = Waewaekoura Mihipeka = HIPIRINI
HERETAUNGA
TONIHI = Ngaputu Manuariki WEROHI

A Ngaparu- = PANAPA TE Wiripine = HAIRA Te Mata
KI paru NIHOTAHI

Tauri ERU KAPUAIWAHO Pipi TUPUNAUIA TE POHUE

Ngaparuparu with her hus-
band Panapa te Nihotahi and
family Tauri and Eru.

4

5 Heretaunga
6 Wiripine with her
husband Haira, and
family.

5 6

Maramena with her hus-
band Wiari, and children
Pipi, Tupunauia, and
Te Pohue.

7

Rihari, his wife Wae
waekoura, Tonihi an
wife Ngaputu, an
daughter Te Mata.

8

HAKAREWAREWA ABOUT 1880   (I, II). See pp. 45, 56-7.

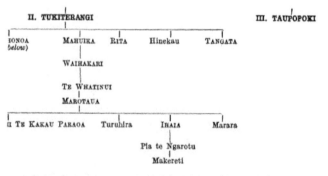

II. TUKITERANGI   III. TAUPOPOKI

IONOA MAHUIKA RITA Hinekau TANGATA
below)
WAIHAKARI
TE WHATINUI
MAROTAUA

a TE KAKAU PARAOA Turuhira IHAIA Marara
Pia te Ngarotu
Makereti

Makereti with her Koroua and Kuia, Maihi te Kakau Paraoa and Marara.

1

III. TAUPOPOK

(II)

Relationship terms

In the chapter about children, I have described how the older people taught the children their genealogy, along with the history and legends of their race. Genealogies were of great importance, and quite young children knew their exact relationship to all the people about them, and their connexion with them for many generations back. Though they used the same term to cover many more relationships than an Englishman would include in any one term, they of course knew exactly how the various people included under one name were connected with them, just as an Englishman when he uses the term cousin or uncle knows the different ways in which cousins or uncles are related to him. A study of the genealogy of the village on pages 40–1, 45, 56–7 will show

how closely its members were related to each other. When one considers too how the Maori never did anything alone, and how all worked together, their use of classificatory terms seems reasonable.

"Blood relations." Tuakana, taina, tungane, tuahine

A man *may* use the word *tuahine* for his sisters, and for his female cousins on his mother's and on his father's side. A woman will always use the word *tuakana* for elder sisters, and *taina* or *teina* for younger sisters.

A woman *may* use the word *tungane* for her brothers, and for her male cousins on her mother's and on her father's side. A man would always use the word *tuakana* for elder brothers, and *taina* or *teina* for younger brothers.

Elder and younger

The words *tuakana* and *taina* (or *teina*) are of even wider application. They can be used for all time, as long as a common ancestor can be traced, and the children are of the same generation. For example, the descendants (including myself) of Kahumatamomoe, who lived eighteen generations ago, would speak of the descendants of Tuhoromatakaka his elder brother, as my tuakana, or tuakana whanaunga, and the descendants of Tuhoromatakaka would speak of the descendants of Kahumatamomoe as their taina, or taina whanaunga.

Tuakana and taina with relation to marriage

In the chapter on marriage, two examples are given of a type of marriage which the Maori allowed, but disapproved.[1] As Paora was tuakana or elder brother of Ihipera,[2] because Katerina was born before Makereta, so Te Wiremu was tuakana or elder brother to Ngahina, because Parewahaika was tuakana or elder brother to Maata. Te Wiremu was of the same generation as Ngahina on his father's side, and therefore tuakana to her, though she was of the fourth generation on her mother's side from Katerina and Makereta. Although in both of these cases the woman married on the "elder side" there was no rule or custom requiring the husband to be tuakana in such marriages. A woman can marry a man who might be referred to as a "younger brother" or taina.

It might be asked how marriage between elder and younger lines affected the use of the terms tuakana and taina in subsequent generations. If my "elder brother" or tuakana married my "younger sister" or taina, their children would be tuakana, i.e. elder brothers and sisters to my children. In the same way, if my "elder sister" or tuakana married my "younger brother" or taina, their children would also be tuakana, or elder brothers and sisters to my children. It makes no difference whether the elder is male or female; if either is elder to me, the children are elder to my children.

Karangarua

If my "elder brother" on my father's side married my "younger sister" on my mother's side, the children would be *karangarua*, i.e. doubly related to my children. This term would be used whenever a "brother" on one side married a "sister" on the other.

Tuakana, taina

Cousins may be termed *tuakana turanga whanau*, or *taina turanga whanau*, as well as tuakana or taina. For example, my father's or mother's elder brother's children are tuakana, or tuakana turanga whanau to me, and their younger brother's children are taina, or taina turanga whanau to me. The same is true of my father's or mother's elder and younger sister's children. The distinction between the elder and younger branches is always maintained. To give a further example, this time from second cousins, a father's father's elder brother's children's children would be my tuakana, while a father's father's younger brother's children's children would be my taina.

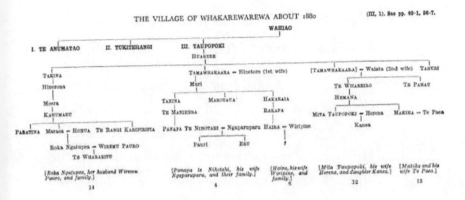

THE VILLAGE OF WHAKAREWAREWA ABOUT 1880   (III, 1). See pp. 40-1, 56-7.

Once again, a man can use the word tuahine of these female relations, but if they are male, he will use the words tuakana or taina, and a woman can use the word tungane of these male relations, but if they are female, she will use the words tuakana or taina.

Pāpā, whaea, etc.

The word *matua* is used of parents. One's father is called *pāpā, koro, hakoro, matua,* or *matua tane.* The name *pāpā* is also given to the father's brothers, the mother's brothers, and to the father's and mother's male relatives of the same generation as the father and mother. Another term for father's and mother's brothers is *pāpā keke.* The name for a foster parent is *matua whangai,* and for a step-father, *pāpā whakaangi.*

The words *whaea, koka, kokara,* or *hakui,* are used in referring to one's mother, and also to one's mother's sisters and father's sisters, and to the father's and mother's female relatives of the same generation as the father and mother. A

35

step-mother is called *whaea whakaangi*.

All these are terms of reference and not of address

The relatives whom I call pāpā and whaea, apart from my own father and mother, are called tuakana or taina, tungane or tuahine, by my father and mother. When I say "called", I should say "referred to", for these terms are all used in referring to relations. When you speak to a Maori, you call him by his name.

Koroua, kuia, tipuna, etc.

The words *koroua, tipuna,* or *tupuna* were employed in referring to one's grandfather on the father's and on the mother's side, and to his brothers and male relatives of the same generation, and the words *kuia, tipuna,* or *tupuna* were used in referring to one's grandmother on the father's and on the mother's side, and to her sisters and female relatives of the same generation as herself. Great-grandparents, their brothers and sisters, and male and female relatives of the same generation, were called *tipuna* or *tupuna*.

Aku tamariki

I should use the expression *aku tamariki*, i.e. my children, in referring to my own children, the children of my brothers and sisters, and the children of all the male and female relations to whom I should refer as tuakana or taina.

Aku mokopuna

In the same way I should say *aku mokopuna*, my grandchildren, of my own grandchildren, and of the grandchildren of my brothers and sisters, and of all the male and female relatives to whom I should refer as tuakana or taina. Great grandchildren counted after the same fashion were also termed aku mokopuna.

Concrete examples

It may be as well to give here two genealogies illustrating these relationships, before passing on to the description of relationships incurred by marriage.

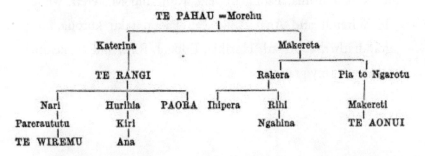

Katerina would refer to the children of Makereta as aku tamariki, my children, and Makereta would use the same term for Katerina's children. Te Rangi would call Rakera or Pia te Ngarotu his tuahine, and Rakera and Pia te Ngarotu would call Te Rangi their tungane. Te Rangi would say aku tamariki of the children of Rakera and Pia te Ngarotu, just as he would of his own, and Rakera and Pia te Ngarotu would call Nari, Hurihia, and Paora their tamariki, just as they would Ihipera, Rihi, and Makereti. Nari, Hurihia, and Paora would be tuakana to Ihipera, Rihi, and Makereti, and the three last would be taina to the other three. All of the girls in this generation would refer to Paora as their tungane. Pareraututu, daughter of Nari, would also be *tamahine* (daughter) to Hurihia, Paora, Ihipera, Rihi, and Makereti, and she, as well as Kiri, Ngahina, and Te Aonui, would refer to Paora as pāpā, and to Nari, Hurihia, Ihipera, Rihi, and Makereti, as whaea or koka. Pareraututu's son (*tama*) Te Wiremu, and Ana, daughter of Kiri, would be tamariki to Ngahina and Te Aonui as well. Te Wiremu and Ana would be mokopuna (grandchildren) to Nari, Hurihia, Paora, Ihipera, Rihi, and Makereti, while Te Wiremu and Ana would call Paora, taku koroua, my grandfather, and Nari, Hurihia, Ihipera, Rihi, and Makereti, taku kuia, my grandmother.

THE CHIEFS TAMA TE KAPUA, NGATOROIRANGI, HEI, AND IKA, WHO CAME OVER IN THE ARAWA CANOE ABOUT 1350

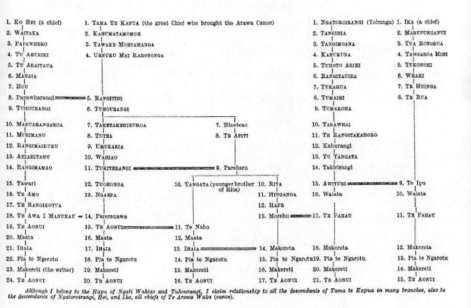

Although I belong to the Hapu of Ngati Wahiao and Tuhourangi, I claim relationship to all the descendants of Tama te Kapua in many branches, also to the descendants of Ngatoroirangi, Hei, and Ika, all chiefs of Te Arawa Waka (canoe).

Another example shows the *whanau*, family group, of Tamawhakaara.

TAMAWHAKAARA — Waiata

TE WHAREIRO	TE KOHURU	TE PAHAU
HEMANA	TE NGAHA	Makereta
MITA TAUPOPOKI	WIKITARI	Rakera Te Ngarotu

Tamawhakaara and Waiata would use the term aku tamariki (my children) for Te Whareiro, Te Kohuru, and Te Pahau, and the term aku mokopuna (my grandchildren) for Hemana, Te

39

Ngaha, and Makereta. For their great grandchildren Mita Taupopoki, Wikitari, Rakera, and Te Ngarotu, Tamawhakaara and Waiata would also use the term aku mokopuna.

If anyone else were speaking of these grandchildren, and of following generations, they would use the words *mokopuna* or *uri o Tamawhakaara*, which is to say, grandchildren or descendants of Tamawhakaara.

Mita Taupopoki would use the term taina for Wikitari, and taina or tuahine for Rakera and Te Ngarotu, while Rakera and Te Ngarotu would use the term tungane or tuakana for Mita Taupopoki and Wikitari. Rakera and Te Ngarotu would use the term pāpā for Hemana and Te Ngaha, and whaea for Makereti. Finally, Mita Taupopoki, Wikitari, Rakera, and Te Ngarotu would use the terms koroua or tupuna for Te Whareiro, Te Kohuro, and Te Pahau, horoua or tupuna for Tamawhakaara, and kuia or tupuna for Waiata.

Iramutu

The word *iramutu* is sometimes used in speaking of a brother's or sister's son, but it is not a word which was much used in days gone by.

A very common word for a child, especially the youngest, is *potiki*. If a child were hurt, a mother would exclaim Aue! taku potiki! O! O! my child!

First-born, youngest, adopted, or foster children

A first-born son or daughter would be termed *matamua,*
muanga, or *hamua,* and if the first-born were of a tino (very)
rangatira family, he or she would be termed *ariki.* A youngest
child was *muringa* or *whakapakanga,* and an adopted or foster
child was *tamaiti whangai* or *tamaiti taurima,* tamaiti being
the word for child, and tamariki its plural.

"Relations by marriage"

The word used for husband was *tane, hoa tane,* or *mâkâu,* and
for wife, *wahine,* or *hoa wahine.* In referring to a husband's or
wife's relations generally, a man or woman might use the term
taku pāākuha, i.e. my connexions by marriage, but if a blood
relationship exists, either a husband or wife will prefer it to a
term which shows the connexion by marriage. For example,
if any of my husband's people were related to me in my own
genealogical tree, I should use the term which expressed
that relationship rather than the term which expressed our
connexion by marriage.

Husband and wife

Otherwise, I might speak of my husband's pāpā or whaea,
his koroua or kuia, or his mokopuna or tamariki, they being
counted by him just as my own are counted by me. Or I might
speak of my husband's father or grandfather as *hunngawai*
tane, and of his mother or grandmother as *hungawai wahine.*

41

Father- and mother-in-law

For father-in-law and mother-in-law or their "brothers and sisters", either a man or a woman would use the terms *hungawai, hungarei, hunarere, hunarei,* or *hungoi.*

Sons- and daughters-in-law, etc.

My own sons-in-law and daughters-in-law, and those of my brothers and sisters, would be referred to as *hunaonga.*

Taokete, etc.

For a wife's brothers, and also for her sisters, a man would use the word *taokete.* For her sisters generally, he might use the word *auwahine,* and for her elder sisters *tuakana wahine,* and for her younger, *taina wahine.* For a husband's brothers and sisters, a woman would use the word *taokete.* For brothers-in-law generally, she might use the word *autane,* and for a husband's elder brothers the words *tuakana tane,* and for his younger brothers, *taina tane.*

Hoahoa

A woman might use the term *hoahoa* for her brother's wife, or for her husband's second wife, or for her husband's brother's wife, the term showing that the other woman was of the same position or standing as herself.

Examples

The following table shows the marriage of Waaka te Rohu and Parerautic, giving the whanau of each, and the terms which Parerautic would use in speaking of her husband's relations, as well as the terms which Waaka te Rohu would use in speaking of his wife's relatives. It was not easy to recall two groups which possessed all the relatives necessary to make a complete table on both sides.

Blood relationship mentioned rather than connexion by marriage

It must be remembered too, that if relations by marriage are also relations by blood, the husband or wife would always use the terms expressing the blood relationship, or the connexion in their own genealogical tree. This I tried to make clear on.

MARRIAGE OF WAAKA TE ROHU AND PARERAUTUTU

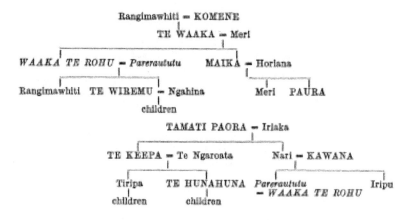

Parerautu refers to Maika as her taina tane or taokete, and to Horiana as her hoahoa, because the two of them married two brothers. She might refer to Meri and Paura as aku tamariki (our children), or as iramutu of Waaka te Rohu. Te Waaka and Meri are her hungawai, and she would refer to Rangimawhiti and Komere as our horoua and kuia, or as Waaka te Rohu's koroua and kuia. Ngahina is her hunaonga, and Ngahina's children are her mokopuna.

Waaka te Rohu would refer to Iripu as his taina wahine, and to Tiripa and Te Hunahuna as tuakana of Parerautu. Nari and Kawana, are his hungawai, and he would refer to Te Keepa and his wife as Hungawai also. Tamati Paora and his wife would be our koroua and kuia, or Parerautu's, Ngahina would be his hunaonga, and her children his mokopuna.

Tiripa's and Te Hunahuna's children would be iramutu (if male) of ParerautUtu, or aku tamariki.

But while Pareraututu could say our tamariki, our mokopuna, etc., of the children and grandchildren of her husband's brothers and sisters, she would be more likely to say So and So's tamariki and mokopuna, and to refer to other connexions by marriage as Waaka te Rohu's pāpā, whaea, etc. The same general rule applies to Waaka te Rohu in referring to his wife's relatives.

Terms of address

So far we have discussed the terms used in referring to relatives. It is now time to consider terms used in addressing relatives and others.

E Pa. If a young man or woman met a man who is married and has a child or children, but is not an old man, he or she would say "E Pa". This term is used even for a young man, if he is a father.

E Whae is similarly used for a young or middle-aged woman if she has had a child or family. Even a young woman is so addressed if she is a mother.

E Koro is how one would address an elderly man with respect.

E Kui is for an elderly woman.

E hine is for a girl of any age before marriage, even after marriage if she has no children.

E ko is for a very young girl.

E tama is for big boys and young men.

E ta is used for a lad or small boy, but is a term often used by one man to another when he suspects him of "pulling his leg".

E hoa (O friend!) is used by male or female, but is generally used by men to each other, and sometimes has the same meaning as *E ta*.

E Kare is also used by male and female to each other, but is generally used by women to each other.

E Moi or *E Moia* is an affectionate term used by a mother to any of her children when small, or to a grown-up daughter. An older sister would use it to a younger sister at any age.

E Riki would be used by an elderly woman when addressing a matamua (eldest child) of a family of an elder line to her own. She might use it for any member of such a family as well. She would say *E Riki* or *Taku Ariki* (my Ariki).

Forms used by tribes other than Te Arawa

There are of course other forms of greeting used by other tribes. Besides the ones given, in Ngapuhi, the Bay of Islands, for example, *E Mara* would be the term of greeting to a man, *E Kara* to an elderly man, while the Whanganui people also use *E Weke* in greeting an old man. *E hika* is used in greeting by the Ngati Porou on the East Coast, and by Ngati Kahuhunu in Hawke's Bay, and others, but not by Te Arawa.

General methods of meeting and greeting

In the old days when one Maori met another by the wayside, each would say "Tena koe", press noses, and pass on. They might never have met before, and might not know each other, but this greeting alone would be given before passing on, and no other word would be spoken, nor questions asked. If one person met two Maori in this manner, he would greet them with "Tena korua", hongi (press noses), and pass on as before. When three or more persons were met, the greeting would be "Tena koutou" and the proceeding the same. It was bad form to ask a stranger who he was, or any other questions. There was only one thing you would do.

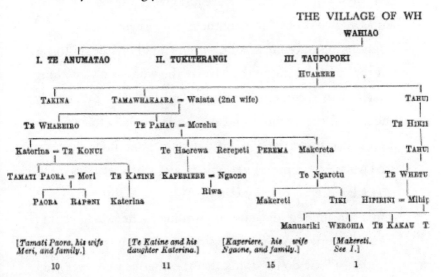

THE VILLAGE OF WH

WAHIAO

If your home was somewhere near, you would say, "Hoaki ki te kainga," or "Haeremai ki te kainga," Come, let us go to the kainga (village or home). You would not go with him yourself, but ahead of him, to arrange for his welcome. The rule of hospitality was so strong, that even if a man were your enemy, you would entertain him. No questions were ever asked of a guest, but if he were a rangatira, he would give his genealogy in replying to the speeches of welcome, and then everybody would know all about him.

Meaning of terms of greeting and farewell

It is difficult to translate these terms of greeting, for the literal translation does now always express the meaning of a Maori word. Take the words "Tena koe", or "Tena koroua" and "Tena koutou" which I have just given. The exact English rendering would be "You are there", or "There you are", and would have no feeling as a European would say them. This is not the real meaning to the Maori. The words are something greater than the mere greeting. A reader must thoroughly understand the Maori language and customs before he can thoroughly understand these greetings, and how they are used when Maori meet one another, and when relatives meet, especially after a long separation. When a Maori used these words, he pressed the nose of whomever he was greeting. To the Maori, hongi (the pressing of noses) was a token of affection. Please do not think that these terms were ever used in the manner in which Europeans say "How do you do?" or "There you are". Such expressions seem very cold to the

Maori, and the way in which he expresses a term of greeting is very different from the tone and expressions of the European using the same form of words.

WAREWA ABOUT 1880   (III, 2). See pp. 40-1, 45.

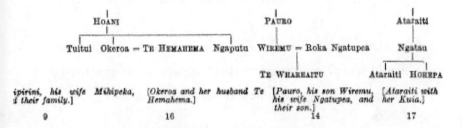

Sometimes the greeting was made even more expressive by adding the word *ra*, and expressing the words in a more emphasized manner. Instead of saying "Tena koutou" (Greetings to you all), the Maori would say "Tena ra koutou".

In parting, a Maori would say "Haerera" to the one who was leaving. This cannot be translated as it should be in English. Its real meaning is in the way it is spoken, as only a Maori can say it, when he bids farewell to a friend, or to his loved ones. This is especially true of days gone by, when everything that the Maori did was expressive, and full of meaning and affection.

To those who remained behind in the kainga, the departing Maori would say "Hai konei ra", or "E noho ra". The meaning was not "Sit down" or "Remain behind", as I have often heard these words translated. They expressed much to the Maori in their partings, and to hear the words used by parents to their children, or by children to parents, or by relatives to relatives, would bring tears to the eyes. But the tears never fell.

There were no tears shed at parting. No matter if the fathers, husbands, and sons went away to fight in a Taua party, there were no tears shed, nor outward expressions of feeling shown.

All this would happen on their return, when a tangi (crying) would take place. A tangi was held too when visitors arrived at a village, as I have explained in another place.

Conversation without words

A great deal of conversation with relatives or other loved ones is carried on without words, but by gestures, expressions of the face, and by inarticulate sounds. One of the most expressive was an m-sound made with closed lips. This sound had a great variety of meanings, and expressed love and grief, and tenderness and affection. I remember when I returned to New Zealand after many years' absence, my old people did not need to speak to me, but as they looked at me, and uttered this voiceless sound, they expressed all the depth of their love for me. This is only one of the many examples which I might write.

[1] The genealogy of Makereti's village is on.

II

MARRIAGE

THE MAORI HAD his rules about marriage from far back ancient times, and these were generally recognized and carried out by the people. He learned what was right at home gradually, as European children do.

Marriages were generally love matches, but sometimes a marriage was arranged between two people of rangatira[1] families. No matter how it took place, though, the two people lived happily together.

Permitted degrees of relationship

There was no objection to a marriage within the whanau (family group) or the hapu (p. 34), as long as the couple were not too closely related. The old Maori was very much against the marriage of close relations, and termed it incestuous, even to the third and fourth generation from a common ancestor. If the two people belonged to the second generation from a common ancestor, they were considered too close to marry, but were allowed to, if they were at least three generations from a common ancestor. The following is an example of a type of marriage which took place, although the parties were considered too closely related to marry, according to the old Maori idea.

TAMA WHAKAARA

Muri — TE WHATINUI   TE PAHAU — Morehu
MAROTAUA — Maata   Makereta
     IHAIA — Makereta

From a European point of view, Marotaua and Makereta would be first cousins, and their children would be second cousins. To the Maori, Marotaua and Makereta would be tungane and tuahine,[1] brother and sister, and the children of Marotaua would be termed tamariki of Makereta, and vice versa. The above genealogy shows that Ihaia married Makereta, he being the third, and she the second generation from a common ancestor. The marriage was considered too close, and was objected to, as Ihaia was marrying his whaea (aunt) according to the Maori point of view.

RELATIONSHIP BETWEEN TE WIREMU AND NGAHINA, BOTH SIDES

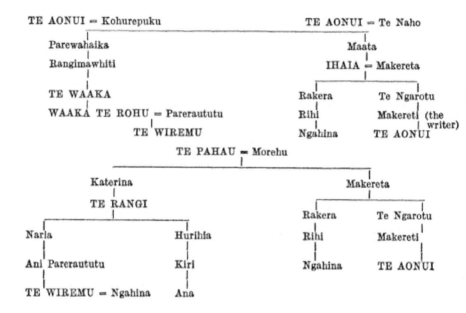

Tungane and tuahine marriage

In this case Te Wiremu of the fifth generation on his father's side married Ngahina of the fourth on his mother's side. This marriage was objected to because they were doubly related, and was always spoken of as a tungane and tuahine (brother and sister) marriage as on his father's side. Although Ngahina was of the fourth generation on her mother's side, such a marriage would always be termed a brother and sister marriage. When any relative asked Ngahina where Te Wiremu was, the question was put, "Kai whea to tungane?" meaning, Where is your brother? i.e. Te Wiremu her husband. The same thing happened when anyone met Te Wiremu and wanted to see Ngahina. He would be asked, "Kai whea to tuahine," i.e. Where is your sister? meaning Ngahina his wife.

Their children would be referred to as aku mokopuna,[1] my grandchildren. I was reminded of this on my last visit to New Zealand a few years ago. One morning I was greeted with "Hello, grandma" by Ana, daughter of Kiri, who was a baby when I had seen her last, but now a grown girl. This sounded most comical to me, especially hearing it said in English, but it was quite a natural thing for her to say, and in Maori would have sounded quite differently. It showed that she knew our relationship, even though she had not seen me since she was quite a small child.

Influence of family affection and contiguity

Te Rangi and his whanau, and my family always kept up our relationship with great affection, just as though my mother was Te Rangi's own sister. When he passed away, Nari and her sisters and brothers carried it on, and my family felt the same affection for them. We were a whanau kotahi (family group) who were descended from Morehu, and in speaking to each other called ourselves Ngati Morehu. When other people saw us together, they would say, "Kongati Morehu," It is the descendants of Morehu. Waaka te Rohu, the father of Te

Wiremu, was also another relative whose family were on close and affectionate terms with my family. From our tupuna, great great grandfather Te Aonui, we were doubly related, as our great great grandmothers Kohurepuku and Te Naho, wives of Te Aonui, were sisters. This bond of affection came down from their generation to us. When quite small, I was told of it by my kuia, great aunt Marara, who brought me up. She explained the relationship, and said, "Kia manaaki i to tungane ia Te Waaka," Always do what you can for your brother Te Waaka. She impressed upon me that I was to uphold him in whatever he did, no matter what it was. She went so far as to leave him part of her shares in the land at Whakarewarewa.[1] This, to anyone who understands the ways of the Maori, goes to show how very much she thought of nga uri, the descendants, of Parewahaika her mother's sister. Through this relationship, and the bond between our families, we looked upon the marriage of Te Wiremu and Ngahina as too close, and considered it as a tungane and tuahine marriage.

Arrangement of marriages

The Maori were very particular in all matters of etiquette, even the smallest points, and most exact in behaviour during any ceremonial. They were a communal people, and in the arranging of a marriage, especially in the rangatira class, the matter had to be discussed by the hapu or the tribe.

Proposal and betrothal

Generally, a kotiro (girl) rangatira would be asked for in marriage by a chief of another clan when she was at a marrying age, that is, about twenty to twenty-five. It might also happen that a chief who had a son born to him, on hearing that a certain chief had got an infant daughter, would pay him a ceremonial visit, and ask that the child might be given to him. At whatever age the kotiro may be, the chief would visit her father in this ceremonial fashion, with a retinue of people from his people from his hapu who would go and visit the hapu to which the girl belonged.

The tangata whenua (people of the village) would welcome and receive them in the manner due to distinguished visitors, and would not even know the object of the visit. After the ceremony of tangi (crying), whaikorero (speech-making), and whiu kai (giving of food), the visitors would enter the wharepuni (meeting house) which was prepared for their accommodation. In the evening there would be an assembly of the tangata whenua to entertain their visitors, and they would occupy the left side of the whatitoka (door), as you enter, the visitors being on the opposite side. More speech-making took place welcoming the visitors, followed by waiata (chants) and dances.

It would be during a speech made by the visiting chief that the reason for their visit would be made known. He would repeat his line of genealogy, which would show how he was related to the resident chief, ending his speech with these words: "I haere mai au ki to tiki mai to taua tamahine (or mokopuna) So and So," I have come to get our daughter (or granddaughter, whatever their relationship may be from some ancestor far back) So and So; "Homai kai au," Give her to me. When he asked for the girl or infant in this manner, the tangata whenua knew that he did not mean her for himself, but for his son or nephew. If he had a grown-up son, he would ask for a girl of a marriageable, or approaching a marriageable age. If he had a small son, he would ask for the chief's baby daughter. He would then lay taonga (presents) on a space near where he was standing. These would go to the girl and her people, but if there were any heirlooms, they would be given to the girl, who would take them with her as taonga for her husband, herself, and their children.

Gifts and heirlooms

After a formal proposal like this, whether it came as a surprise or not, or whether it was welcome or unwelcome, not a word would be uttered by the tangata whenua immediately. The near relatives of the girl would make signs to one another to go out, and would leave one by one, so that they would not be missed. The departure would probably be managed while a waiata or haka (dance) was going on for the entertainment of the visitors. The relatives would meet in another whare (house) for a hurried discussion of this tono (proposal). Whatever their decision, the girl was seldom consulted as to her wishes. If it was the wish of the elders, a kotiro rangatira carried it out. They were like that in the old days.

Consultation by relatives

Then one of the uncles, or the grandfather of the girl would make a speech, and end with "Kua rongo ra e pa ki ta koutou tono i ta tatau tamahine (or mokopuna, as the case may be)", We have heard your proposal with regard to our daughter (or granddaughter); "Waiho i konei ta taua tamahine noho ai mo enei ra," Leave our daughter here a while.

Te Paakuha, and ceremonial handing over of the bride

The visitors would return to their home, and in due course, when the girl reached the age of twenty to twenty-five, the ceremonial handing over of the bride occurred. This was a very important function, and much preparation for it took place at the kainga (village, i.e. home) of the prospective groom, where a marriage feast was made ready, many clans being invited to attend it. The prospective bride would be accompanied by her relatives, people of standing, and they would bring many presents, such as cloaks, weapons, ornaments, and choice food. A kotiro rangatira never went to her husband's people empty handed. The relatives who brought the bride would be spoken of as Te Paakuha by the tangata whenua.

Te Paakuha would arrive with her, fifty, a hundred, or

more people, and a great ceremonial welcome would be given them by the whole tribe of the chief whose son was to be the tane (bridegroom), all assembled on the marae in front of the wharepuni. The cries of Haeremai, Welcome, would be repeated by the women and girls, thirty to fifty or more, holding branchlets in each hand.

As Te Paakuha drew near to the marae, the women receded and mingled with the tangata whenua. A tangi would first take place, then ceremonial speech-making. A chief of the tangata whenua began with a welcoming speech to the visitors. After him would speak a visiting chief, and then chiefs of the tangata whenua and the visitors spoke alternately. All the speeches mentioned the great ceremony which brought all the people together, and each side hoped that the tie would bind the two groups even closer to each other.

Gifts

Te Paakuha would lay the gifts which they had brought on the marae. These would all be very valuable gifts, such as a patu pounamu[1] (short-handled greenstone weapon), or perhaps two, a kotiate (short-handled bone weapon), heitiki, or greenstone neck ornaments, whakakai, ear ornaments, taiaha (long-handled weapons) and other weapons, and various cloaks of korowai, kahu kiwi and other feathers, and whariki (floor-mats). Not far from these would be a heap of presents of food, such as kumara (sweet potatoes), taha huahua (preserved pigeons in calabashes), and other kinaki (relish) such as eels, dried fish, etc.

Ceremony of presentation

All these things were presented to the tangata whenua with great ceremony and speech-making by a close relative of the bride, who walked up and down the marae beside the tahua (heap) of taonga and the tahua kai (heap of food). He would end his whaikorero with his staff in his right hand pointing to the tahua and shouting, "Ara ra kia ngati mea," To the descendants of, or hapu of So and So, giving the name of the hapu of the tangata whenua. If there were other clans present with the tangata whenua to whom the bridegroom was related, these hapu would be mentioned in the presentation. None of these hapu would be left out even if only a few people represented them. The presentation in this case was only a matter of form. These hapu, although they were relatives who had come to support the tangata whenua by bringing much food of all kinds for the marae of their kinsfolk, and by being there to help them in welcoming and entertaining the Paakuha and other visiting clans, would not dream of taking the offered gifts. But they liked the relationship to be recognized, especially at an important ceremonial function like this, in which they felt themselves a part, through their relationship to the bridegroom. They knew that these valuable gifts should go to the chief who was father of the groom, and to his family group and hapu.

The tahua taonga (heap of valuable presents or treasures) and the tahua kai would remain on the marae for the best part of the day, and would be the centre of many speeches, words of which brought to mind other ceremonial functions in the past. The speakers praised at length the valuable presents in the tahua before them, these taonga given at this marriage ceremony. In doing these things they were only carrying on the old customs o nga koeke (of the old people). "Kia manaaki i nga tikanga a o tatau koeke," the speaker would say, Keep in mind and respect the customs of our old people.

Discussion of other matters

At these meetings many important things were discussed on the marae, things which affected the hapu and the tribe. Such discussions occurred whenever there was a hui (gathering) of the various hapu or of the tribe.

Acceptance of gifts

When the proper time came for the chief of the tangata whenua to make a ceremonial speech accepting the gifts, many of his people were round him. The chief would stand up with his taiaha (staff) in his right hand, and whaikorero, a long ceremonial speech, as only a Maori chief can, for they were wonderful orators. He would end his speech by presenting the two heaps of gifts to the hapu present who had come to support him, and who were relatives of his son, both on his father's and on his mother's side. Every speech ended with an appropriate waiata, sung in chorus by the people standing.

Recognition of relationship by presentation and return of gifts

The hapu to whom the tahua had been presented by the chief would arrange for one special chief from among the hapu to make a final speech on their behalf with regard to the taonga (valuable presents). During his speech, he would say that he was speaking for all the hapu present who had been mentioned in the presentation of the taonga, and express how very much they appreciated the taonga which had been presented to them. He would end thus: "Kua kite iho ra i o tatau taonga," We have seen these valuable gifts which have been presented to us; "Kua naomia iho," We have handled them; "Kua kakahu ria," We have put them on, and had the pleasure of owning them; "Ma te aha tenei?" What is greater than this? Then, on behalf of all present, the chief would mention his hapu and all the hapu to whom the gifts had been presented, and say, "E whaka hokia atu ana nga taonga nei ki a mea, me tana whanau," We are returning these valuable gifts to So and So (giving the name of the chief of the tangata whenua, father of the bridegroom) and to his whanau (family group).

The bride and groom

On the day of the ceremony, te wahine (the bride) was prepared and dressed for the occasion. She bathed in a stream, and rubbed herself with the sweet-scented oil of the titoki berries, further scented by putting in sweet-smelling leaves and gum. Round her neck was a hei which held a small bag of the scented karehu (Hierochloe redolens). She wore an ornamented maro (apron) which was tied round her waist and came down to her knees. This would be decorated with the red feathers of the kaka (parrot), and the white feathers of the kereru (pigeon). Round her shoulders would be a korowai (Plate X), koro-hunga,[1] or kinikini cloak (Plate IX), made from the fibre of phormium tenax; the top of this cloak would be passed under her right arm-pit, and tied over her left shoulder. She would have whakakai pounamu, ear ornaments of greenstone hanging from the lobes of her ears, or perhaps ear ornaments of mako (shark's teeth). In her hair would be the tail-feather or feathers of the huia bird, or of the toroa (albatross), or perhaps both together. Her hair would hang loosely over her shoulders, and would be anointed with scented oil. The Maori women had beautiful thick long hair.

The man would also be dressed for the ceremony with a rapaki (loin-cloth) of a small kakahu (cloak), or perhaps a piupiu, or flax skirt, down to his knees. A fine kahu kiwi (cloak of kiwi feathers) or kahu kura (cloak made of the red feathers of the kaka and the white of the kereru pigeon) covered his body. Or he might wear a kaitaka (Plate VIII) with an ornamental taniko round the border. His cloak might be tied over his right shoulder with the strings on either side of the cloak, or it might be pinned together with an aurei, that is, a curved whalebone pin. Sometimes a bunch of these aurei would be suspended where the cloak was pinned. Only people of high rank would use them.

The feast

A great feast would be prepared where there was choice food in plenty, with kinaki (relish) of various kinds. This was made ready by the women of the marae, who formed themselves into groups for doing the different things to be done. Whatever they did was always accompanied by pao (love songs), and they always entered into their work with great joy. When the food was cooked and the marriage feast was ready, the food was laid before the many guests with great ceremonial dances and songs. The young couple and their close relatives were served with food that had been specially cooked in a separate hangi (oven) and they were served at a short distance away from the gathering of people.

Special arrangements for young couple and their near relatives

Occasional and special ritual by Tohunga as part of marriage ceremony

Sometimes, but not often, among the rangatira class ritual was performed over the couple who wished to be married. A Tohunga would karakia[1] over them the karakia whakapiri (to stick), which bound them together for always. Another karakia[1] was performed for their happiness, so that the woman would bear many children to carry on the kawai (line), and so that the man would be good to his wife and take care of her for all time, no matter what happened. His genealogical lines would be repeated from far back Chaos right down to him. The wife's genealogical tree would also be repeated, mentioning distinguished ancestors down. to herself. She was advised to stick to her husband always, no matter what happened.

General account of the hui

When a marriage took place between two rangatira people, either by ritual, or Paakuha, or by arrangement between two people of the same hapu who belonged to the same kainga (village, or home), there were always the ceremonial festivities of a hui, that is, gathering, of all the relatives in various hapu who would be invited. The couple would sit together throughout the hui ceremony and during the marriage feast, and as I have said, they and their close relatives would have their food specially cooked in a separate hangi, and would be served with it at a little distance away from the other people. This great marriage feast had taken many moons to prepare the food for it, and each hapu who came to the hui brought a plentiful supply of all the choice foods which helped to feed the big gathering of people who were present at the ceremony. The guests were not fed solely by the tangata whenua (people of the kainga), and the people of the kainga were not impoverished by the people who came to the ceremony just for the sake of what they could get to eat, as many ignorant writers have stated.

Contribution of food from visiting hapu

Invitation by hapu and not for individuals

No individual persons were invited to a ceremony like this, but a hapu would be asked, and those who attended would represent their hapu. It would be said that Ngati So and So, i.e. the descendants or hapu of So and So, would attend the hui, and it would be known how many different hapu were represented. Each hapu of course had a chief or chiefs, for no hapu would attend a big function without one. The hapu had to be well represented, if they were to uphold their mana, and the more who went, the better, especially to a hui which took place to discuss the affairs of the tribe.

It was generally an important set of men and women who attended and represented their hapu, and they were generally related to either the bride or the bridegroom. The men must be good orators, able to waiata (chant songs) and do all the haka, or dances, required of them. They must also have all the other accomplishments necessary for such a gathering. The women must be able to waiata, or chant and join in the songs, and dance the poi (the poi is a small ball of raupo), a dance performed by the girls who hold the poi balls (Plate XI) by the string in their hands, and swing them with a rhythm to the accompaniment of song and graceful movements of the body. Men and women must be fit to compete in all the events which took place during the evening of the hui, when each hapu tried to outshine the other. This competition was very important to a visiting hapu.

Addresses to bride and groom

In the evening all the people gathered in the wharepuni and outside it, and the early part would be taken up with more speeches. The whaikorero of the Paakuha would be directed mainly towards the young couple, who would be seated with the husband's people. Each chief who stood up to make a speech would address the young couple at the end of his whaikorero with words full of advice and good wishes for their future happiness. The relatives would address the bride, one repeating her genealogy and expressing the hope that she would always remember her distinguished ancestors, and never bring disgrace on her husband and his people, for this would bring disgrace on her people too, as all that she did affected them also. She was reminded that she now belonged to her husband's people till death parted them. To the husband these words would be addressed: "E moe korua ko to wahine; manaaki tia e koe," You and your wife are now one; take care of her. Then all the people would join in a waiata suitable for the occasion.

Final entertainment and departure of guests

After this the entertainment began with the tangata whenua doing poi dances and hakas. Then the visiting hapu would also dance, and so the different clans would compete with each other all through the night. The couple would watch the dancing from the moenga (sleeping place) by the side of his parents. Often they would fall asleep in the midst of it all.

The next morning the visitors would probably depart, with the exception of the girl's family, who might stay on for a few days. When they left for the journey home, there were no parting tears, only a farewell hongi (pressing of noses).

The married couple and their mode of life

Sometimes a whare was built for the young couple, but generally they lived with his parents, and slept in the wharepuni with them. The bride would be waited on in everything by her hungawai (mother-in-law), who saw to all her needs, and she was surrounded with love and kindness by her husband's family and relatives.

The power of love in family life and in the whole society

It was almost an unknown thing in the old days for a man to leave his wife and children. The Maori woman was a faithful and affectionate wife, who lived for her husband and family and hapu. There was great love between a couple who were married, and they generally lived happily to the end of their lives. The love they bore their children was very great. Indeed this love for their children was one of the most wonderful things in the character of the Maori. It seemed to bind the whole family together, even to the whole family group, and beyond that again to the hapu. The life of a Maori was surrounded with love from his infancy, and this love continued through the whole of his life. A person has to realize this thoroughly, and understand all the Maori's customs, knowing why he does certain things and not others, before he can sit down and write about the Maori. Otherwise his criticisms lack understanding.

Special position of heirlooms among the other gifts and return of gifts in kind

With regard to taonga paakuha (gifts at a Pakuwha marriage) although they have been presented, it is an understood thing that some day, either during the life-time of the givers or in the next generation when occasion arises, these gifts will be returned in kind. The heirlooms, if any, go to the young couple. These would never become the property of the husband, even though he might have them in his possession and use them all his life. They belong to his wife's family. If they have children, these taonga will pass on to them. Should the couple not have children, and the wife dies before her husband, the heirlooms will go back to her family. They would be returned in a ceremonial manner. The general thing would be this. If the wife died, and her hapu came to tangi (mourn) over her, they would during a speech make the request that her body be taken back to their kainga for burial. If the husband and his people consented, they would go in great numbers to take the body to her home. In this case the husband's family would discuss a return in kind of the gifts of the Paakuha, which had been presented at her marriage. The heirlooms, and many other gifts, would be used as kopaki to wrap round her and cover her body as she lay in state. Again, if the husband and his people did not consent to having the body removed, she was buried at her husband's kainga. Nga taonga would remain with his people until later years, when it would be arranged for the wife's bones to be exhumed and returned to her people with great ceremony. Nga taonga would then be used as a kopaki, and would be returned with her to her people, together with other things of value presented by the husband and his family.[1]

Kopaki

Marriage among ordinary people

Very little ceremony was observed in marriages among the ordinary people of a hapu. If a couple fell in love, the parents were consulted, and if there was no opposition, the man took the girl to his parents' house, and they slept together there. There may be no ceremony, but the mere fact that he had taken her to his father's house and kua moe raua (they had slept together, or become husband and wife) was binding. Sometimes the couple went to the girl's people, and so lived with them. Even if the parents did not think it a suitable match, when once kua moe raua, either in his father's or her father's house, objections were generally overruled. They were husband and wife. In most cases the parents were consulted, but sometimes when the parents objected to the match, the couple would go to a relative's house a ka moe i reira and would sleep together there. If her parents objected, they would take her away, but if she still persisted in going back to him, objections would be withdrawn, and the couple would be sent for to return either to his or to her people. This would also happen if she was going to have a child.

Marriage by arrangement; sucessful courtship

Position of whanau

Generally, if a boy and girl fell in love, he would make known his wishes to his parents. The parents would make their wishes known to her family, who would gather together the family group and discuss the matter. Each member of the family group liked to have his say. The girl would be with her family while all this was taking place. Should both family groups be agreed, the girl would be taken over to the boy's place, where a formal handing over occurred. After speeches, she was left with her tane's family, where the couple occupied a sleeping place prepared for them in the wharepuni with his people.

Unsuccessful courtship

There were of course cases in which a couple fell in love and were not allowed to marry. In some instances, the couple were separated, and made to marry others.

Elopements

But sometimes a couple ran away either to the bush or to some place unknown, and as the Maori had great love for their children, the couple were usually forgiven and asked to come back and live either with his or her people. This did not happen among people of rank, as girls generally did what their parents wanted.

Whakamomori

Sometimes a wahine rangatira (woman of rank) fell in love with a tangata rangatira (man of rank) of another hapu which her parents did not approve of, and nothing could persuade them to agree to her marrying him, as they wanted her to marry someone else. Because her love was so great, and she was not allowed to marry him, she would whakamomori (die). She just pined away and ate nothing and died of a broken heart. There have been a number of these cases, and their songs, most pathetic and beautiful, are sung to this day. Some of them are of my own relatives.

Names

When a woman married, she did not take the name of her husband, but kept her own name, and her husband kept his. Each child had its own name, and did not take either the mother's or the father's. The giving of a name to an infant of rangatira parents was generally done by the grandparents and the family group, and seldom by the parents. The child might be named after an ancestor, or more often after some great event which happened at the time of birth. Te Huinga is an example, meaning "the great gathering", probably for some important function at the time. Pipi, Shell-Fish, is another. Perhaps an invalid relative asked for it before his or her death at about the time when the child was born. Both these names would be for a female child. If a great chief died and was mourned by many people who attended the tangi, the child would be called Tangirau. He might receive this name after an erruption where many people were killed. Tangirau means the weeping of hundreds, or of many. If at the time a noted relative was drowned at sea, the child would be called Moananui, that is to say, The Ocean, or Te Ngaru, The Waves, or, if the wind that caused the storm was a west wind, the child would be called Hauauru.

Marriage and relationship

When a woman of one hapu marries a man of another hapu, their children will be related to all members of both hapu[1]; that is to say that the children of a marriage between two hapu would establish a relationship and connect the genealogical trees of both hapu, as shown in the chapter about social organization.

Monogamy and Polygyny

Polyandry was never a custom of the Maori at any time, Monogamy was the general rule among them. It was only among tangata tino rangatira, men of very high rank, that polygyny was practised. It was not the custom to buy a wife. When a man took to himself a wife, he looked upon her as his possession, and she was tapu. He and his people looked after her, and if she bore him children, he esteemed her more. One of the most important things in the married life of the Maori was to have children, as many as they could have, and especially a son who would carry on the family tree and help his father in battle, and in everything he did. Such sons married women of standing who bore them many children, who, in doing brave deeds, became famous, and were spoken of as the sons of So and So, who did such and such a thing. If a wahine matua (first wife) was pukupa, i.e. barren, she encouraged her husband to take another wife, so that she could bear him children, and the first wife would rear and love those children as her own, and speak of them as her own. It was a great blow to a tangata rangatira not to have a son to carry on his kawai (line), and it was mainly for this reason that a chief took more than one wife, and *not*, as is often stated by writers, for the purpose of showing his importance and status. The number of wives made no difference to this, nor did it make a man a rangatira. A tangata rangatira, i.e. a chief of high rank, was important in his very self, by means of his high birth. It was his own greatness which gave him mana, and made him important in the eyes of the people, and made his reo (voice) heard and obeyed. His importance had nothing whatever to do with the number of wives he had.

A chief's herehere wives

In general, a chief's wives were of high rank only, but a chief had two wives of high rank, with one or two others who had been herehere, that is, captured in war, and these would do the menial work for the family. The first wife would be termed wahine matua, and if he had a second one, the two wives would be termed punarua, a pair, or the two wives of one husband. In speaking of each other, either wife would say "taku hoahoa", i.e. one of the wives of the same husband. The word hoahoa is also used by two women who are married to two brothers, or by two men who are married to two sisters, when speaking of each other.

Punarua

Hoahoa (V. also cap. I, p. 52).

Inheritance

All the children of the wives shared whatever property or land the father possessed or the mother possessed, even the children of women who had been taken in war. They all shared alike. Many of the women taken in war were of the rangatira class.

Marriages to cement peace or form alliances between clans or tribes

Sometimes a chief would offer his daughter to a victorious chief of an enemy tribe to cement peace after a battle in which he had been defeated, or after continuous fighting over a period. It was always a defeated chief who gave his daughter to cement peace. Sometimes a chief who had a daughter of marriageable age, wishing to make a certain alliance, would pay the chief a ceremonial visit, and offer his daughter as a wife for him. In a case of this sort, which did not often happen, the chief could not refuse to take the girl. Indeed it would be considered ungracious to do so, and such a refusal would give rise to the term whakahawea (despised). It would be said, "I whaka hawea tia a mea," So and So has been despised, and the girl would whakamomori, i.e. die of shame.

Resort to "white magic"

Sometimes a man desires a certain girl for his wife, and she refuses his proposal. The man then may visit a Tohunga atahu, taking with him something which belongs to the woman. The Tohunga repeats a karakia to try to make the woman aroha (affectionate) towards him. After the karakia, the man takes the article back, and puts it under her moenga (sleeping place). This often succeeds in making her return his affections. The same procedure was followed when a man had been left by his wife, or a woman by her husband. A Tohunga atahu would karakia and try to get the wife back to her husband, or the husband to his wife, and it was wonderful how often this influence worked. Again, if a man and woman love each other very much, and their people object to the marriage, the man will visit a Tohunga atahu who is a wise man in the art of wehe ki te wai, separating or withdrawing with water. This used to be done to soften the pain of separation, and to withdraw the love from the heart. The ritual was performed by a Tohunga in a stream, standing in the water up to his pito (navel). He held some kokowai (red ochre) in his hand, and mixed it with a little water and fat, and rubbed them together in the palm of his hand. He then rubbed this mixture across the eyes and face of the love-sick man, and next over his chest. While the Tohunga is mixing water and fat with the kokowai, he repeats a karakia, and when he rubs the mixture over the man's face and breast, a different karakia is repeated. The Tohunga makes two mounds of sand by the stream, and on them the man places his feet, standing the while. The Tohunga has a green stick which he has broken off a growing karamu tree. With this stick he first strikes the water, repeating a karakia wehe, appealing to the Atua (gods) to withdraw this great love from the man's heart, and to lessen his pain. This was done in the case of my pāpā[1] Mita Taupopoki, when it was arranged by the people that Herena was to be his wife. A Tohunga atahu performed this ceremony over him to lessen the pain and the aroha he felt for his first wife.

Marriage between rangatira and ordinary people

A tangata rangatira can marry a woman of the ordinary class if consent has been obtained, or a wahine rangatira can marry a man of the ordinary class in the same way.

Adopted children

Children who were adopted were looked upon as brothers and sisters of the children of the people who adopted them. There was no law to prevent them from marrying, as long as the relationship of the adopted child was not too close to that of the children born of the people who adopted him or her. I have never heard of a marriage between a girl and her brother by adoption, nor between a boy and his sister by adoption. A boy generally looked upon an adopted girl as a true sister, and treated her as such, while a girl looked upon an adopted boy as a true brother.

Punarua

Widows

Two sisters often married two brothers, and if one lost her husband, the husband's family would ask that she should become the wife of one of her husband's brothers, or become a punarua with her sister. This proposal would be made with ceremonial speech-making during the tangi (mourning) when the widow's people would be present, especially if she belonged to another hapu. This proposal would not bind the widow in any way. If she had a large family, her people would ask for one or two of the children, so that they could bring them up and keep the family ties closer, if the widow should decide to go to live with her husband's people. If she had no children, and wished to return to her own people after the death of her husband, there was nothing to prevent it. But in a case like this, the husband's people generally asked her to be the wife of one of the family, or to remain with them, and later, she could marry if she wished to, or she could return to her own people if she preferred to do so. Some time would elapse before this was carried out. There was no such thing as a widow and her children being left unprovided for, as among Europeans. She and her children were all looked after by her husband's or her own relatives.

Intertribal marriage and its difficulties

Sometimes marriages were arranged with other tribes,[1] but not often, as there was very little intercourse between them. They lived long distances apart, and there was no means of transit. Such marriages were arranged sometimes after continuous wars when a tribe wanted to make peace. Generally the chief of the defeated tribe would give his daughter in marriage to the victorious chief to cement it.

Insulting language

In this kind of marriage between people of different tribes, no matter how arranged, the husband and wife had to be very careful about what they said when they were angry. Should the wife be living with her husband's people, and he, or any of his people, call her or speak of her as a pokohohua or taurekareka (slave or low-born), it is a terrible thing, and not only an insult to her, but to all her people, and often a cause of war. The news of the insult would be taken to the wife's people by some relative of hers who was living in the kainga. It may not be the husband who had used these words, but one of his relatives. However, this makes no difference; the words have been uttered, and their utterance to the wife affects all her relatives. It is a great breach of etiquette, and they all feel the insult. The matter will be taken up by her people, who will visit the husband's kainga and take her away. Her people will pay a ceremonial visit, and although the matter is a quarrel, they will be received in a ceremonial fashion and treated with great hospitality. First of all on their arrival, a taua will take place, demanding payment for the insult, and the return of the wife to her people. This taua had to be paid, and she would have to return. But if, after she has gone to her people, she and her husband find that they cannot live apart, he will pay a ceremonial visit to her parents and ask for her to be given back to him. Afterwards they will remain with her people, or they may return to his home later. Should she not return to her husband, and later marry some other man, her husband's people will come and taua her and her people. This would be considered a taua puremu (demanding payment for adultery) as she still was her first husband's wife in the eyes of the Maori. However, after the taua have taken place, she is free to marry if she wishes.

Taua demanding payment for insult

Separation

Taua puremn

Occasions for meeting future husbands or wives

Marriage between two people of different hapu often took'place after a hui or gathering, when many people gathered together at a kainga to discuss various matters of state. At these meetings there were many entertainments and competitions among the younger members of the various hapu. Just as Hinemoa and Tutanekai met at these meetings and eventually fell in love with each other, so also were many other matches made between others of the rangatira class, as well as between those of the ordinary people. Some matches are made when people gather at a tangi, to mourn for the dead, or at any other important meeting.

Mothers-in-law

A mother-in-law was never looked on as among Europeans, but was generally loved and looked up to. Indeed she always proved to be the best friend of her hunaonga, whether it was the wife or the husband. If the husband was her son, she saw to the welfare of her hunaonga (daughter-in-law), and in fact tried to do everything for her comfort so that she was free to enjoy herself if she wished. She saw to it that her hunaonga was looked after in every way by the family. If she was the wife's mother, she proved a good friend to her hunaonga (son-in-law) all his life. She saw to his needs, and especially saw that he was treated with the greatest respect. Indeed she was his best friend. Sometimes a girl hunaonga was one who loved to be busy and do things. She would be to the fore in all manner of work and in entertaining the visitors at the ceremonies which took place at the marae of her hunarere (father-in-law), and she would be a great help to her mother-in-law.

Marriages between people of unequal rank

If a wahine rangatira married a man from another hapu of lower rank than herself, and her husband came to live with her people, she would retain her mana. Generally she would never do anything to make him feel his position. Her husband would never order her to do anything. He might be a great warrior who had done noble deeds. His wife liked him to take his stand with her family as a general thing, and she would probably be very proud of him if he was good at the ceremonials which took place on a marae, apart from his deeds of war. But he never presumed, although he would be taken to the hearts of his wife's people. One of his best friends was his hungawai (mother-in-law).

Holding the tie of affection

When a woman married into another hapu, her parents or relatives would ask for one or two of her children, whom they would bring up among themselves. In cases like this the parents never interfered with anything arranged for them, even when they grew up. Often relatives belonging to other hapu would ask for a child to be given to them, either for a short period, or for all time. This was done hai pupuri i te aroha, to hold the tie of affection.

Position of husband and wife in general run of marriages

If both the tane and his hoa wahine (husband and wife) were of high rank, the husband held the mana over the family, nor would the wife have had it otherwise. A wife generally looked up to her tane, and upheld him in all that he did. Maori women were like this, and generally carried out the wishes of their old people. A Maori woman knew before her marriage what would be expected of her at her husband's marae. She was to be hospitable and karanga tangata (call and welcome people). The Maori was most hospitable. She was to see that there was plenty of food and kinaki for the marae, so that when visitors arrived unexpectedly, there was food at hand to be prepared for them. Although she might live happily all her life in her husband's home, she would never actually become a member of his hapu, except that she would have all the privileges, and especially if she had children, would have some of the mana as their mother. Nor does a man ever become a member of his wife's hapu, if he marries into another tribe or hapu and goes to live with his wife's people, even if he lives with them all his life. But through being the father of his children, he has all the privileges, and generally the great support of his mother-in-law.

Marriages between two people of different hapu

Herehere

Herehere, prisoners of war, are often spoken of mistakenly as slaves. In many cases these prisoners were men of high standing and exceedingly good looking. They were treated well by the chief and his people, and indeed, often married into the tribe.

Punishment of herehere who misbehaves with a chief's wife

If one of these men so far forgot himself as to carry on illicit love with the wife of one of the chiefs, the punishment was very severe. He was made impotent, not by incision of his sexual glands, but by lesion caused by tension with the kotiate (Plate XXIV, fig. 5). The victim was flung on his back, and was seized and held in such a manner that the scrotum could be entered and held in the orifice on one side of the kotiate. The appendage was then stretched until its membrane could be inserted into the other orifice of the kotiate. The weapon was then given a circular twist and a vigorous upward jerk. This had the effect of severing the spermatic cord, and resulted in the eventual atrophy of the organ.

Puhi a virgin whose husband had to be chosen by the people

Betrothed girl also made a puhi

Generally marriages were love matches, but in some instances among people of rank, a marriage had to be arranged by members of the whanau or hapu. If a girl was made a puhi, a husband of rank had to be chosen for her by the hapu, and the girl had no say at all in the matter. In the case of a taumou (betrothal) when a chief asked for a girl or an infant for his son, the girl became a puhi. She was looked after by her people until such time as she could be taken and handed over to her husband without a blemish to her name, as a puhi should be. If by any chance the puhi broke the rules with regard to her virginity, she was immediately killed. If a girl was a puhi and no husband had been chosen for her, and she fell in love with a man ka moe raua, and married him, her people would take her away from him. Or, if the man was of equal rank with herself, her people might sanction the marriage after the whanau and hapu had discussed it. In the case of Hinemoa, a husband had not yet been chosen for her when she fell in love with Tutanekai and swam across Lake Rotorua to him.

True story of Hinemoa, a famous puhil

Hinemoa was the daughter of a great chief called Umukaria, and her mother was Hinemaru, also a great rangatira. When she was born, Hinemoa was made a puhi (she was made tapu), and a husband had to be chosen by her hapu when she grew up. She was very beautiful, and her fame spread far and wide. People came from distances to see her and ask for her hand in marriage. She lived with her parents and people on the edge of Lake Rotorua at a kainga called Owhata.

On an island called Mokoia which stands in the middle of Lake Rotorua lived another great chief called Whakaue, who had a family of five sons and one daughter. The three eldest sons were Tawake-heimoa, Ngararanui, and Tuteataiti, the younger were Tutanekai and Kopako, and the daughter, the youngest, was Tupa. When the eldest brothers heard of Hinemoa, each thought that he would like her for his wife.

Every year chiefs and members of various hapu living round Lake Rotorua and Rotoiti gathered together to hold a hui at Owhata to discuss matters of state regarding the tribe. At these meetings many young chiefs saw Hinemoa and fell in love with her. She was all that they had heard of, and of course a great rangatira. Many asked for her hand, and among them Whakaue's eldest sons. But the people had not yet chosen a husband for her.

Hinemoa lived in a whare belonging to her father, with her handmaidens who looked after her and waited upon her. She was not allowed to do anything in the way of work.

When the hui took place each year, Whakaue and his sons attended these gatherings, including Tutanekai, a younger son of whom he was very fond. At these meetings Hinemoa and Tutanekai saw each other, and although they never spoke, knew and felt that they were in love. When the different hapu danced the haka (posture dances) and war dances, Tutanekai excelled, as he did in all the games. He was also good to look at, well-built and strong. The hui often lasted many days, and Hinemoa saw Tutanekai each day from a distance on her father's marae (plaza). She thought him the most wonderful man she had ever seen, and her love for him grew until it filled her whole being. Tutanekai would glance at her and wonder if Hinemoa, a puhi, and a great rangatira, would deign to look at him when his elder brothers sought her hand also. He loved Hinemoa, but his love could only be sent by a glance and a look from his eyes.

When the hui ended, Whakaue and his sons returned to

Mokoia. Tutanekai built himself an atamira (high stand) on a rise behind his father's house. He told his father that he wanted Hinemoa, and that his love was returned, and every evening, he and his friend Tiki took their pu (flutes), Tiki the torino, and Tutanekai the koauau, and sitting on the atamiro, played. On a quiet evening the sound of the music floated across the water to Owhata where Hinemoa lived, and she knew that it was her lover playing, and conveying his messages of love through his koauau. Each evening she sat and listened to her lover's music, and felt that she really loved Tutanekai, and could not marry anyone else.

Her people began to suspect this, and thinking that she would go across to Mokoia, dragged the canoes up each evening so that she could not paddle across. But one evening as she listened to the koauau, she could almost hear the message asking her to go across, and felt that she could not live any longer while Tutanekai was eating his heart away on his island home. As the canoes were well guarded, there was only one thing that she could do, and that was to swim across. "E kore ranei au e whiti ki te kau hoe?" Cannot I get across by swimming?

She then told her maidens that she was going to the whare tapere, the house where dances were performed and games were played, but instead of doing so, she went into a wharau (cooking house), and took six calabashes. She then rested on a rock called Iri iri kapua, which is there to this day, and after that went to the beach to Wairerewai, where she took off her clothes and left them before slipping into the water of Lake Rotorua with the six empty calabashes tied together, three under each arm. It was growing dark when she got into the water, but the sound of the flute gave her the direction of the island. After swimming for a time, she came to a tumu, a stump in the lake, called Hinewhata, which her father Umukaria used for tying his tanga (long fishing nets) on, and a bunch of fern to which the small fish toitoi and the koura (crayfish) stuck. She held on to the tumu and rested, as she was beginning to feel the strain. When the tired feeling left her shoulders, she started swimming again, guided by the sound of her lover's music in the darkness, which took her across to Waikimihia, a warm bath on the edge of Mokoia Island by the lake. Hinemoa knew that above Waikimihia was Tutanekai's home. She got into the warm pool, for she was shivering with cold. She also shivered through being whakama (shy and ashamed), wondering how Tutanekai would look on her action. She also realized that she had no clothes, and this made her very whakama indeed.

Now about the same time that Hinemoa was sitting in the waiariki (warm bath), it happened that Tutanekai felt thirsty, and sent his taurekareka (slave) with a calabash, saying, "Tikina he wai moku," Go and get me water to drink. His taurekareka went to get the water, and had to pass the bath where Hinemoa sat. She asked in a gruff voice, "Mo wai te wai?" For whom is the water? The taurekareka answered, "Mo Tutanekai," It is for Tutanekai. Hinemoa then said, "Homai ki ahau," Give it to me. The calabash was handed to her, and after drinking the water she wanted, she broke the calabash. The slave asked her reason for doing this, but she gave him no answer. He returned to Tutanekai, who asked where the water was which he was sent to fetch. The slave replied, "The calabash is broken." Tutanekai asked, "Na wai i wahi?" Who broke it? The reply came, "Some man did it." Tutanekai asked him to take another calabash, and get him the water. When the taurekareka filled the second calabash with water, and turned to return with it to his master, Hinemoa asked again in a gruff voice whom the water was for, and the reply was that it was for Tutanekai. She asked him, still in a gruff voice, to hand her the calabash, which he did. Hinemoa again drank some water, and then broke the calabash by knocking it on the stone formation by the side of the pool. The taurekareka returned and told Tutanekai what had happened, and Tutanekai asked who had done this thing. The slave replied that he did not know the man, and that he must be a stranger. This made Tutanekai very angry, as the stranger knew that the water was for him, yet had dared to insult him by breaking his two calabashes.

He then dressed himself in his rapaki with a kahakaha cloak round his shoulders, and a tawaru cloak outside that, and with a patu pounamu (short-handled weapon) in his right hand, went forward to fight the stranger who had dared to break his calabashes.

When he reached the bath, he cried, "Kei whea te tangata i wahi nei i aku kiaka?" Where is the man who has dared to break my calabashes? Hine-moa knew the voice to be that of the love of her heart, and moved under an overhanging ledge of rock, for she did not want to be seen yet. She rejoiced within her heart to think that what she had done had brought out her lover to her, without her having to go to his house, having no clothes. Tutanekai felt round the edge of the bath until at last he caught her dripping hair and pulled her from under the ledge of rock, saying, "Ko wai tenei?" Who is this? Hinemoa answered, "Ko ahau, Tutanekai." It is I, Tutanekai. Tutanekai said, "Ko wai koe?" Who are you? She answered, "Ko au ko, Hinemoa," It is I, Hinemoa. Tutanekai exclaimed, "E! E! Hoake taua ki te whare," Come, let us go home. She replied, "Ae," Yes.

He took her hand and led her out of the bath. He saw how very beautiful she was. Her skin was like the tapukoraki,[1] and when she stood out of the water she was like a kotuku[1]. Tutanekai then took off one of his cloaks and covered her with it, and they walked to his house and slept there. This to the Maori signified marriage.

In the morning early the people rose to work and get ready the hangi to cook their food. After their food they missed Tutanekai, for he was still in his whare. His father said, "Katahi a te ata o Tutanekai, i moe roa ae," This is the first time that Tutanekai has slept so long. Perhaps my child is ill; go and call Tutanekai, that he may have some food.

A messenger went to call him. He slid the pihanga, that is the small wooden window, of the house, and looked in. He saw that Tutanekai had a companion, and wondered who it was, and hurried to tell Whakaue, who sent him back to make sure that he had made not a mistake. The messenger returned to Tutanekai's whare, and saw and recognised Hinemoa, and with that shouted, "Ko Hinemoa, ko Hinemoa te hoa o Tutanekai," Hinemoa, it is Hinemoa with Tutanekai!

When his elder brothers heard this, they would not believe it, and said, "He hori, he hori," for they were very jealous of Tutanekai.

Just then, Tutanekai came forth from his whare, with Hinemoa beside him. His people could hardly believe their own eyes, but when they looked across the lake, they saw several war canoes coming from the direction of Owhata. They knew it was Umu-karia, Hinemoa's father, with his people, coming across, as they thought, to take Hinemoa away. They expected war, but when Umukaria and his people came, instead of war, there was great rejoicing, and peace was made.

Hinemoa and Tutanekai lived happily ever after, and many of the people who live in and around Rotorua and the near lakes are descended from them. My own genealogy from Hinemoa is as follows:

```
          TAMATEKAPUA (chief and captain of the canoe Arawa in the
                |                              great migration)
          KAHUMATOMOMOE
                |
          TAWAKEMOETAHANGA
                |
          RANGITIHI
                |
          TUHOURANGI
                |
          TAKETAKEHIKUROA
                |
          TUTEA
                |
          UMUKARIA = Hinemaru
                |
  _____
  |                        |
WAHIAO              Hinemoa (a famous Puhi) = TUTANEKAI
                                                  |
                                          TE WHATUMAIRANGI
                                                  |
                                          HURUNGATERANGI
                                                  |
                                          WHATUMAIRANGI II
                                                  |
                                          MOKEMOKE
                                                  |
                                          TE AWAIMANUKAU
                                                  |
                                          TE AONUI
                                                  |
                                          Maata
                                                  |
                                          IHAIA
                                                  |
                                          Pia te Ngarotu
                                                  |
                                          Makereti (the writer)
                                                  |
                                          TE AONUI
```

There was great love between Hinemoa and Tutanekai, and many years afterwards, when Tutanekai passed away, Hinemoa sang her broken-hearted waiata for her lover husband who was always dear to her, a song sung to this day at a tangi when a descendant of hers has lost a husband.

HE TANGI NA HINEMOA MO TANA TANE MO TUTANEKAI

Te tau, e, te tau a te rau, ka wehe ia au, e,

Aha i wehe ai? Ka uru kei roto, te niho o Mokoroa,

Rarahu tuana, i ona peke ngaruhu,

Tangi ana, te wheoro, ki te tuakiri,

He whana taua nei, te wa o te mamae,

Tikina mai au, whaka waireka tia,

Kia hoki ake ai, te korou, ki te ao; e,

E kore hoki ake, he ngati mate pea; e,

Keria mai au, ki te ruahaeroa, e,

A ngaro ai ra, te wairua.

Ritual defloration

In days gone by when a puhi, a girl of very high family, was given in marriage, ritual defloration was practised on her, generally by her kuia.[1] In my possession is a whakakai (ear ornament) called "Ahi-wharau", which was owned by Maihi te Kakau-paraoa, my old koroua,[1] and which he always wore in his ear. This whakakai was used in ritual defloration on several female members of our family, in days gone by, when they were given in marriage.

Moral tone of family life

There was no law against cohabiting before marriage, and

because of this, it seldom happened. The Maori man was not lustful. It was the usual thing for a family and other relatives to sleep together in one whare. There was no privacy in a Maori home, such as is known in an English home. Conditions made it imperative that the children should sleep in the same room as their parents, and probably their grandparents. But I should like to emphasize the fact that this did not result, as strangers often suppose, in any lowering of the moral tone. The reason for this is that children were not curious about things which were treated in a matter-of-fact way. Every phase of life was freely discussed by the parents in the presence of the children, even things which western people deem most intimate. This could be so because there was no such thing as mock modesty among the Maori people. In their vocabulary there was no word considered rude; in the body there was nothing unclean; no bodily functions were treated as being unworthy of mention in plain language. To this admirable frankness, the high moral standing of the people is probably traceable. The morality of the race was high, and as already written, the marriage ceremony was just a ceremonial handing over of the bride. But in spite of this, misconduct after marriage was extremely rare, and universally censured.

No prostitution

Various misunderstandings

The Maori had no practice equivalent to that which is among Europeans called prostitution. I have seen it written by people who did not know the language or customs of the Maori that Maori women have sold themselves. I say, and with emphasis, that this is absolutely untrue. A Maori woman would never have sold herself for money, never! She might give herself to a man if she loved him, for there was no law against this, but never for any other reason. In the far back days of the early visits of the pakeha (European) to New Zealand, a pakeha rangatira has asked a chief for his daughter, and he has handed her over with ceremony to him to be his wife. The pakeha no doubt laid down a present when he asked for her, being told that it was the custom of the people. When the girl was handed over to him, the presents that accompanied her would be of much greater value than anything that had been given. It does not mean, that because the pakeha made a present of a few nails or an axe, that he was buying the girl. The reader has only to read our marriage customs to see this. These early writers spoke of things that they did not understand. The old chiefs treated a pakeha rangatira with the great respect due to his rank, and treated him as they would treat one of their own chiefs. The pakeha did not know the customs of the language of the Maori, and judged the Maori according to European customs.

Much has also been written about the Maori and the sailors of the early days. A Maori girl would not have anything to do with a sailor or any other man unless she got to know him and they became friends. This friendship would have ripened into something more before she would have any intercourse with him. She would probably mention the matter to her parents, and with their consent, her father would hand her over to the man, treating him as he would one of his own people. To the Maori, kua moe raua, they were husband and wife. That girl would not dream of having any other man than the one she slept with. She would not give herself to any pakeha who came along. The Maori did not do this. Such behaviour may occur to-day under the deteriorating influence of western civilization, but to suggest that such a thing was done in the time of our old people—I emphatically say No! I feel sure, knowing my people as I do, that even at the present day, our Maori women would not sell themselves for money. There are many pakeha rangatira to-day who know and love the Maori who will bear me out in what I say, and only the people who do not know the Maori and his customs will make such false assertions. It is not any more difficult to defend the way of living of certain types in those old days than it would be to defend that of certain of the European women in Limehouse to-day. Morality is not confined to any one race. Some of the lower type of Maori may have consorted with sailors of a like nature as certain English women with foreign seamen in this country. One does not form an opinion of the womanhood of England from the conduct of these unfortunates.

A Maori custom misunderstood by some writers and other Europeans

It is the custom for Maori friends to sit with their arms around each other, two girls, or a girl with a boy or man, and they treated their pakeha friends in the same way out of pure friendship. The pakeha rangatira understood them thoroughly, and never dream of taking any liberties with them. The ignorant pakeha man or woman, not usually a rangatira, observing this custom, often drew wrong conclusions, and likened the Maori to themselves. They condemned us as utterly lost and beyond redemption, without first finding out what the customs of the Maori were.

The incident of Bishop Selwyn misconstrued by later writers

Much has been written about the courtesy shown by the chief Manunui towards Bishop Selwyn. The chief looked upon the Bishop as a Tohunga[1] who was very tapu, and sent handmaidens to look after him and feed him. When the handmaidens went to attend the Bishop, they found him praying, and waited until he had finished. When he arose from his knees and saw them, he was horrified, thinking that they had been sent as wives. He did not know the Maori custom, nor did the Maori know his. The chief, thinking that he had made a mistake in sending only two to wait upon so great a Tohunga, sent four or five. The chief acted in good faith and so did the Bishop in sending the girls away. The assignment of domestics and handmaidens by our old Maori hosts to their guests was merely an act of courtesy not dissimilar to that of the English host whose servants and family wait upon the pleasure of a guest. It is unfortunate that this action of the chief inspired by the dictates of courtesy should have been misinterpreted by baser minds. The old Maori was a gentleman, and assumed that his guests were no less. But from some of the things that have been written, it might appear that he was wrong in his assumption.

Taua Puremu

When a woman was married, she was tapu. It was seldom that she forgot it, but if she did, especially if she was a wahine rangatira, the utu, i.e. payment for this sin, was generally her life. For this was considered a very great crime indeed, the puremu (adultery) of a wahine maronui (married woman). In many instances the man was also killed by the husband. The husband's people would hold a taua at the home of the woman, and her whanau and hapu would give payment for the hara (sin). A taua puremu, that is a raiding party for the adultery of a married woman, had to be paid with big things such as her life, land, green-stone weapons and ornaments, various cloaks, and other valuables. Many taua parties might come, relatives of the husband who belong to other hapu. Taonga, and many taonga had to be given, not only by the woman's hapu, but by the man's hapu. A puremu like this of a wahine maronui who was a rangatira often caused a war.

When such a taua happened, her hapu would be stripped of all the valuables they possessed, but they never murmured. They gave what they had freely to try to wipe out this debt of honour. No matter what the raiding parties did or said, her people said nothing in her defence. They just welcomed the taua parties in the usual way, and treated them with great hospitality, as was their custom, and gave them of the best in the larder. Through their relatives committing this sin, the disgrace came upon them all.

Account of an eye-witness

In the old days taua puremu seldom happened. I saw one as a small child, and did not see another for many years afterwards. The one I saw as quite a small child at Te Awa a te Atua was unforgettable.

In the early morning the cry went round the kainga, "Kua puremu tia a mea," So and So has committed adultery with So and So. Long before daylight the stamping of feet could be heard keeping time to the takitaki, the leading song of a woman who led the taua party of a hundred people or more. There were the women in front. Then came the injured husband who was naked, with only two long plaits of torori (plaited tobacco leaf) hanging in front suspended from a cord of fibre which circled his waist. His face was traced with charcoal, he wore feathers in his hair, and in his right hand was his patu pounamu. The women had their skirts tucked above their knees, and as they led the haka taua, it was a terrifying sight, yet a wonderful one.

With movements of the body, pukana (eyes rolling), and tongue out, the taua party advance, all the while doing the haka movements led by the women, keeping rhythmic time with their feet and hands, and joining in words repeated in answer to their leader—words appropriate to the hara (sin) committed. The taua advance on the marae, where the tangata whenua all gathered together in front of the wharepuni, greet them with cries of "Haeremai, haeremai!" Welcome, welcome! As the party draw nearer, they repeat the haka appropriate for the occasion, demanding to know the reason why this woman had done this great wrong in giving her sacred body to another man. "He aha te take? He aha te take?" What is the reason? why? why?

The people of the kainga look on in silence and shame for this awful thing which had been done by a woman belonging to them. Although she committed the offence, the disgrace covers all her hapu, and is felt by them. So the taua goes on until at last the taua party have said all they wish to say and have sung all the songs they wish to sing and have danced all the haka dances for a taua.

Then the chiefs of the tangata whenua make speeches welcoming the visitors, while the women bring taonga (valuable presents) and lay them in heaps on the marae until there is a large heap, perhaps two large heaps. Men bring weapons and lay them on the whariki (floor-mats) beside the other taonga. Others call out in a loud voice that their whanau is giving so much land in such and such a place. Many heirlooms are given, and the presentation goes on until many taonga of great value are given.

After the taua party is served with food, it returns home with the taonga. Several taua parties come from different hapu to which the husband belongs, and in such a case, the wife's people are stripped of all their valuable possessions.

It was very seldom that a married woman puremu. When it did happen, and taua occurred, the marriage tie was broken. The dissolution of a Maori marriage was done by the taua. After a taua both parties were free to marry someone else. If there were children, they decided themselves as to whom they should go. There was no law making them go to one or the other party, and neither the father nor mother would influence them in making their decision.

Children of divorced parents

Pakeha marriage

Many rangatira Englishmen, Scotchmen, and Irishmen married wahine rangatira in the old days after the custom of the Maori people, from about 1840, the time of the treaty of Waitangi, or a little earlier. A pakeha rangatira would fall in love with a chief's daughter and ask the chief for her hand, and hearing of the custom of giving presents, would present blankets, axes, and other things. The chief would discuss the matter with his whanau, and if the girl was willing, she was handed over with ceremony with presents of cloaks, greenstone ornaments, weapons, and many acres of valuable land. There were many such marriages, and although the ceremony was just a handing over of the bride, the couple lived together very happily until the end of their days, often rearing a large family. The Maori woman was a most affectionate and faithful wife, and generally lived for her husband and children. There were and are many of these rangatira Englishmen who belong to noble families in England who have married Maori wives and they and their wives have been devotedly attached to each other for fifty, sixty, or more years.

Children

The children of such a union are a fine type, the girls being pretty, and many beautiful with olive skin, rosy cheeks, and brown eyes and hair. Some of them have very fair complexions with blue eyes and flaxen hair, the hair becoming brown as the child grows older. The boys have the same complexions and hair, and are generally very good looking, with fine physique, and strong and healthy. They are fond of sport. The children are quick to learn, and many of them hold important and high positions in New Zealand in the social and political world.

There are also marriages between ordinary pakeha and Maori women which are very happy and which last for life. These men also had families and made good husbands.

Maori men and pakeha women

In all the pakeha and Maori marriages, it was the woman who married a pakeha. The Maori man would not have anything to do with a wahine pakeha. Such marriages were very rare. One case which I know is that of the chief from Ngapuhi, who visited England, and before he returned, married a pakeha woman. I never heard of one case among Te Arawa people. I often asked my uncles why this did not happen, and their answers were very funny. English people would not understand the reason, even if I wrote it.

A pakeha man, whether a rangatira, or not,[1] would, if he was enterprising, build a home for himself and his wife on the land that she brought him, and they would get on in the world. There were some of course who would not work, but lived on the Maori in the kainga. They sometimes drank to excess, and taught their Maori wife and her people to drink. This was very sad in the old days.

Then there were the men who went to New Zealand and settled for a few years, and married Maori women according to Maori custom. The pakeha would know and think that this was only a temporary affair, but to the Maori woman, he was her tane (husband) for all time. In due course, he would return to his own country with promises that he would soon return. He would leave without making any provision for his wife or family, but the wife would not think of this. All she thought of was that her husband should have enough for his wants on the journey back to his country so that he could travel comfortably. Indeed she often sold things belonging to her to help him. Of herself she never thought, or her children. She knew that her people would never let them want. There were many such cases, when the wife after years of waiting died of a broken heart.

The pakeha husband learned the Maori language from his wife, and more important still, learned from her what not to do, according to Maori custom. This was really important, because such ignorance of Maori custom was the cause of many of the troubles in the old days between the pakeha and the Maori. A man's wife's people backed him up in all that he did, but he did not always try to help the Maori.

The pakeha husband often taught his Maori wife the ways of attending to a pakeha house, of cooking his food, and how to understand, and sometimes to speak his language. In most instances, the wahine Maori tried her very best to carry out his wishes, and in many cases she succeeded.

The marriages nowadays are different. The husband and wife are joined together by the laws of the pakeha. But I doubt if these marriages are happier than those of the old days, or more binding than the old Maori custom of handing over the bride with ceremonial.

[1] Rangatira, i.e. chiefs, well-born, people of standing and worth in the community.

[1] V. cap. I, p. 43.

[1] V. cap. I, p. 47.

[1] V. cap. IV, p. 166, 172.

[1] V. cap. VII, p. 322, and pp. 11–14.

[1] Border on ends larger than at sides.

[1] Incantation or make an incantation.

[1] A Woman's body may remain in her husband's country, so long as any of his family live there.

[1] V. cap. I, p. 49.

[1] See p. 46.

[1] For definition of tribe, hapu, and whanau, v. cap. I, pp. 33 ff.

[1] She was fair and graceful. Tapukoraki is the name of a bird;

te kotuku is the white heron.

[1] For kuia and koroua, v. cap. I p. 47.

[1] Priestly expert.

[1] Some of the pakeha in the old days were tino rora, pretty low down. Some were sailors who deserted their ships, and some wanted to settle down and start in a new country. A Maori would claim one of these as his pakeha, thinking that he might help him to deal with the pakeha traders. The pakeha would be free in personal matters, but in anything which affected the hapu, he had to conform to the rules of the kainga. He was a pakeha Maori, and one of them. Then there were the pakeha tino taurekareka (very low down indeed) who visited New Zealand in whaling vessels in the very earliest days. For the most part they congregated at Kororareka in the North, and in Cook's Straits on the North Island side. Their behaviour shocked the Maori although he was called a savage. Their drunken orgies, debauchery, filthy language, immorality, and vileness were a disgrace to the pakeha. If these vile creatures were the type of pakeha which the Maori of those parts saw, can you wonder that he classed all pakeha as such? Is it to be wondered at that some of the Maori learned to drink, and to use vile the words which he thought were the proper language of the pakeha?

I must apologize to the reader for what I am about to say, but in view of what one writer has published, I feel that I must discuss the subject frankly, in order to answer him adequately. This writer publishes the mistakes which a Maori makes when he tries to speak the English language. What a lot of fun they make of the poor uncivilized Maori, and how they take him off! These people forget that the Maori did much better in trying to speak English than many Englishmen who tried to speak the Maori tongue; only we don't publish these things nor make fun of the pakeha. Rangatira people don't do this sort of thing. With pride is published the fact that a South Island man in replying to questions gave replies full of the word "bloody", a word learned from the pakeha. Some place was named Bloody Jack's Island after him. The writer should have added that "bloody" was not a Maori word, but a word frequently used by the people he met, people whose every other word was a vile oath. The writer also forgot to mention that the Maori hearing nothing but "Bugger yer" every few seconds, and repeated so often by the pakeha when speaking to him, felt sure that the expression was something very important to the white man, and so christened him pakeha, which is the nearest that he could get to the expression with the consonants and vowels at his disposal. There may be other reasons why the white man is called pakeha, but I have often heard from my old people that this is the reason for the name.

III

CHILDREN

Child-birth Whakawhanau

WHEN A MARRIAGE took place in the old days, one of the most important things in the minds of the couple was the children they would have. The Maori were anxious to have children, as many as they could have. Whether boys or girls, they were all welcomed, no matter to what class they belonged. If it happened that a wahine rangatira (woman of rank, who was married to a tangata rangatira (man of rank) became hapu (pregnant) with her first child, this important event was hailed with great rejoicing and ceremonial feasting. Gifts were brought and presented to the young mother, in the way of choice foods, so that she might feed her child that it might be born strong and healthy. If she longed for any kind of food, it was procured for her, no matter how difficult it was to get. Sometimes this meant expeditions to a distant part of the forest or country, and in the old days these expeditions were difficult, as there were no conveyances, and in many cases, no roads. These foods, although procured for the mother, were really for the child. If she lived by the sea, she might long for inland foods such as kereru (pigeon) or other birds, or inanga and other small fish from the lakes. This food not only helped to feed the child, but helped the mother to get plenty of milk in her breasts.

Care of mother

Whakawhanau

Generally whakawhanau or giving birth to a child was not a matter to worry over, and a Maori woman of the old days did not suffer or go through the same painful experience as the wahine pakeha (European woman). She lived a natural life and generally went about doing her ordinary duties up to a few days before her confinement, when she left the kainga to live in a small temporary place which was built for her. Here she would live with someone who saw to her wants in carrying food from the kainga. The food would be brought halfway from the kainga by someone who had cooked it, and the attendant would get the food from there. A woman was considered tapu (unclean) for a certain time before and after confinement, that is, until after the Tua or Tohi had taken place about seven or eight days after the birth of the child.

Tapu condition of mother

When the time came for the mother to whakamamae, have

labour pains, her mother, grandmother, and other relatives were with her, especially if it were her first child. They would sit close to her as she knelt in front of the hunga whaka whanau iaia, the one who was attending to her. The attendant sat on the ground of the whare (a temporary structure) with her knees up to her chin. The young mother knelt in front of her with her legs apart, while the attendant pressed her knees lightly on the upper part of the poho (abdomen) of the patient, thus helping to force the child downward. As each pain comes, the attendant puts her arms round the body of the the patient, and pulls her forward gently against her knees. As the pains get stronger, she presses her knees in harder, encouraging her with the words "Kia kaha e whae", Be brave, O mother. And the relatives looking on say the same. Not a murmur comes from the patient, no matter how great the pain, for what is pain but nothing, when she is giving her husband the son or daughter which he so desires? The presence of her mother and relatives close to her helps her greatly to bear the pain. She must be brave just as they were, and her forbears before her. And when the great moment comes and the child is born, she will say, "He aha ai?" What is it? But whether it is a boy or a girl, it is welcomed.

The new-born child

The infant is then shaken with its feet up and its head down to loosen the nanu (secretion) in its mouth and nose. The attendant or one of the relatives would then draw out any remaining nanu by placing her mouth over the nose or mouth of the infant, and taking a deep inward breath. This relieved the infant of all the thick fluid which might be in its nose and mouth, and prevented the child from having an ihu hupe or secretion in its nose, or from being whango (having a husky voice) when it grew up. If a child does not cry when it is born, it is shaken to make it cry. If anything was needed to soften the pito, which sometimes looks sore, a piece of soft cloth was soaked in the oil from the kernel of the titoki berry, and placed over the pito before wrapping the child in old pueru cloth. The soft old cloth would be an old woven korowai[1] or korohunga.[1]

Early care

A Maori infant did not use the clothes which are needed for pakeha children. Indeed there was only one garment used, and that was the one wrapped round his little body. The child was then placed on the whariki, floor mat, without mattress or pillow, and was quite happy and comfortable.

The mother

The placenta

When the attendant has finished with the infant, she turns her attention again to the mother, who in the meantime has been waiting for the whenua, i.e. the placenta, to come away. During the short time that the attendant was spending with the child, one of the relatives would support the young mother until she was ready. Sometimes the afterbirth comes quickly, and in some cases takes a long time. When it comes away the whenua is taken by the mother, aunt, or other close relative to a secret place already chosen and ready to receive it. It is there buried. If the whenua does not come away as it should, the patient is sometimes taken to a running stream—she would walk herself—and here she would lie in shallow water, and the attendant would stand on her poho, first on one foot and then on the other till the whenua and all the parapara (blood) has come away. She would then walk back to the whare where her relatives were. After this she would be considered well enough to attend to the infant and to herself.

Infants brought up at the breast

Her û (breasts) which had received special attention during the months of her pregnancy would have the waiu (milk) flowing easily, and so the child is fed from the breast soon after it is born. In the old days the û were mirimiri, massaged, and also the matamata, nipples, and a Maori mother never had the difficulty of the women who have come in contact with civilization. When a woman became hapu, her breasts were attended to from three months after right up to the birth of the child.

An infant was always brought up on its mother's breast in the old days unless the mother died, and then a foster mother who also had an infant was looked for, and she would bring up the two babies.

Whare ngaro

Sometimes of course a child is born dead. This would mean that the mother had broken some law of tapu, or it might be a case of makutu (witchcraft). When a woman loses all her children at birth, and none are born alive, it is called a whare ngaro, a house extinct or a lost house, and with the very rangatira people, this is considered a terrible tragedy. A Tohunga would be in attendance to perform karakia at each birth, and if it should happen that a child was born alive, it would be taken right away from the mother, and brought up by a foster mother. With my mother's family it was like this. Several of the children of Makereta my grandmother died at birth or soon after, and when Rakera, the ninth child, was born alive, she was taken away by Maihi Te Kakauparaoa and his wife, who brought her up, and the same thing happened later when my mother was born, and also Hoana who came after her. They were taken away from the mother by her father's brother and his wife, who in later years took me when I was born, and brought me up.

Care of children

A Maori woman generally suckled her child till it was able to run about, and sometimes long after this. I have known children still at the breast when over two years old.

Illegitimacy

The old Maori did not look on illegitimacy as the European did. It was not a common occurrence among the old Maori, but if a child should happen to be a poriro, he would not be thought less of than other members of a family. If a man knew that a girl was hapu, and he was unmarried, he took her as his wife, as cases like this only happened when the parents had not consented. Thus the child would be born in wedlock, as the pakeha say. A man never deserted a girl who had a child by him, even if he were married. Either he or his people would take the child, or she would bring it up herself. But in any case the father generally claimed it. Other members of the whanau (family group) might take the child and bring it up, and it would be well looked after, and would own shares in land and property like the other children.

Attendants only for first child

In the old days women could attend to themselves if need be, and were able to stand a great deal more than they can now under the altered conditions. In many cases a woman was attended to only with her first child, when she learned what to do. It was not always possible to have someone to attend her during confinement. Women were quite capable of attending to themselves even up to quite recent times. My mother's sister Hoana married into another hapu (see *hapu* page 34 in chapter on Social Organization), and when she was hapu and getting near her time of whakawhanau, she came home to my kuia and koroua at Whakarewarewa. She was attended for her first child only. But after that she came home as usual, and no one ever attended to her, and no one knew anything about it until she appeared with her infant after a few hours' absence in a whare. It was the same with her daughter Karaihe who died only a few years ago. She, like her mother, had all the necessary things ready, the kakahi shell with which to cut the umbilical cord, and the string for tying it. Whereas in the old days a woman would have a branch of a tree to help her, Karaihe had an empty box which she placed by the side of the whare. She tipped the case so that the top edge would come on to the top of her poho (abdomen). As each pain came she pressed herself against the edge of the box until the child came. She then attended to cutting the cord and tying it, and after making the infant comfortable, attended to herself, the most important thing being the whenua (placenta) which should all come away with the parapara. She had all of her children in this way except the first one, and then the last. But the story of her last child is too long and sad to repeat here.

118

Hine-te-iwaiwa and Hine-Korako

Child-birth and everything connected with it were under the care of the beings Hine-te-iwaiwa and Hine-Korako, who personified the moon. In the old days when a woman was matewahine or mate marama (monthly sickness), she was considered tapu or unclean, and this term was also used when a woman was going to give birth to a child, and up to seven or eight days after.

Matewahine

Frequency of children

A Maori woman did not have children quickly as Europeans do, and was generally married two or three years or more before having her first child, and there would be about the same number of years between successive children.

If a first-born child died in infancy, the parents would ask a Tohunga to perform karakia over the next one when it was born, so as to save its life.

Love of children

From the time of its birth and all through life till his death, the life of a Maori was surrounded with racial and family traditions. The Maori had very great love for their children. It was a great unselfish love which nothing could weaken. I doubt if any other race could surpass them in their love for their children.

Number of children

I have never heard of a Maori having triplets or more children. They occasionally had mahanga (twins), and sometimes a huatahi (only child). Years ago it was not a common thing for a married couple to have no children. It has become more common since there has been contact with civilization.

The old Maori had no method to prevent children coming, such as those practised by civilized peoples. When a woman had a very large family, a Tohunga would be asked to speak a karakia over her to prevent any more children coming. This was known as the tuapa rite. I have heard that women who were childless (pukupa) carried and nursed a kind of wooden dummy made in the shape of a child, and sang lullabies over it as they would to living children. I have read what writers have written about their nursing the pig as a child and suckling it. I do not think this is possible, as pigs were killed and eaten.[1]

Childless women

The hei-tiki was supposed to be worn in the very old days for the purpose of causing a woman to conceive. The hei-tiki was always worn by a wahine rangatira, a woman of high birth, in the very old days hidden under her cloak or other garment. Most of these heirlooms were never seen. A woman who was childless would also stand astride over the whenua (placenta) of a newly born infant so that she might conceive. If she wanted a son, she would stand over the whenua of a male infant. When Tane took Hinetitama the Dawn Maid as a wife, he recited a long karakia so that it would cause her to conceive. This is a very old karakia.

Difficult or premature births

In the case of a difficult birth, a karakia was repeated by a Tohunga. The first karakia repeated over a difficult birth was repeated over Hine-te-iwaiwa, and was called "Ko te Tuku O Hine-te-iwaiwa". It was often repeated over a wahine rangatira when having difficult birth. This karakia was repeated over Rangiuru, the wife of Whakaue, the chief who lived on Mokoia Island, when she was giving birth to Tutanekai who married Hinemoa. A case of premature birth seldom happened in the old days, and when it did, was supposed to be caused by the mother's breaking the laws of tapu. A Tohunga then had to perform a karakia Takutaku over the woman to send away the wairua (spirit) of the unformed child, which was supposed to fly about in space—or it might enter a mokomoko (lizard)—and do harm to living people. A wairua of this kind, having never been properly formed, would never know any feeling of affection or love, and so would only try to do harm. It was the belief that in far back ancient times a child who was born dead or through whakatake (miscarriage) was thrown in the water, and fish ate of it, and became harmful atua to men, women, and children. The woman was again pregnant, and the child was dead within her, and there was a miscarriage. This child was buried in the ground, and its flesh was eaten by the things who live in the ground and by the birds from the heavens. These beings remain as atua, the beings who do great harm to living men, women, and children, although they are not important gods.

Various beliefs about children

Sometimes a child would be born feet first. He would be called a whanau waewae (born feet first), and was sure to grow up mischievous and full of tricks. In old times a woman was often able to tell the sex of her child before birth through its movements during pregnancy. The movements of a male child were vigorous and quite different from the movements of a female child. If the dark parts of the breasts extended only a short distance from the nipples, it would be a boy; if they extended much further, it would be a girl.

Deformity

Sometimes a deformed child would be born, such as a tuara hake, hunch-back, or waewae hape, with deformed or turned in feet, but this did not often happen. I have only known two cases of deformed feet in the whole of my own hapu of Tuhourangi. (See the genealogy[1] and the account of hapu in my chapter on Social Organization.)

Urukehu, the red haired children with fair skin

Among children who are born there are the Urukehu who have very fair skin and reddish coloured hair. The Urukehu is a very old strain among the Maori, and was brought with them from Hawaiki (the distant home) by our ancestors. The origin of it is not known to the Maori of to-day. This strain still goes through certain families.

In my hapu of Ngati Wahiao we have one family, whose picture is shown in Plate XIII. Tonihi is an Urukehu, but his wife is not, and yet all their children are Urukehu like the one in the picture. Rihari Te Taru, father of Tonihi, was also an Urukehu. The child of Tonihi by his first marriage was not Urukehu, but every one of the several children by his second wife was Urukehu.

Albinism

Albinism also occurred among the Maori, but very seldom. I knew of one case when I was a child. She came from Ngapuhi. She always spoke of her father as an atua, a Turehu, one of the fair-haired people who live in the mist. Her mother was an ordinary Maori. The girl used to hold conversations with her Turehu father, an unseen being, during the night, a thing which terrified me. These Turehu (albino) children are supposed to be born of an ordinary Maori mother and a patupaiarehe father, and are termed Turehu. Patupaiarehe is sometimes termed Turehu, and Urukehu is sometimes termed

Turehu, but patupaiarehe and Urukehu are generally the words used in each case, and Turehu is sometimes used. The patupaiarehe spoken of to me by my kuia are supernatural children of the mist. They are seen in indistinct form in the passing mist. Their principal dwelling places are on the high mountains where they live in great numbers. These dimly seen beings passing in the mist are seen to advantage after the rain has stopped. They are fair, and are clothed in flimsy white like the web of the pungaiwerewere (spider).

Patupaiarehe

Modesty

It was very difficult in the past to get a Maori woman to allow a pakeha doctor to attend her in any illness, and almost impossible in a case of childbirth, as no one but her husband must touch a Maori woman. She would rather die than allow a doctor to touch her. The Maori woman was very modest, although I have seen it written by some "pokokohua pakeha"[1] that she was otherwise. This I say again, and emphasize the fact, that a Maori woman of the old order would die rather than let a man see her puke, or feel her, unless the man were her husband. I can name many who have died rather than allow a doctor to touch them. One of my own relatives, a beautiful girl who lived three generations ago, comes to my mind. Because she would not have a man who wanted her as his wife, the man lay in wait for a chance of seeing her, thinking that if he saw her puke she might have him. His chance came, and he did see her, but she whakamomori, died rather than see him. She could not survive the shame of the thought that a man had seen her virgin puke. The people of old were like that. My old kuia Marara told me of this, and of many other things with regard to our tupuna (ancestors) and relatives of her mother's time, and of others before her.

Tua or Tohi

When an infant was seven or eight days old, or when the pito (cord)[1] fell away, the tua or tohi took place. This was a cleansing ceremony, or taking away of the tapu from the mother and child, and was also a dedication of the infant to the care of the gods. The tohi was not a baptismal ceremony as used by Europeans at the christening of a child, although the naming of the child occurred at the end of the ceremony. Through this tohi ceremony a male child was made tapu, and this tapu was greater than the tapu of a female infant. The tohi for one was not the same as that for the other. Just as there was one whakatuputupu repeated over a male infant to make him grow strong, so was there a different whakatuputupu repeated for a female child. There was a karakia pure repeated over a male child, and a different pure was repeated over a female child. The tohi or tua repeated over a male child made him very tapu, as he was endowed with tapu and mana which

125

came direct from the gods, and the many heavenly beings who dwelt in the heavens, and the many beings from above, from Tawhirimatea, and from the many beings below, and from the many many beings in Hawaiki. This tapu prevented a man from doing many things which were only done by the women, a fact which caused many ignorant writers to say how lazy our men were, and how the women were made to work. The tua repeated over a female infant was different. She received only part of the mana from nga atua, the gods, half from the heavenly beings in the heavens, and half from the many many beings in Hawaiki. A female infant was made noa, so that she was able to carry food on her back, to cook food, to gather shell-fish from the sea sand, and to do many things which the men were unable to do on account of their tapu.

For a male child

For a female

The tohi was repeated over all infants, but if the infant was the first-born son of tangata rangatira,[1] i.e. people of high rank, there was much ceremonial attached to it, even from the time that the mother became hapu. She was waited upon by her husband's people, if she lived with them, and was not allowed to do any hard work. There was general rejoicing in the hapu. When the time came for her to whaka whanau (bear her child), a special whare (temporary house) was made for

126

her to move into, and there she would stay with one or two women relatives who attended to all her needs. When her child was seven or eight days old, the Tohunga (Plate XIV) would perform the tua or tohi over it.

The ceremony

The ceremony took place in the early morning, before anyone had partaken of food, in a running stream, at some hidden spot which faced the rising sun. The people who attended the ceremony were the parents, grandparents and near relatives of the child, and one or two Tohunga. When they reached the place arranged for, the parents would stand in front by the stream, with their parent behind them, and so on. The Tohunga, who had taken off his kakahu (cloak), went into the stream wearing only a rapaki (apron) of green leaves, until the water reached his pito, navel. He held branches of the green karamu (Coprosma robusta) in his right hand, and with his ringa maui (left hand) which he formed into a cup, he took up some water and began to karakia, telling Parawhenua, the personified form of water, that he now stood as one with her.[1] Then a karakia was directed to Io-matua, i.e. Io the parent, saying that he was a tapu and learned person in all ritual matters, and that he was now a qualified person to carry out this tapu ceremony, and that he places the child under the mana of the gods. He then dips the karamu branch in the water for a moment, then turns to take the infant from the mother who has been holding the child with its head resting on her right arm. He and the child turn and face the rising sun, and he repeats the karakia that the child he holds is now dedicated to nga atua in the heavens, at these waimatua virgin waters of Tawhirimatea of Ihorangi, of Papa-tu-amiku, and of Para-whenua-mea. After this he repeats the name which has been given to the infant. With his left hand the Tohunga covers the mouth and nostrils of the child, then slips down in the water for a moment so that he and the child are covered. When the child went under the water with the Tohunga, he was freed from all the evil influences of the earth, and was directly under the mana of the gods.

This ends the tua ceremony, and the Tohunga hands the child to its father, who hands it to the mother who stands on his left. The party then return to the kainga (village), and as they get near to the kainga, the assistant Tohunga repeats the whakaaraara which tells the people at the kainga that the tua ceremony is over. Cries of "Haeremai, haeremai", Welcome, welcome, rend the air from the many people at the kainga who have all gathered to prepare a ceremonial feast. After the arrival, the Tohunga repeats another karakia asking that the child may have of the best in future, and in this the people join in a short response at the end. Then there is a ceremonial feast in which the parents, grandparents, and near relatives eat their foot apart from the other people.

Karakia

The following karakia was one which a Tohunga would repeat during the tua or tohi, a cleansing and dedication ceremony, while standing in the water. All these karakia are very archaic, and it is beyond one's power to translate them into English, as so many of the words are obsolete, and the meaning not now known. It would be wrong to attempt a word for word translation, but I will give some idea of what this karakia meant. It was said so that the child might be endowed with health, courage, and strength, so that he would catch the enemy, be able to climb mountains, to fight and to hold the enemy, to kill the enemy, to storm a fortified pa, to rise and kill the enemy, to fight in a field of battle where many men are killed, to be brave and to be able to hold and use a stone patu (short weapon), to be able to use and wield the taiaha (long-handled weapon), to be able to go up great mountains, to climb proud trees, the great proud trees of the forest, to brave the great high waves of the ocean, and overcome the dangers of the sea.

Then, as though addressing the infant, To work and get yourself food, to make a large house for yourself, to make a war canoe, to be hospitable and call visitors to your marae (plaza), to make fishing nets for yourself, to trawl for fish, to surround yourself with plenty of work.[1]

Such is the general meaning of the following karakia, KO TE TUA, MO TE TANE, tua or tohi repeated over a male child.

For a male child

Tohi ki te wai no Tu;

Whano koe.

Tangaengae.

Ki te hopu tangata

Tangaengae.

Ki te piki maunga,

Tangaengae.

Me homai, tangaengae,

Mo te tama nei.

Whano koe.

Tangaengae.

Kia riri, ai,

Tangaengae.

Kia niwha ai,

Tangaengae.

Ki te patu tangata,

Tangaengae.

Ki te tomo pa,

Tangaengae.

Ki te patu whakaara,

Tangaengae.

Ki te tu parekura.

Tangaengae.

Kia riri ai

Tangaengae.

Kia toa ai,

Tangaengae.

Ki te mau patu Kowhatu,

Tangaengae.

     Ki te mau taiaha

Tangaengae

Me ho mai, Tangaengae.

Hei whakatupu Tangaengae,

Mo te tama nei.

     Whano koe.

Tangaengae.

Ki nga maunga nunui,

Tangaengae.

Ki nga rakau whakahihi,

Tangaengae.

Ki nga rakau whakahihi o te wao.

Tangaengae.

Me ho mai Tangaengae.

Hei whakatupu tangaengae,

Mo te tama nei.

Whano koe,

Tangaengae.

Ki nga ngaru teitei, o te moana,

Tangaengae.

Kia turakina i tai,

Tangaengae.

Me ho mai tangaengae,

Hei whakatupu tangaengae,

Mo te Tama nei.

Whano koe,

Tangaengae.

Ki te mahi kai, mau.

Tangaengae.

Ki te hanga whare nui, mou

Tangaengae.

Ki te hanga waka taua,

Tangaengae.

Ki te Karanga pahi,

Tangaengae.

Ki te whakatupu kupenga, mau,

Tangaengae.

Ki te hi ika, mau,

Tangaengae.

Ki te hao mahi, mau,

Tangaengae.

Me homai tangaengae

Hei whakatupu tangaengae

Mo te tama nei.

    E ahua mai ra

Te toro, i a kiharoa,

Hei kawe rawa, i a au,

Ki te one, i Rangaunu,

Kei te rerenga, ki te Po;

Ko wai au ka kite,

Karakia kia ora ai, kia toa ai, kia kaha ai.

For a girl

If the infant was a girl, this was the tua repeated over her.

KO TE TUA MO TE WAHINE

Tohi ki te wai no Tu.

Whano koe.

Tangaengae

Ki te mahi kai mau

Tangaengae

Ki te whatu pueru mou

Tangaengae.

Ki te karanga pahi

Tangaengae.

Ki te waha watui mau

Tangaengae

Ki te keri mataitai mau

Tangaengae

Me homai tangaengae

Hei whakatupu tangaengae

Mo te tapairu nei.

E ahua mai ra

Te toro ia kiharoa

Hei kawe rawa ia hau

Ke te one Rangaunu

Kei te rerenga ki te Po

Kowai au ka kite.

This karakia was repeated over a female infant so that she might be endowed with health so as to be able to work and gather in food, to be able to weave the clothing, to be hospitable so that her voice was heard in welcoming visitors to the marae (plaza), to be able to carry loads of firewood on her back, to dig in the sand and gather shell-fish, etc.[1]

Dread of the line dying out

As I said before, one of the greatest things in the life of a couple was children, and plenty of them. It was a terrible thing for a man of high rank to let his kawai (line of descent) die out. For this reason, a chief of high standing sometimes had two, three, or more wives, and not, as is often stated, to show his importance and status. The number of wives he had made no difference to this, nor would the number of wives make him a rangatira. A tangata rangatira, i.e. a chief of high birth, was always an important person, and he was important in his very self. It was his own mana that made him important in the eyes of the people and made his reo (voice) heard. His importance had nothing whatever to do with the number of wives he had. If all her children die, a woman will ask her husband to take another wife so that she may bear him children. Should this happen, and the children come, the first wife will love the children as her own and help to bring them up. It was because the Maori had a great dread of his line of descent dying out that polygyny occurred among the very high chieftain class.

Polygyny

Care of infants

A Maori mother tends her baby from the day it is born, though she has many offers of help from relatives. She need never bring up any of her children, as the grandmothers and grandaunts always want to do it for her.[1] If the mother died, the baby would be fed from the breast of a relative who also had a young baby. The mother, as I have said, suckles her infant on the breast, sometimes until it is a year or even two years old. When weaning it, she sometimes rubs her breasts with the sap of the kawakawa (Somaria fluvialis), a fern which has a bitter taste.

The head, arms, legs, and body of the infant were massaged so that they would have a good shape, and the joints were massaged to make them supple. The fingers were bent backwards and forwards, and a female infant had the first joint of both thumbs pressed backwards, to make it easier for her to whatu, .e. weave clothing when she grew up. All Maori fingers have an upward turn from the palm, and are tapered and well shaped. The nose was pressed gently between the thumb and first finger from time to time to prevent the child from being parehe (flat-nosed). The legs were bandaged together fairly tightly to prevent them from being crooked, and the body was bound in the pueru (cloak) to keep the back straight. It was an unknown thing to see a round-shouldered or bow-legged Maori.

From a day old, the child is carried straight up on its mother's back. A pueru is passed round the child and crossed in front of the mother, and the ends are tied at the back under the child's tou, so that he sits against them. Sometimes, if the mother is doing nothing, she will hold the ends of the cloak in front. This way of carrying the child is very comfortable for the child and for the mother, and enables the mother to carry on her work with the child on her back.

An infant was taught to be clean from its birth, when it would be held out by an attendant or by its mother. The child soon learnt what was expected of it.

A mother could not bear to hear her child cry, especially at night. She would take it up in her arms and croon over it, singing oriori, or lullaby songs, to soothe it. The Maori had many of these songs, and some mothers made up their own, some being very beautiful and poetic. Their oriori over their dead children are most heart-rending, expressing the intensity of the grief they feel for the loss of their little ones. Many such songs have been made up by fathers.

First teaching

The first teaching is given when the child begins to crawl and walk. It will first try to get up by holding on to its mother's or grandmother's knee while she is sitting on the ground. The Maori always sat on the ground, the men tailor fashion, and the women with their knees up to their chins, or with the knees bent and almost touching the ground and their feet to the left underneath them, or with one knee up to the chin, and the other leg bent underneath. Sometimes a small enclosure with a rounded top was made in which the child might learn to use his limbs and to stand and walk, but this was seldom used.

Food

A child would still be at its mother's breast when it began to walk, and sometimes for a long time afterwards. A woman first gives the child food when it is nine months or more old, unless she has not much milk, then earlier. But a mother nearly always had plenty of milk for her child. When she gives ordinary food to her baby she is careful of what she gives it, and masticates it well before giving it to the child, either straight from her own mouth to the child's, or taken from her mouth with the two first fingers and thumb, and so given to the child. This method might be used until the child was weaned, and sometimes afterwards. The mortality among children was not high in pre-pakeha days. Only the weak ones perished, as the life the Maori led was a hard one.

Names

The first word a baby would learn would be its mother's name, and then its father's. Each parent had his or her name, and the child had its own name. There were no surnames. Sometimes a child would be called by the same name as his father, but this was seldom done, unless the father died. A son might take the name on the death of his father, but this was not usual. For example, a son's name might be Wahiao and his father's Umukaria, and all his descendants would have their own names, but never the same as his or his father's until, probably many generations later, the name might reappear. Children never said "mother", "father", "uncle", etc., like European children, but always addressed their relatives by their own names.

Care and early teaching

Maori children did not wear any clothes except the maro, an apron, which a boy wore from about the age of five or six or more, and a girl from about the age of five. They wore nothing on their feet or on their heads. An infant's hair was not cut. Its nails were not cut, but bitten off by its mother, and buried or hidden where no one could get at them.

The Maori never beat their children, but were always kind to them, and this seemed to strengthen the bond of affection which remains among Maori throughout life. Between the ages of three and nine, children enjoy a great deal of freedom. A child is free to play when and where he likes, and always has companions on the marae in front of the whare (house). It is extraordinary how a Maori child knows the danger of fire or boiling water. Although he is free to wander where he likes, and even plays with fire and goes among the boiling pools, you will scarcely ever hear of a child being burnt or scalded. The children were fond of takaro (play). They had few toys, yet they amused themselves making mud pies, playing hunahuna (hide and seek), punga, and many other games. It was a wonderful sight to see a little Maori child eating various kinds of foods with his fingers, and never making a mess or making his fingers dirty.

Piercing the ears

Their ears were pierced when they were quite small. A sharp thin pointed manuka needle was used, bent into V-shape, with several thicknesses of muka fibre in it. The ear was first mirimiri, i.e. rubbed between the thumb and first finger. The sharp ends of the manuka are placed together, and pushed through the ear with the muka fibre. The pierced ear lobes are bathed every day, and the fibre moved from side to side, and as the ear heals, pulled backwards and forwards. In a few weeks the ear is ready for a whakakai or ear ornament. Children usually had only the muka fibre until they were grown up, and were always taught to keep something in the ear so that the hole would not close. The ears were never torn intentionally. A girl had both ear lobes pierced, and a boy had one ear pierced, but sometimes both.

Girls

When girls are old enough to understand what is said to them, their mother begins to tell them how they should behave in the kainga. She teaches them to take care of their good name, and speaks freely of the time when they will be mate wahine, or mate marama, so that they will know what to do when it happens. When a girl reached that age, she knew all about it, as it had been explained to her by her mother, grandmother, or other close relative. She knew just what to do for herself, although her mother might show her at first what to do. It was important for a girl to know, because when she was mate wahine there were many things which she must not do because she was tapu (unclean) in the eyes of the old Maori. During this period she used a whaka aupuru (diaper) of woven fibre, with soft moss on the inner side, and this was replaced from time to time, while the used moss was buried by the girl in a secret place where no one would ever find it. On no account could the moss or whaka aupuru be thrown anywhere. When a girl is in this condition she is careful not

141

to step over a man who is lying down or over a man's sleeping place, nor to sit where a man sleeps, especially where his head rests, and she must not get into a bathing pool where men bathe, and she must not dare to rinse anything she may have used in that water. Any of these things would desecrate the laws of tapu, and in the old days, she would not dream of desecrating such laws. No eyes but her own must look upon her whaka aupuru or anything else that she used. She could not prepare a hangi (oven) or cook tawa berries. If she did, they would not be cooked. She would not gather shell-fish, as this would make them all go to another part of the coast. Nor would she go on cultivated ground, as the crops would be a failure. And she had to be careful in many ways too numerous to mention in this chapter. When she reached the age of mate wahine, she was supposed to be grown up and to have sense. A Maori girl matured earlier than a European, and was generally mata wahine at fourteen or fifteen, or even much earlier. It was seldom that she became ill at such a time. Her natural life prevented this. She went about as usual in the rain and did various work, other than that which she was prohibited from doing. A man would have nothing to do with his wife during this period. When the change of life came, a woman in the old days did not suffer at all. It all took its course in the natural way, without any laying up. She worked as usual on the things which she could do, such as getting flax and firewood, and preparing flax for, and making baskets, mats, etc.

Mate wahine (period of menstruation)

Unselfishness

There is much teaching to inculcate unselfishness. When there is not much kinaki (relish) at a meal, the little girl is asked to share hers, no matter how small it is, with other members of the family. Much of this was arranged by the mother to teach the little girl to be thoughtful for others. She was taught not to let the old people go to the spring to fetch water, but to bring it to them in calabashes. No child was ever ordered, but was always asked in a kindly way to help. I am sure that this is the reason why children looked on work as a pleasure in the old days.

Work

She was quick to learn all the duties which her mother performed. By the age of eight or ten or more, she liked to show her parents what she could do, and would get up early to light the fire, getting the hot embers together with a stick and putting a few dry sticks on and scraping away the ashes, then blowing the embers with her breath until the fire burnt up and she could put on thicker pieces of wood. She would not be waked, or made to get up. A Maori child of eight looked as old as a European child of eleven or twelve.

House work was not hard. There was no furniture. For the sleeping place in the whare, there was a quantity of rarauhe fern or raupo (bulrush), over which whariki, or sleeping-mats, were spread. If the day was wet, the mats were rolled up towards the head of the bed against the wall. On other days, these floor-mats were taken out and put in the sun, and the bed was often remade of fresh fern.

She learned to waruwaru, i.e. scrape kumara and taro to prepare it for cooking in a hangi. Little girls learn to prepare a hangi when quite young, but do not actually prepare it themselves until they are grown up. They go to the forest with their mother and gather sticks for firewood, making them into kawenga, that is, bundles on their backs with ropes of fibre or flax fixed round them like braces at the back and front. The girl puts each arm through the brace in front of the kawenga, which rests on a mound, or even on the ground, and carries it home on her back. This is a very easy way of carrying large bundles of wood or baskets of kumara, which often had to be carried several miles, for the plantations were often a long way from the kainga, and the Maori often had to go a long way for aruhe (fern root), or berries from the forest.

Girls soon learned how to clear away the weeds among the plants and between the rows, for weeding was generally done by women, and how to loosen the ground with a timo, an implement for grubbing. They helped their mothers to cut and carry bundles of flax to the kainga, and how to prepare flax for making rourou, the baskets from which food was eaten, taka, the mats on which kumara and taro might be served when it was ready for eating, rough kete (baskets) for holding kumara, taro, and other foods, whariki, the floor-mats on which they slept, and tuwhara, the rough or more coarsely made mats which were put under the whariki, and were also used for the kauta or wharau (cooking shed).

A little girl will carry the baby on her back to relieve her mother, and it is her ambition to grow up and be able to do all the things that her mother does. Girls join in all the games, swimming, running, poi dances, tititorea, and matemate. The children, like all Maori, are very modest. They bathe together, yet never see anything, and many will sleep side by side along the sleeping side of a whare, and nothing wrong enters their minds. They went to bed at sunset and rose at sunrise, and when they lay down on the whariki, the children heard from their elders the history of their people, their folk-lore, and other stories, which delighted them until they fell asleep.

Teaching

At about fourteen to eighteen, girls were taught to pukana (roll the eyes), and walk with a parepare movement of the hips. This moving gait of the hips, which was so wonderful in the old Maori, is the same as that practised by the modern civilized girl, only more marked. They were taught to do the ordinary haka and to sing pao and waiata, though they learned the waiata later. Singing came naturally to the Maori. They nearly always sang when walking or working or paddling a canoe, or going through a bush or lonely road. Many of them have beautiful voices.

Boys

Boys were massaged on the head, face and limbs with the romiromi massage to get them into form so that they would be strong when they grew up to fight, to do the war dances, peruperu, and whaka tu waewae, i.e. dance with long pointed sticks before a battle. They were taught to use weapons of stone, greenstone, and wood, and especially the whakahoro or use of arms, and the art of karo, the parrying of weapons. Upoko-titi was a favourite game of children, played with both hands. Each one crooked his koiti (little finger) over the next finger, and the same with the next, till all are bunched together.

Teaching

From the age of six to that of fifteen or sixteen, the father undertook the boy's training, and the grandfather took a great part as well. They taught him to be hospitable and generous, and to share any delicacy he might be eating. A parent would ask for a portion so as to teach the boy unselfishness, though if there were only a little kinaki, or relish, parents liked to give it to their children, who ate with them. Parents did many things and devised many methods to teach children good habits and a generous nature. The boy was taught to see that everyone had kinaki before eating his.

As he grew up, he was taught all the things that his father did. He accompanied him to the cultivations, and learned to use the ko (see page 187) in planting the kumara, and the songs which accompanied the movements of the workers. He learned the planting of kumara and taro, and how to build the whata,[1] the open store-house on posts, and the making of the pataka[1] (closed store-house), and how to dig the rua, the pit in the ground for storing kumara. He learned how to hunt and snare birds, of which there were more than two hundred species, and how to make hinaki, traps for eels, nets for sea fishing, and nets for catching inanga and pahore, the small fish in the lakes, and how to dive for koura and kakahi, the crayfish and fresh-water mussels. By the time he was eight or nine, he had learned a good deal about these and other methods of procuring food.

He accompanied his father and relatives to the forest, and watched them cutting down trees and preparing logs for the houses, or hewing them out for canoes, all laborious work which took a long time with their primitive implements, and learned how to choose trees for a canoe or house, and to cut them down and take them long distances to the kainga, or to the river or lake. He learned how to cut timber for the whare (houses) and for building the pa, fortified villages.

PLATE I

MAKERETI. ABOUT 1893

PLATE II

MAKERETI. ABOUT 1908

PLATE III

MAKERETI. ABOUT 1922

PLATE IV

MAKERETI WEAVING. ABOUT 1926

PLATE V

THE CHIEF, MITA TAUPOPOKI

PLATE VI

MAKERETI. WITH MEMBERS OF HER KAINGA

PLATE VII

FEATHER CLOAKS

PLATE VIII

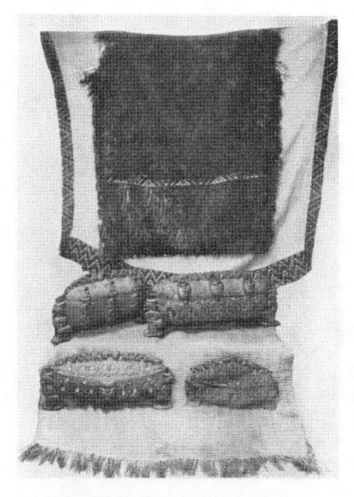

CLOAKS AND CARVED BOXES

PLATE IX

KORIRANGI OR KINIKINI

RAHOKUIA

PLATE X

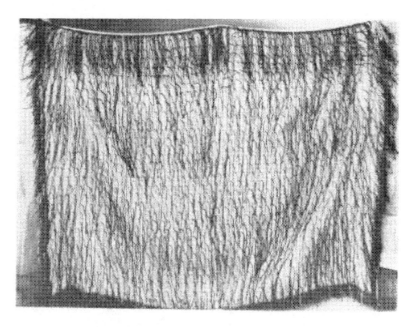

KOROWAI CLOAK

PAKE OR PORA, RAIN-CLOAK

PLATE XI

PIUPIU AND POI BALLS

PLATE XII

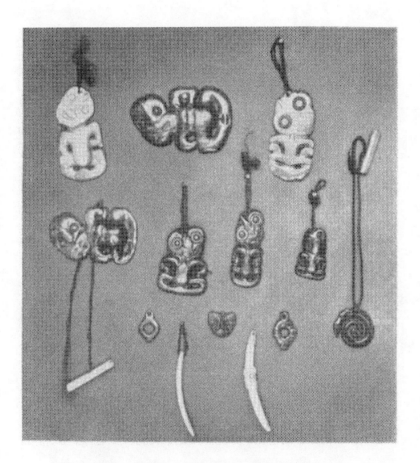

TIKI AND OTHER ORNAMENTS

PLATE XIII

RUHIO.   PUTIPUTI,   TONUI?

URUKEHU

PLATE XIV

THE TOHUNGA, TUTANEKAI

PLATE XV

OLD CARVED PATAKA

PLATE XVI

OLD CARVED PATAKA, BACK AND FRONT

PLATE XVII

OLD CARVED PATAKA, VERGE-BOARDS, SIDES,
TEKOTEKO

PLATE XVIII

BASKETS FOR FOOD

PLATE XIX

MALE AND FEMALE HUIA BIRDS

PLATE XX

TUHOROMATAKAKA EXTERIOR

PLATE XXI

MAKING PLAT-WORK PANELS FOR THE INTERIOR
OF A HOUSE

PLATE XXII

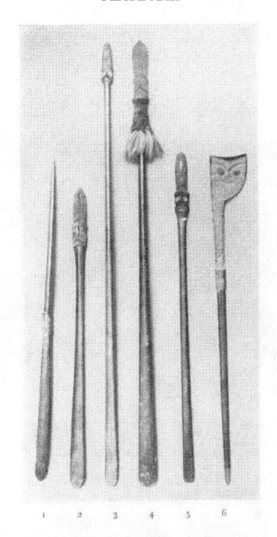

TWO-HANDED WEAPONS
1. Pouwhenua (p. 319) 2–5 Taiaha (p. 316)
6. Tewhatewha (p. 319)

PLATE XXIII

TE RANGI WITH TAIAHA
1. Popotahi 2. Whakarehu 3. Huanui

PLATE XXIV

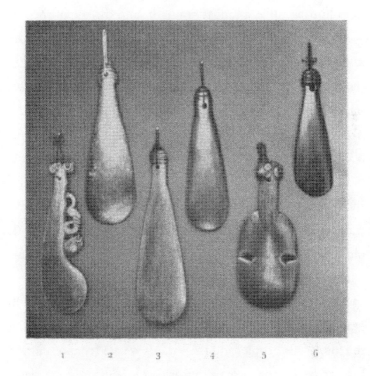

PATU

1. Wahaika 2. 4. 6. Patu pounamu

3. Patu paraoa 5. Kotiate

He was taught the customs and arts of his people, whaka tu waewae, a war dance, with the taiha or tewhatewha or pouwhenua (Plate XXII), and koikoi.[1] He learned how to hold himself up as a rangatira ought, and the use of the long two-handed weapon, each with his own way of tripping and killing the enemy. He was taught to use a patu pounamu or short-handled stone weapon for close combat, which was most important for a warrior, as all their fighting was hand to hand. Beside this, he learned the haka, or war dances which occurred when they approached the enemy, with distorted faces, eyes pukana (rolling), and arero whetero, tongue out to show defiance (Plate VI, man at back. Plate XXIII). He was trained in the use of all war weapons when quite young by the old men, and his training went on all through his life, at first with harmless sticks, and then with weapons.

At night when he lay down to sleep, his father, or often his grandfather, would tell him the thrilling deeds of his ancestors, the lore of his people, and the various waiata (chants) suitable for war, peace, and welcoming visitors for deaths or marriages, many of them composed by his own forebears. This would go on night after night until the lad fell asleep. He would be taught the names of the various stars and comets, and the different signs appearing in the sky or mountain, showing them when not to go to war, when not to go to sea, or when not to go to a certain place, for the Maori is full of superstition from his infancy and all his life. He learned the seasons for various work in the summer when a good deal of hard work is done from daylight to sunset, when the season was open, and when it was closed for bird snaring and fishing. All these things the Maori observed and was taught from childhood. He was taught not to desecrate tapu, and especially the tapu of burial places, a most important thing not to do.

Tapu

Games

Many games and haka kept them fit. They were taught very young to swim, and were great swimmers and divers and quite at home in the water. They practised canoe racing, jumping, wrestling, kite flying, racing, potaka spinning, morere, and swinging, and watched with interest all that went on about them, for nothing was hidden from Maori children, and all conversation was open before them. Yet they were most modest, and there was nothing vulgar about them. They were fearless, for they met with love everywhere, and in their homes they were petted and loved by their parents and relatives. In many families, the old people bring up the children when one or two more babies come, and children were taught to respect the old people.

Moral atmosphere

General teaching about tapu

They were taught never to put their hands over the head of a tapu person, nor to pass food over the head of a chief, Tohunga, an older member of the family, or anyone else who is tapu. A younger member of a family must not pass food over the head of an elder brother or sister. If a child inadvertently did so, the food had to be thrown right away or buried. They were taught never to put hair in the fire. Should this be done, the fire must be put out at once, as the person whose hair it was would die.

Early teaching of children

Parents never made their children work, but they naturally accompanied them to their work in cultivating the soil or anything else, and could join in or not as they liked. They were not paid for any work that they did, but soon came to enjoy it like the older people, joining in the songs as they worked. One would start a song, and the rest would join in. There was generally one who started the songs, which would be appropriate for whatever they were doing, and they were much enjoyed

Various types of children

There were of course naughty children as well, and there were quarrels, as among children everywhere. A quarrelsome child was termed a tamaiti whekiki, and one who was the opposite was called a tamaiti ngawari or humaria. One who was well formed and able to do much for his age was termed a tamaiti pakari. An industrious child was called a tamaiti pukumahi, and a lazy one, tamaiti mangere. Many of the terms were of course applied to grown-ups as well, but in the old days so much time was taken up by work that there was little room for idleness.

Terms of endearment

A mother speaking to a child in endearing terms would say Taku mokai, taku mokaikai, moi, E moia, taku potiki, taku potikitiki, or if it were a boy, she might also say Taku tama, taku tahae, or E ta. A girl might also be addressed Taku kohine, E hine aku, or E hine.

Illness

In the old days it was a case of the survival of the fittest. Children went about in all weathers without clothes until they were six or eight years old. There were few ailments before Europeans visited Aotearoa (New Zealand), but soon after Captain Cook came, the first epidemic swept over our land, and according to our traditions many thousands of men, women and children perished. It was called by the Maori Te Upoko o te rewharewha. Each vessel that visited us left an epidemic of some kind, which wiped out many children as well as grown up people. Though I could mention various epidemics, here I merely want to say that before Europeans came, there was comparatively little illness.

Treatment

Much has been written about the callous and indifferent way in which the Maori treated their children when ill. This is a libel. The writer forgets that the Maori of pre-pakeha days was free from illness as a rule, and if any did assail him, he believed that it was became some law of tapu had been infringed. If a child was ill, it was through something done by the mother or father in the way of desecrating tapu. The child was taken to a Tohunga, who took it to a stream and repeated appropriate karakia over him. The child often got well, and sometimes died, but this was not a common occurrence, nor was it looked on as neglect. When the pakeha brought his epidemics and laid the Maori low with fevers, influenza, and colds and measles, it was natural that the Maori should go to the Tohunga to find comfort and relief for his child. He knew nothing of these strange diseases, and still less how to deal with them. Even in England with all the doctors falling over each other, it is not always possible to cope with these diseases which were altogether new to the Maori. He tried to cope with them as he and his ancestors had done, by karakia at an isolated and tapu place, and if the child was in a high fever, he was put into a cold bath. Sometimes a patient lived, and sometimes he died, but he was never treated with neglect. The

European must not judge the Maori to be callous because he does not understand his methods of treating illness. He was never indifferent to anyone who was ill or dying. I have yet to deal with the subject of sickness and death,[1] and so will not speak further here.

Infants were not washed in basins every day, but cold water would be poured out of a calabash into the cupped right hand of the mother, who would then wash the eyes, face, and the rest of the child's body. Where there were hot springs, the infant was put into the warm water each day, and held by the mother or other relative, by both hands, the left hand below the waist, and the right under the head and shoulders. The infant was quite happy in the water. Children often suffered from toretore in the eyes, and were unable to open them in the morning. The eyes were then bathed in cold or warm water to open them. A Maori child went through the time of teething like any other child. The mother generally rubbed the gums with her little finger.

The pito

I spoke earlier of the performance of the tohi rite when the pito or iho dropped off. This was sometimes taken to the place where the tua or tohi was performed, and in some cases was tied on to the karamu branch used by the Tohunga, and afterwards put into a wooden or stone box and buried. In many cases it was buried in a secret place, or placed in the hollow of a tree or hole in the fork of a tree, or it might be buried on the boundary line of the tribal lands. There were many ways of disposing of the iho, but it was never left at a public place where it could be seen. The great reason for hiding it was to prevent anyone from placing makutu (witchcraft) on it, and so doing harm to the child, or even causing its death.

Early teaching

Children slept all together in the same whare as their parents and sometimes their grandparents from the age of three until they were grown up. Going to rest was always a great joy to the children, especially to those who were with their grandparents. When they lay down on the whariki (floor-mats, they had no pillows), their grandfather or granduncle, or whomever they might be with, would tell them stories of the brave deeds of some of their ancestors, the various battles they fought and won, the battles they lost, and the reasons for these wars. Probably a famous ancestor was killed and a party went and avenged his death. The old man would teach them their line of descent from that ancestor, and from other noted ancestors back to the time of the arrival of the great fleet of canoes in New Zealand about six hundred years ago, repeating the genealogical tree from the different members of the canoe down to himself night after night until the child could say them from memory, and repeat them all by the time that he was ten years old. If an ancestor was mentioned, he would know how many generations back he had lived, and how he was related to his other descendants. From these old people, the children learn much in the way of folk-lore, legend, genealogy, and tradition.

Genealogy

The old people told them stories of the patupaiarehe, the fairies who moved past in the mist of early morning, or in the mist after the rain, the fairies who sometimes came down from their homes on the tops of historic mountains. They told the children how dear their home and lands were to them, and to their fathers before them, and tried to make the children feel the same. They taught them the names of the birds of the forest, and of the different trees and shrubs and plants, all the names of which the old people knew, and wonderful stories of the mountains, rivers, and streams, as though they were living human beings. They tried to impress on the childish mind the ways of the unknown which the Maori observed, for the old Maori was familiar with the stars and knew their names, Kopu the morning star, and Matariki the Pleiades. They spoke of the comets and other signs which appeared as omens in the sky, those which were good and those which were not. Everything was personified to the Maori, as he was very near to Nature.

History

Then the old people would tell them how their bold

adventurous seafaring ancestors came from Hawaiki, the distant home, in their historic canoes across the great ocean of Kiwa about the fourteenth century, and sailed across that vast ocean without a compass, believing only in the power of their atua (gods) to help them. They relied on the regular trade-winds to guide them by day, and on the stars and the rolling waves to help them at night. And they sailed on and on for many days to find Aotearoa, the beautiful land which their ancestors first visited two hundred years before their great migration to it.

At night then, they talked of these and many other things until the little people fell asleep. And so they grew up with the stories and deeds of their ancestors until the boys reached the age when they entered the whare kura, the sacred school of learning where they learned from the Tohunga all the karakia and everything that was tapu and not taught outside the whare kura. Games taught them sharpness of eye and quickness of movement. In the winter of an evening they gathered in the wharetapere, a house where games were played, or in the wharepuni (meeting house), and played games and practised the haka posture dances, and peruperu and other war dances, which they all enjoyed. They learned whai, i.e. cat's cradle, and many other games too numerous to mention.

Games

Children of a chief

After a young boy chief had gone through his time with the Tohunga, if he were successful, he became a leader in all the social functions just as his father and his grandfather before him had been. He was taught how to whaikorero, make speeches, as this was most essential at all the different meetings or gatherings. He had to elaborate a high degree of imagination as an orator, and to become expert in rousing the feelings of his people. With great dignity he paced the marae (plaza) backwards and forwards, slowly at first, then gradually rousing himself and his people to the heights of enthusiasm, ending with an appropriate waiata (chant) in which all the people joined. Through his wonderful gifts of oratory, a chief added to his mana.

A boy was taught to uphold the mana of his chief, whose word was law. Any deed of valour performed by him was a credit to all his people. Indeed the individual was absorbed in the whanau (family group), and the whanau in the hapu. He must avenge an insult offered to one of his whanau, hapu, or tribe, and always be ready when warriors were called to fight. He was taught his different lines of descent from the ancestors who came over in the canoes of the great migration, and from the generations before that.

The whare kura, a sacred school of learning

He grew up knowing these things before he entered the whare kura or whare wananga, the sacred school of learning, at the age of sixteen or seventeen. Here he was in the hands of the great Tohunga and his one or more assistant Tohunga, and learned all the traditions, mythology, and religion. The Maori had no writing, and everything was handed down by word of mouth. Through the tapu school of learning, traditions were kept intact and handed down for many generations without any alterations. The whare wananga was held in high regard by the Maori people. Here the youths passed through a severe test of learning, and had to memorize word for word all their traditions and sacred lore, and the very high tapu karakia of Io the supreme being. Before a youth was allowed to enter the whare kura, he was tested as to his powers of memory. He was generally of very high rank, and was chosen as akonga (pupil) for the very high tapu matters.

Ariki

First born line

The term ariki was used for a first born male or female child of rangatira (high born) parents, and there were several in a hapu or tribe. But Te aho ariki, the first born line of descent, was thought greatly of by the old Maori, and if the child belonged to rangatira parents, he was considered a most important personage. Generally the matamua, the eldest son of such a family of each whaka tupuranga (generation) naturally became the head of his people. An ariki of this kind, if he was descended from many of the important whakapapa through various lines from noted ancestors, was a tino ariki mana nui, a great ariki who had very great mana, and this was the sign of a tangata tino rangatira, a man of the very highest rank. The tohi ceremony over him would be carried out with very great ceremonial indeed, and presents of value would be given to the Tohunga who performed the tohi. There would be many presents brought from the relatives who came to attend the ceremonial feast. This child would have special care taken of him in the way of special foods as he grew up, and he would be taught from childhood the many things which would be expected of him when he grew up. His grandfathers would take special pride and care in training him in the use of arms and everything pertaining to warfare, and to agriculture, fishing, house-building, making canoes, and the many things which a man was supposed to do. But an ariki was expected to excel in all work, games, and war dances, and in oratory he was expected to have great powers to move his people and hold them through his mana, making his reo (voice) heard, and he would have mana to protect the land. Thus it was important that a boy who was an ariki should be taught well all the things necessary to a leader, and when he was old enough, he attended the whare kura, the tapu school of learning, where special care was taken by the Tohunga over his education in all tapu matters. An ariki was a very tapu person. An important personage like this would always travel with a retinue of chiefs and other relatives who guarded him, and if necessary, died to save him. An ariki was born, not made. Should an ariki be born a tatauhea, with not much initiative, it was possible that a younger son would be chosen by his father to follow in his footsteps as a chief, but that eldest son would always be termed an ariki, and if he died without issue, then the mana of the chosen brother would be even greater. But this did not happen often.

Mana of Tuhourangi[1]

The mana of Tuhourangi commenced on the day of Tuhourangi the great ancestor. It was conferred on him by Rangitihi his father above his elder brothers. There were seven older than he by different mothers. Tuhourangi was the youngest son. Their father made them walk under Tuhourangi. They did so with the exception of Ratoroa who escaped the ceremony. Wahiao being male direct descendant from Tuhourangi, the mana was inherited by him. He had a double mana, over the people and over the land.

[1] Food takes away tapu.

[1] Besides the printed genealogies, I have a great number of written genealogies of the descendants of Wahiao. Tuhourangi is sixth from Tama te Kapua who was captain of the Arawa Canoe; Wahiao is tenth and Makereti is nineteenth.

[1] Ill-informed foreigner. The first word applies to the cooking of his head and to an insulting expression. See Tregear.

[1] See *ariki* at end of chapter.

[1] See Appendix to this chapter, also Grey, Sir George, *Konga Moteatea, me nga Hakirara o nga Maor*, Wellington, 1853.

[1] Cf. a version in Maori and English of part of such a karakia in *Te Ika a Maui* by the Rev. Richard Taylor, London and Wanganui, 1870, 2nd ed, also Grey, *op. cit.*.

[1] V. Marriage.

[1] Spear.

[1] This section was not written.

[1] From Makereti's papers, now in my keeping.—EDITOR.

IV

FOOD

The food supply

MUCH NONSENSE HAS been written about the starving
Maori. People have written as though the Maori attended a
meeting or a tangi just for the sake of having a good meal or
overfeeding, and as though he starved or lived in a state of
semi-starvation after it until another feast came along. These
writers often speak as though a Maori made himself poor by
giving a feast for the opening of his house, the marriage of his
daughter, or by the food he supplied for a tangi for his mother
or father or other relative. I am writing enough in this chapter
about the large cultivations of kumara, aruhe, taro, and other
foods of the Maori, about the fishing for sea fish and fresh-
water fish and shell-fish, about the many varieties of fruits
and berries gathered in the forests, and about the birds caught
or snared there, to show that the Maori always had plenty of
food, and that he need never wait for a hui (gathering) to have
a square meal. Indeed, there never was a poor or hungry Maori
before the days of the Europeans, when the Maori left their

kainga to work for Europeans and a necessity for money arose and disorganized their former wonderful method of living.

Effect of European settlement

Method of feeding a great company

Perhaps it would interest the reader to know how food was collected and supplied for a hui, either at a large meeting of the tribes to discuss affairs of state, or at a marriage, or at the opening of a new wharepuni (meeting house), or at any other ceremony of importance. Take as an example an important gathering to discuss affairs of state, given, we will say, at Te Wairoa where Te Keepa Te Rangipuawhe, a chief, lived with his hapu Tuhourangi. Although the hui would be spoken of as being arranged by the chief Te Rangipuawhe, the food collected to feed the various members of the hapu attending was not supplied only by the people of Tuhourangi who lived at Te Wairoa. All the hapu of Tuhourangi, and they were many, when they heard that there would be a hui, began at once to collect food to help feed the multitude. A hapu living near the sea began getting fish and preparing them a year or more beforehand, and clans living near a forest collected birds and berries and fruits. Extra cultivations of kumara, taro, and hue would be planted, and aruhe would be collected in quantities. These foods would be brought to Te Wairoa as they were ready, and stored, and greater quantities were brought by the many hapu when they arrived a week or two before the meeting. This may show that the expense of the hui was not borne entirely by the hapu of Tuhourangi who were supporting their chief, and that his hapu was not made poor as a result of the gathering. In addition, all of the other hapu or tribes who attended never came without a presentation of food to help the ceremony, and the expense, being so evenly distributed among a great many people, would scarcely be felt by any of them.

Expense distributed among many people

Again, take the opening of my own whare (house) Tuhoromatakaka, named after my ancestor Tuhoromatakaka, eldest son of Tama te Kapua who was captain of the Arawa canoe which brought my ancestors to New Zealand. Many hapu attended the whaikawa (opening ceremony), and there was a hui, which is described in my chapter on houses. Here then I will simply speak of the food supplied for this ceremony at Whakarewarewa. I did not supply it, and the ceremony cost me very little. My relatives in the hapu descended from Wahiao supplied the necessary food, and attended to the preparation and cooking and giving the food (whiu kai), as I have described it later in this chapter. Here again the cost of entertainment was spread over so many people that it was scarcely felt by anyone. Yet we had food and to spare for the hundreds of visitors who attended the ceremony. (Plate XX.)

Cooking

Cooking was never done in a dwelling house, but in the open, or in a wharau or kauta (cooking sheds). They were shaped like a whare with uprights and rafters of wood. The sides were split boles of kaponga, tree fern, with a small space between each. The roof was generally of the same material, or of nikau palm which was used as a thatch. The door was usually in the middle of one side, and there was no window. Smoke escaped through the door and the spaces between the uprights. Each dwelling house had a small wharau, and a large one was attached to the principal house of the kainga. This was used by the community for preparing food for visitors or for a great gathering.

Sheds for cooking

Who may and may not cook

Cooking was done by women and pononga (slaves), but mainly by the women, who waruwaru (scraped) the kumara and prepared the other vegetable food, and very often prepared the hangi, or cooking oven. No woman may cook tawa berries, and some other foods, during menstruation, neither must she prepare a hangi while in that condition. It was believed that the food would not get cooked. Tohunga and chiefs must not cook food, for fear of losing their mana. Food must not be passed over the head of a chief, Tohunga, or elders, as the head is very tapu indeed. A young member of a family must not pass food over an elder brother's or elder sister's head, nor over the head of an ariki (first born), for the head was tapu. The food must be thrown right away or buried.

Preservation and storage of food

Whata

Food was preserved or stored in whata, two open work shelves, one above the other, supported on four uprights. The lower was about five feet from the ground, and the upper about ten or twelve from the ground. The shelves were reached by an arawhata, step-ladder, which was a tree trunk or pole with notches cut out to hold the front part of the foot. The shelves were used for drying fish, and as a larder for human flesh, or dog flesh which was to be eaten shortly.

Pataka

The pataka (Plates XV-XVII) was a permanent store house whose shape was identical with that of a whare, but the sides were much lower. The door, also a sliding slab, was in the centre, and there were no windows, except in very large ones. But this was very rare. The size varied from 4 by 2 feet or 6 by 3 feet, up to that of a good-sized whare 20—24 feet long or more. The pataka was raised on posts, one, two, four, or more, according to size. These posts pass through inverted cones of wood to prevent rats from climbing up. There were many ways of keeping rats out, but a favourite way was to cut lengths from an old disused canoe, and invert them over the tops of the posts. Sometimes the post was cut so as to leave a projection all round the top, and again, a straight plank might be placed on the top of the post. The side walls were generally of large planks, 2 or 3 feet wide and 2 or 3 inches thick, and carved with manaia[1] figures. They were placed in a horizontal position. The pataka was approached by a permanent arawhata, step-ladder, a log with notches cut out for the foot to step on. There were two kinds of pataka, the small private one belonging to a whanau (family group), and the large one, generally elaborately carved, the public property of the hapu which was attached to the wharepuni (meeting house). A large pataka was sometimes used as a whare for sleeping. The large ones were most elaborately carved with some of the finest carving that the Maori did. This carving was usually confined to the front part, the threshold plank, the verge boards and their vertical supporting planks, and the interior of the porch. The walls were of planks, and the roof was thatched.

Hangi, cooking ovens

Food was cooked in hangi. A rounded hollow was dug in the ground, usually circular, and with a diameter of 2 feet or more and a depth of I foot at the deepest part, the size varying according to the number of people for whom food was to be cooked. A fire was built in this hollow. Small wood and logs were arranged in a cone, and a layer of hard stones (kohatu) about the size of cricket balls was placed on the fire. When the stones were red hot, the unburnt parts of the logs were removed, leaving only embers below the stones. Water was sprinkled on the stones to make steam. The sides of the hangi were then lined with fern leaves tied together with flax. This lining had been dipped in water. Meat or fish was wrapped in wet leaves and placed on the stones, and kumara (sweet potato) which were already scraped and placed in water, were taken up with both hands and placed wet over the meat or stones. More water was then sprinkled over the whole hangi, and layers of korokio fern leaves were placed all over the food to cover it well. Then a taka made of rough flax was placed on the top, and earth was heaped over the whole, which was left an hour or more to cook. Food was beautiful cooked in this way. When the food was cooked, the earth was scraped off with a flat piece of wood, and left in a heap by the hangi ready for the next time. Hangi in kainga (villages) were permanent, but temporary ones were often made as occasion required, for instance, in the bush. When there was a large gathering and many people had to be fed, many large hangi were made, of a long rectangular shape.

Meals

Two meals were taken each day, the first about 9 a.m.,

194

and the other about 4 p.m. The members of a household ate together. A Tohunga had his meals alone. There was only one course, but this consisted of a variety of dishes served together. The food was served in rourou baskets made of flax, or on a taka of plaited flax. Much work was done in the early morning before breakfast, as the Maori was an early riser.

Feasts

Feasts were held for a marriage, a victory in war, a tangi, a burial, the entertainment of visitors, the opening of a meeting house, the opening of a fortified pa, or the completion of a waka taua (war canoe). During a feast the men and women who have done the cooking, with others who are not partaking of the feast, entertain the visitors with songs and dances. Invited guests have places of honour, and help themselves first. The food is brought in in pieces in rourou baskets. There are generally three or four rourou for each person, containing different foods. The rourou are placed on a long narrow plaited tuwhara, i.e. a strip of coarsely woven flax 3 or 4 feet wide and in 20 foot lengths, which forms a kind of table-cloth on the ground.

Whiu kai, the giving of food

When the rourou kai are placed on the tuwhara, the head man of the cooking party, holding a stick in his hand, touches different parts of the tuwhara, saying, "Ara ra kia ngati mea!"

This is for the people or descendants of So-and-so, and thus apportions the feast to the members of the different tribes present. The visitors may then sit down and begin to eat.

Family meals

A family of two to four or so would have their food served on a taka. The taka would be taken to the hangi and filled with the kumara, taro or hue (gourds) and the relish would be placed on top of the food. The taka would be carried to the place where the food was to be eaten, and the family would eat their food without forks or knives. Food was picked up between the thumb and first finger of the right hand. It was only in dividing a bird or any other relish which might be on the food that the thumb and first finger of the left hand would be used. The hands as a whole did not come into use unless a penu (mash) was wanted, when the third finger could be used. Thus the hands did not get dirty. The Maori was generally careful how he picked up his food. He liked to look at it, if it was a tasty relish. If there was not much relish, the parents would not have any themselves, but pass it on to be shared among the children or old people. No word was spoken during a meal, and all meals were eaten in silence.

Position during meals

A Maori sat on the ground close to where the food was laid. A man sat with his legs crossed tailor fashion, and a woman with her left leg bent so that her knee came up near to her chin, and with her right leg bent underneath her. Boys usually sat tailor fashion, and girls with both legs bent sideways. A woman sometimes sat like this when eating.

A Tohunga's meals

A Tohunga had his meals cooked with other food except on tapu occasions, but his food was served in a special rourou or taka made for his own use of prepared flax. A Tohunga was not allowed to touch food with his hands for fear of losing his mana. Generally a boy six or seven years old, a relative, carried his rourou or taka of food to him, and with a purau, a long stick 12 or 18 inches long with two prongs at the end, placed the food in the mouth of the Tohunga. Water was generally poured from a calabash into his open mouth if he needed a drink. Liquid food was served in the same way, or poured down through a funnel into his mouth.

Cooking in boiling or steam holes

In parts of the thermal district, food was cooked in the boiling or steam holes. At Whakarewarewa where I lived with my koroua Maihi te Kakauparaoa and his sister Marara who brought me up, we never had any fires at all. All the food was either boiled or steamed. Kumara, potatoes, or taro would be placed in a tukohu, a basket made for this purpose from the leaves of the toetoe (pampas grass), and the plaited string at the top would be pulled, so closing its mouth (Plate XVIII). This would then be placed in the parekohuru (boiling spring), and the end of the string would be tied to a peg in the ground near the edge of the hole. After a quarter of an hour or so, the tukohu would be lifted out and placed in a hangi, or natural steam oven dug and prepared in the ground, and left for about ten minutes to steam. The basket of kumara or potatoes could also be rinsed through the boiling hole and put into the steam hole straight away without boiling. Food cooked in these hot springs was very nice to taste. Meat, birds, or fish were generally steamed and tasted good.

Personal recollections

We lived in a wharepuni made in the real old style. The slabs of totara were all put into the ground about three feet deep, and shone with age. The floor was of earth which was slightly warm, and the place where we slept was covered with lycopodium, waewaekahu, then tuwhara and whariki (sleeping mats) were placed on top. The inside of the house was lined with kakaho reeds, and the heke were beautifully fitted. Everything was made well. The house was about 25 feet long and 14 feet wide, and stood about 10 yards from the rahui (ground belonging to us) where we had our cooking holes, baths, etc.

How well I remember my young days when I lived at Whakarewarewa with my koroua Maihi te Kakauparaoa and my kuia Marara his sister, those two fine old people of the old order who lived their good and simple life, not knowing a word of English. We lived mostly at Whakarewarewa during the winter season, going to Parekarangi now and then to get potatoes and other foods, as nothing was grown at Whakarewarewa owing to the heat of the ground. We had a rua kai (food pit) on the site where the government now have a so-called model pa, for we owned the land then.

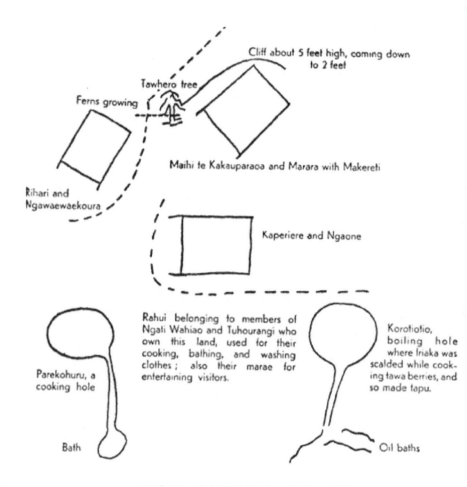

Cliff about 5 feet high, coming down to 2 feet

Tawhero tree

Ferns growing

Maihi te Kakauparaoa and Marara with Makereti

Rihari and Ngawaewaekoura

Kaperiere and Ngaone

Parekohuru, a cooking hole

Rahui belonging to members of Ngati Wahiao and Tuhourangi who own this land, used for their cooking, bathing, and washing clothes ; also their marae for entertaining visitors.

Korotiotio, boiling hole where Iriaka was scalded while cooking tawa berries, and so made tapu.

Bath

Oil baths

1. HOME AT WHAKAREWAREWA

The two baskets of potatoes brought from Parekarangi would be emptied into the storage pit, and my kuia would take a supply on to the kainga which was not far away, for our immediate use. Sometimes after the hauhake (the digging up of the food), my mother or other relatives helped to carry the

200

baskets of potatoes from Parekarangi to Whakarewarewa to be placed in the pit there, while the greater part of the mara kai (crop) was gathered and placed in a pit at Parekarangi, to be taken out from time to time as we needed them. In later years pack horses were used for fetching potatoes.

When I was older, and able to walk longer distances and not be carried on my kuia's back, I enjoyed those journeys backward and forward. The stream Puarenga had to be crossed before arriving at the kainga. This the people waded, generally knee deep, but after heavy rain, it became deeper in parts, and the current was strong. I crossed this stream on the back of my kuia till I was big enough to look after myself. The place where we crossed was from fifteen to twenty yards wide, shallow in most parts, then deep under the steep bank on the other side. A path was made in a cutting down this steep bank.

How well I remember sitting on the taumata, the brow of the hill above this Whakawhitinga (crossing), looking down on that dear old kainga and on the fine old people who occupied it, that old generation who have nearly all passed away. I close my eyes, and I am there again, sometimes alone, and sometimes with my relatives and playmate Ataraiti, companion of my childhood.

Songs by Makereti and Ataraiti

It was on this taumata that we concocted the haka (songs) for Repora and Taranaki, when we were about nine years old, songs which are sung to this day at meetings and tangi.

HE HAKA PAO. NA MAKERETI RAUA KO ATARAITI

> Kai whea Taranaki ka ngaro nei ia hau
> Kai te Mahi ruri tika moku ka ai.
>
> Ma wai e kau te awa nei Puarenga
> Ma taku tau kuiairehe ka ai.
>
> He hui nga he memenga ki roto o teneti
> Waiho a Repora tangi raho ka ai.
>
> Kihai koe e Naki i ki mai kia hau
> Kai whea he whare ai tanga moku ka ai.

When Repora heard us singing them, she chased us, but could not catch us. The taumata we sat on looked down on the Puarenga stream, and not far from the opposite bank was where Repora and her sister lived with their mother Mareti. They were all my own relations, and I have mentioned them in the genealogy of Wahiao when I tried to show the people who were living at Whakarewarewa in the early eighties. These people were called Ngati Wahiao, and were made up of sub-hapu of Wahiao, being Ngati Huarere, N. Tukiterangi, N. Tuohonoa, N. Te Amo, N. Taoi, N. Waihakari, N. Te Anumato, N. Umukaria, and others.[1]

Preparation of food for cooking at Whakarewarewa

In preparing a meal at Whakarewarewa, the women would first scrape the sweet potatoes (kumara) or potatoes (riwai) with the half of a kakahi (freshwater mussel shell), the potato being held between the thumb and the first and second fingers, and the shell between the thumb and first two fingers of the right hand, about midway of the shell. A woman would waruwaru (scrape) a basketful in a very short time. Hue (a gourd) would be put into a different basket, and not put into a cooking hole until later than the potatoes, as it did not take long to cook. The tukohu (basket) of potatoes was drawn at the top as I have described, and carried by its long tau, plaited string, to the edge of Parekohuru, the large cooking hole, and dropped in, then drawn out and gently dropped up and down on the smooth stone edge of the cauldron, and afterwards put back into the water for a final rinse before tying the string on to a stake near the edge. The basket might also be put straight into the steam hole a few feet away. In the old days the sides of these hangi, or natural steam cookers, were made of slabs of wood, and the bottom of the hole had a plank or two with holes between to let the steam through. They were very hot, and one had to be careful of the steam. The holes were covered over to keep the steam in while cooking, and potatoes would cook in twenty to twenty-five minutes. The boiling spring was a little quicker. Puwha (Sonchus oleraceus. var., rather like sow thistle) would be left in the boiling water for about ten minutes. It could be steamed, but boiling was preferred. Hue was cooked either way. Meat would be steamed, and would take longer than vegetables. Koura (crayfish) would be placed in a tukohu and dropped into the boiling water for a few seconds, then taken straight out and eaten, or the crayfish might be put into the steam hole for two or three minutes. Koura cooked in this way were beautiful. Fish was generally steamed in a hangi, either in a tukohu or in a vessel, and meat or birds were also cooked in these steam holes. Koeaea (whitebait), like koura, needed very little cooking, and might be put for a minute or two in the boiling water, or steamed in a tukohu, or put into a vessel and stood in the steam hole, or in the shallow part of Parekohuru, the boiling hole, close to the edge.

Cooking in boiling or steam holes

It was a fascinating sight to see the great numbers of tukohu belonging to several families hanging one over the other about a yard or two from the top of the cooking hole, with all their strings tied on to a large stake in the ground a yard or so from the edge. Each person knew her own tukohu by the string, and there was never any difficulty in finding one's own. If I had two or three in one hangi, I would tie their strings together outside the hangi.

Parekohuru

When I was a small child at Whakarewarewa, the cauldron

for boiling the food was Parekohuru, a bottomless pit of clear boiling mineral water which boiled up to the surface from somewhere in the bowels of the earth. It was nearly round, about fifteen or twenty feet across, and had a small outlet at one end to let the water flow away.

Other kainga, and cultivations

Although we lived at Whakarewarewa, we had other kainga, and spent much time at Parekarangi, where we had our cultivations, about six miles from Whakarewarewa, just as my other relatives who lived at Whaka, or in other districts belonging to Tuhourangi and Ngati Wahiao. Each whanau (family group) at Parekarangi had a whare close to its cultivation. My koroua Maihi te Kakauparaoa had a wharepuni and a pataka standing on our land there, and on one side of us were Mohi and his Makarena, and on the other side were Haira and his wife Wiripine with their family, and so on. We all lived up there during the cultivating season, only going to Whaka occasionally for a few days to have baths, and the old Koroua generally had something that he wanted to do there. How well I remember these journeys, always on foot, and without shoes or stockings.

No food was grown at Whakarewarewa, and it all had to be taken from Parekarangi. My kuia Marara would carry it in a kawenga, rope of fibre, on her back. A large basket would be filled with potatoes, then covered with bracken. A long piece of flax would be threaded crossways through the loops at the top of the basket to draw the sides together. After arranging the kawenga on the ground, she would sit down with her back against the basket, and put her arms through the flax ropes on each side, but nearer the middle really, and raise herself gently with the load on her back. We would start off on our six-mile walk, with me beside her. But I soon got tired, and she would rest against a low bank beside the track, and allow me to climb on to the basket and place my feet over each of her shoulders. Thus I was carried home on top of the kete riwai (basket of potatoes), an extra burden to the dear old soul, who thought nothing of it. So for the next five miles I sat on the basket, sometimes two baskets.

The journey home

On our extreme right, we passed Haparangi, which rises to a height of 2,808 feet, and on our left many cultivations of the clans of Wahiao at Ngapeho, Te Waikorowhiti, and Waitaruna, looking towards Kapapiko on our right and Waipa. Then we passed Te Rua ki o Koko, and through Te Hemo gorge where the road passed round the cutting, with the Puarenga stream rushing down the valley on its way through Papakura Whakarewarewa, Turikore, and Ngapuna, before joining Lake Rotorua. The view after passing the gorge is wonderful. In the distance is Rotorua Lake with Mokoia Island rising up near the centre, the island home of our ancestors in days long past, the home of Tutanekai, son of Whakaue, for whom my ancestress Hinemoa left her home on the mainland, and swam over to him from Owhata; Mokoia, where brave chiefs lived and are buried, where Tohunga keep the tapu places tapu, especially the top of the island where so many of my ancestors are buried; Mokoia, where was Te Atua Matuatonga, which the Arawa people brought over from Hawaiki, the distant home, in the canoe Arawa!

Mokoia

Then there was Ngongotaha Maunga to the left, on the west shore of the lake, rising to a height of 2,554 feet. On the top was Te Tuahu o te Atua. From here one saw the other lakes beyond Rotorua, and the view took in the sea and the coast from Tauranga to Maketu, about forty miles away.

We passed on by the side of Puarenga, with Pohaturoa hill on its other side, and looked down upon the many boiling springs and mud holes at Papakura, Waikite, Pohutu, the old sites of Te Puia Pa and Puke a te Ruahina, the old pa and homes of dead ancestors, famous warriors of bygone days.

Then we arrived at our destination Whakarewarewa, where so much of my youth was spent, when we were not at dear old Parekarangi. The journey from Parekarangi was generally begun after the morning meal somewhere about ten or eleven, and we arrived at about two o'clock.

If Marara carried only one basket of potatoes, it was taken

to the kainga for our immediate use. If she carried two, most of them would be emptied into a storage pit just before we reached Whaka.

On arrival, the kete taewa and hue and puwha would be placed on logs at the foot of the tawhero tree which stood near the front of the whare on the left side of the entrance. On its branches would hang two, three, or four tukohu of different sizes, used for cooking food in the boiling or steam holes. These were made of toetoe, pampas grass, plaited by the women. Flax was not used because it gives a taste to the food. Baskets of flax were used only when pork was being cooked at a meeting, when the very large parts were cooked in one piece. Pork would be placed in a large but *old* flax kete (basket). Green flax would seldom be used, as it gave food a bitter taste.

Tukohu

The various foods described separately

Kumara, sweet potatoes

I te wa o mua, in days long past, the Maori cultivated kumara in large areas all over New Zealand. It was one of their principal foods, and could be eaten either raw or cooked.

Tapu origin

It was thought much of because of its tapu origin, as it was brought from the heavens. All work done in connexion with growing it up to the time of taking it from the ground and storing it in pits was done with karakia and great ceremonial. It was an old belief, told me by my old people, that although the kumara was produced by Whanui, the star Vega, it was through Rongonui-maui and his wife Pani-tinikau that we have it on this earth. But when the kumara tuber is planted in its mound of earth, it is from Whanui that it receives help in growing.

Rongonui-maui, when he heard of the kumara, thought he would visit his elder brother Whanui who lived in the heavens, and ask him to let him have some to bring back to earth. So he ascended to the heavens, and repeated this karakia:

"E Para E! Tukua atu au kia puta ki tawhangawhanga nui no Rangi, no Papa; he aio."

This was a karakia asking for help to enable him to ascend through the great spaces in safety to the heavens on his way to see his elder brother Whanui.

When Rongo arrived, he made known his reason for coming, saying to Whanui, "I haere mai au ki tetahi o ta taua whanau kia riro ia au ki Raro, ki Mataroa," I have come to ask you to let me take one of our family below with me to Mataroa. And Whanui replied, "Kaore au e whakaae kia riro atu tetahi o wa taua tamariki ia koe," I will not agree that you should take any of our children with you.

So Rongo turned as if to go away, but hid behind a whare, and then approached the family of kumara unknown to Whanui, and took some of the seed with him. This seed he hid in his body (huna e Rongo ki roto i tona ure), and then returned to Mataroa and slept with his wife Pani-tinikau, who became hapu (pregnant) and brought forth the kumara.

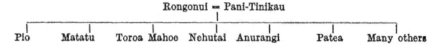

So from Rongonui-maui and Pani-tinikau came all the varieties of kumara which were used by the people of old, and which have now almost disappeared.

Different ovens for Tohunga, chiefs, and people

When the kumara family were born to Pani, her husband Rongo asked her to prepare te umu tapu (a sacred oven) in which to cook them, so that the tapu might be removed. This is the beginning of the tapu ceremonial cooking oven on this earth, and thus we have Waharoa, Kirikahu, and Kohu-kohu used for priests, chiefs, and the people. Through Rongo taking the kumara seed in secret and without the permission of Whanui in whose care it was, theft was started in this world.

Origin of theft

Pests

When Whanui found that Rongo had taken the kumara against his wishes, he was very angry, and as a punishment, he sent pests to destroy the growing kumara, in the shape of anuhe, the caterpillar, and thus made it difficult to grow. This is why there is so much difficulty in growing it, and why the large caterpillar swarms to eat it, and gives the people so much trouble. Rongo was the god of the kumara, and also the god of peace.

There are other stories relating to the kumara, but this is the one told to me by my old people.

Planting

The cultivation of kumara was arranged and carried out with great ceremonial in the old days, and the planting was done by the men, and much tapu was connected with it. No woman was allowed to do this work. It was planted at a chosen time, not always the same time, as it was colder in some parts than in others. But planting generally occurred in the spring and early summer, September, October, or November according to the English months. The men turned out in great numbers at sunrise. They would all be under tapu, so that no food would be eaten till the end of the day's work, when the tapu was lifted off by a Tohunga, and no cooking was done in the kainga. No woman could take part, for fear of polluting the tapu, which would be a great insult to Rongo.

Tapu nature of work

Bringing kumara and other plants to New Zealand

Our traditions show how food plants were carried from place to place by our ancestors in their canoes during their sea voyages. Many plants were brought from the west, and are now growing over most of the Polynesian Islands. When our ancestors left Polynesia in the great migration about six hundred years ago, they brought kumara (Impomoea batatas), taro (Colocasia antiquorum), hue (Lagenaria vulgaris,) and other foods, many of which did not grow. Kumara, taro, and hue were planted, and with the help of great labour, kumara grew in great cultivations and formed one of the most important foods of our people down to the arrival of the pakeha (European). My old people told me that the first kumara was brought to New Zealand by my ancestress Whakaotirangi, in the Arawa canoe. When the canoe arrived off the shore of Aoteroa, they saw a plant which they thought was kumara growing in quantities in the distance. The women said that it was of no use to keep their seed tubers longer, and gave them to their children to eat. But Whakaotirangi tied up her seven in a small basket, and tied the string round her neck. As the people got nearer the land and the tide came in, they saw that the plants were covered, and they were very upset. But Whakaotirangi held on to her seven kumara, and when the Arawa landed, she planted them at Para-wai. From these few seeds came all the kumara.

Whakaotirangi

Cultivation

Choice of ground

Cultivation was very hard work with the primitive Maori tools. The men had first to choose a suitable place for the cultivation. They preferred a large flat open space on high ground, open to the warmth of the sun. Damp or swampy ground would not do, and the field must not lie at the foot of a high hill where rain water would rush down in torrents and so spoil the mara (cultivation). Sandy soil was chosen if possible, or gravelly, and where the land was heavy, gravel or sand was taken up with the tikoko and brought in baskets and mixed with the soil. The people of the Bay of Plenty were favoured, for they had access to sand along the coast, and here kumara grew plentifully. Manure was never used, only ashes.

Sand bought to mix with soil

Clearing the ground

If the chosen place was near a forest, all young plants, shrubs and ferns were cleared with toki (axes), and left to dry. A little time before planting, a fire would be made at the head of the waerenga (clearing) and this would spread and burn all the wood and bracken, leaving pungarehu (ashes) all over the field. If the mara had no trees or shrubs, manuka would be cut in quantities and laid all over the mara in heaps and left to dry. On a very calm day it would be burned. This was only done when the soil was not sandy, or needed help. If planting did not follow at once, layers of cut branches of manuka would be laid over the field to prevent the ashes from being blown away.

Burning

Windscreens

The ground was generally rough and often covered with stones and scoriae, and these had to be carried some distance away, or piled in heaps at the edge of the mara. Then shelters had to be put up to protect the plants from the cold wind.

Mauri, or tapu life-principle

When planting commenced, a mauri would be placed in

the ground on the east side of the cultivation, in the form of a stone or stone image or carved stick. Or it might be a green branch of the mapou (Myrsine urvillei) which was to give life to the mara. Mokoia Island in the middle of Lake Rotorua belonged to Ngati Whakaue and Ngati Uenuku-Kopako, and had splendid sandy, fertile soil for the growing of kumara, and the kumara was abundant and some of the best I ever tasted. My relations who lived there told me that this was because of Matuatonga the kumara god which was brought over from Hawaiki in the Arawa canoe and buried there. He was the mauri, the tapu life-principle of the kumara there, and had great mana in the growing of the kumara. And they did grow. To the old Maori, not only human beings, but everything, such as trees and all plants in the forest, fish, birds, animals, mountains, and rivers, had a mauri or life-principle. With human beings it was likened to a soul. The Maori believed that nothing in this earth existed without its mauri, and that if this were violated in any way, its physical foundation was open to peril or exposed to great risk. If the mauri of a forest were violated, the trees and plants would not be able to produce in abundance, but fruits would be scarce, and there would be very few birds. With the mauri ora of man, if this is violated in any way, the thought is that with the loss of spiritual mauri, he is left without protection, and can be attacked by the bad influences of the many evil beings which float in space, by makutu (witchcraft), etc.

215

Matuatonga Atua Kumara

Matuatonga[1] the kumara god, a rude stone image, was believed to have great mana with which it had been endowed by the many Tohunga of old from far back times. It was believed to preserve the life of the cultivated kumara, and to make the tubers grow, and it also helped to protect the cultivation from the power of evil influence or magic art. Matuatonga was brought over in the Arawa canoe, and belonged to the Arawa people. Other tribes had their kumara gods. These images represented Rongo, the patron of the kumara. This stone had protecting powers over a mara kumara, for it served as a mauri, through which certain karakia pertaining to the kumara would be repeated.

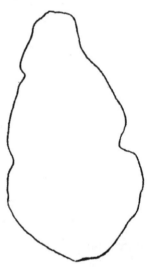

2. MATUA-TONGA

First fruit

A small piece of ground was sometimes planted and set aside, and the tubers were planted in it as an offering to the gods. Or the first fruits gathered would be given as an offering to the gods.

Planting

Much ceremony occurred when the planting was going to begin. Te Ohu, the people who undertook the various work on a maru (cultivation), gathered together at daybreak, and went to the cultivation. When the sun appeared, Te Ohu would turn and face it, while the Tohunga repeated the karakia to Rongomarae-roa, one of the children of Rangi and Papa, who had charge of all cultivated foods. Nga pura-pura, the seed tubers, which had been kept in a rua whakaahu, were carried with great care to the cultivation. The men who carried the ko, the digging implements with their long handles six to ten feet long, led the procession. They were called Kiake, and were followed by nga tangata tuahu, the men who broke up the soil with their hands, working the ashes and gravel into it, and making to puke mounds for the tubers. These were followed by a ropu (gang) of men who placed each tuber on a mound, and after them came the company who planted the tubers in the mounds already made.

Work by ropu, or companies

Tapu nature of cultivation

The workers were all under tapu, and took no food until the day's work was over. When te ohu began their digging, the whole cultivation was placed under the tapu of the gods, and the tapu remained until after the hauhakenga when the kumara was dug up and gathered into the rua kumara, or kumara pits. The first kumara planted was made an offering to the gods by the Tohunga, so that good crops might be forthcoming. All of these operations from the time of planting to the taking up of the crops were under the direction of the Tohunga.

First planted an offering to the gods

Communal nature of work

A European would go to work with his family, or even alone, but the Maori never did this. They always worked in companies. Their life was communal, and everything was for the community and not for the individual. They went to work with the chief, and worked together and moved together, sometimes to the accompaniment of song, as when using the ko. They did not look on their labours as hard work, but sang their ancient songs with joy, asking that their work would be productive and bear fruit.

The ko

It was indeed a fine sight to see an ohu at work on a large kumara cultivation, with their long-handled ko decorated with bunches of feathers near the top, working and moving in unison to the accompaniment of a chant sung by a man who acted as leader of the party, the workers joining in from time to time. Here is the chant used when men were working the cultivation with the ko.

HE WHAKATAPATAPA KUMARA[1]

Kapakapa, kapakapa, tu taku wairua, ki te ao

    Tapiritu, he maunga,

    Hekeheke iho i runga o Rehia,

    Tuhi te uira,

    Ko anahau.

Ki te hau ia, ki te hau ia,

    Ka tangi to pu, ka tangi to pu,

    Ka taupu nui a Weka uea,

    Uea te taua iti,

    Uea te taua rahi,

    Kia tutangatanga, te ara ki Mokoia.

Whakaatu manunu, whakaatu manunu

> Hara na nunu,
>
> E whia aku mate,
>
> Kei taku tua,
>
> Kei taku aro.
>
> Pihapiha manawa o te ika kua riro
>
> I hara te taua
>
> Koia ru
>
> Koia whe
>
> Koia potipoti
>
> Koia rakahua
>
> Te tama i torua
>
> Whakuia e koe
>
> Ki Waerota

Te tau mai ai tohu-ahura tiwatiwa,

> Horahia ori ka mate tama ki te wai whana,
>
> Kaore hoki nga uhi nei

Nga kai nei

> Nga taro nei
>
> Ka marere tia e te tikitiki o Wahieroa,
>
> Te tapa mai e koe taku ika nei,

Ko Hahaururoa,

Ko tutoki hau-nui,

Hauroa,

Mahuta runga,

Mahuta runga,

Mahuto raro,

He Kapua ke hoki

To te atiru,

To te atiru i tau ki whea?

I tau ki Maunganui,

Ki Maungaroa

Taku manawa ka irihia nei,

E Tupetane,

I-o.

Tenei au e Tupetane

Ko Whiti-te-marama au e Tupetane

Ko Tama-te-ahu-iho,

Ko Tama-te-ahu-ake

Ko Whitiau-te-toki

Ko Tama-i-ahua-rorowai,

Taku paenga ruwai e Apo e,

E Apo e

I-o.

Kapua hekeheke iho i runga o Rehia,

Tuhi te Uira,

Rapa te Uira,

Ko anahau,

Ki tahau ia,

Tenei koa te mokopuwananga, te tu mai nei,

Koia kia toia,

Kia tokoua, ki te kauwhau ariki,

Rongo putuputu

Rongo te mangia

Rongo te rakau ohi,

Ko tana kuru motu

E puhi e kei tai

Kei te whakarua koia,

Hutia, hutia,

Hutia te kura i o taringa,

Taku rei, taku rei,

Taku rei ka whati

He toroa, he toroa, he ta

I-o.

Reasons against translation

It would be wrong for me to attempt to translate the karakia. I cannot do it, nor is it likely that anyone else alive to-day could give its real meaning. In the first place, the words of the different karakia are very ancient, and the words used are obsolete. In the second place, religious formulae depend for their meaning on a knowledge of the religious background and history of a people over a long period, and though some lines might be translated to give a certain meaning, it is more than likely that the translation would not give the true meaning known to the old Tohunga, for only the old Tohunga knew the inner meaning of the words. Therefore it would be sacrilege for me to attempt to translate these sacred karakia.

Action in harmony with chant

When the chant begins, each man places his right foot on the foot-rest of his ko, forcing its point into the soil; then he presses the handle down and backwards to loosen the earth. The ko is pulled out, and he puts the point in again a little distance from the first hole, then turns his body, putting his left foot on the foot-rest and pushing the ko into the ground, and loosening the earth as before. He thus forms a small mound in which the kumara tuber will be planted. When this is done, the row of men who are using the ko take one step back, and repeat the performance, until the whole mara is ready for planting.

The ko

The ko, or digging-stick, was the most important digging implement of the Maori, and when it was used in the tapu ceremony of planting the kumara, it would be decorated with bunches or streamers of feathers, especially the one used by the Tohunga who led the ceremony of planting.

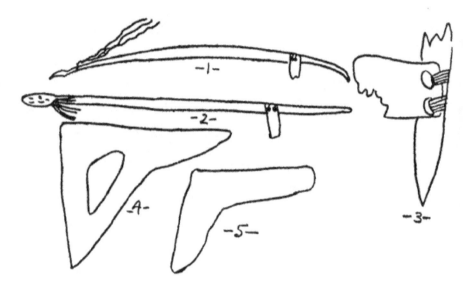

3. Digging Sticks.

The first two figures show the Ko Whakaara, ornamented with the birds' feathers. One of them is curved. The fourth and fifth show the teka, foot-rests. Sometimes this foot-rest was made in one piece with the ko, but usually the foot-rest was fastened on as shown in the third figure. The binding was of plaited flax fibre, and fitted into grooves made on each side of the ko. Some of these teka were decorated with very fine carving.

Setting the tubers

The men with the ko made the mounds, and were followed by another company of men who broke up the soil of each mound and mixed it with gravel, sand, or ashes, ready for the man who followed. This man carried the seed tubers in a basket, and placed one on each mound, and he knew beforehand how many tubers he had to carry for each row. If the row was a very large one, two baskets were used, and one of them would be carried and left in the awa, space between the rows, half way along the line. When the seed tubers were placed in a basket, the basket was kept open by sticks placed across the top, so that the sprouts would not be broken. Very great care was taken not to bruise the tubers or break the sprouts.

Planting the tubers

The tuber is placed on the left side of the mound, in the hollow space on the left side of the row. The man who follows the setter does the planting, but before he plants, he must stand so that he faces the rising sun, and also the rows of mounds which are ready to receive the tubers. He starts at Te Upoko, the head of the mara, standing in the awa (space) between the rows of puke (mounds). He plants the tubers in the rows on his left side. Taking a tuber in his left hand, he makes a hole in the mound and places the seed in it with the sprouting part upward towards the East. With both hands he covers the tuber but not the sprout, and so continues until the whole row on his left is planted. One side of the mara is called Te Upoko, the head, and the head should face the sun; the opposite end is called Te Remu, the tail. The rows run east and west; if they ran north and south there would be a poor crop. The rows were so arranged that whichever way you looked at the plantation, there was a straight row.

Karakia for planting

When the kumara tuber was being planted, this karakia[1] was repeated:

> Torona tou Kakano
>
> Whiti tua
>
> Whiti taro
>
> Whiti haha
>
> Ka tupu te wai,
>
> Ka ora te wai,
>
> > Ohi
> >
> > > Ko te wai ora o muri.

The ground was not dug all over like a European plantation, but only where the plants were to go in.

Care while growing

The leaves were looked after carefully while the plant was growing, for if they were hurt, the roots would be poor. If possible, gravel was placed under the leaves, for it helped to improve the kumara, and also allowed the air to pass through the soil while the sun covered the whole centre of the mound. This gravel was carried in kete, baskets, made of harakeke (phormium), with two handles, one on each side. The man who carried it left a heap of gravel between each two mounds all along the row, and half the gravel was scraped on to one mound, and half on to the other.

Weeding

Weeds were taken up as soon as they appeared, and our cultivations were a wonderful sight in bygone days. Even the early voyagers remarked on this. Weeding was usually done by women, and in a squatting position. I have already mentioned the fact that the planting and lifting of the kumara were very tapu ceremonies, performed only by men who knew their work well. I will now mention other implements used in agriculture, beside the ko.

Implements used in agriculture

Another implement known to my old koroua and kuia was the tima, timo, or timotimo, which was used, generally by the women, for grubbing and loosening the soil. This is a forked branch of very hard wood, mairi, titoki, or manuka, hardened in the fire. The blade is about 2$\frac{1}{2}$ inches wide, and is as long as the handle or even longer. The handle is round, and the blade gradually comes to a sharp point at the end. The handle is held in both hands, the right just above the left at the end of it. A woman kneels when she uses it, first digging it into the ground in front of her, and then pulling it towards her.

Kaheru was the word used for an English spade, but my koroua said that the old Maori one was more like a paddle. The ones used for weeding, whakaeke kumara, and hauhake (lifting), were shorter than those used for digging, being about 2–2$\frac{1}{2}$ feet long, while those used for digging were 5 or 6 feet long, and were often decorated with feathers at the top.

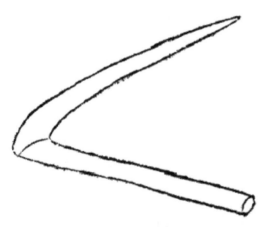

Kaheru

4. Timotimo

Hapara is the Maori form of the English word "shovel", and

I do not remember its being used by the old Maori, although it may have been used in other parts of the island. At any rate my old koroua and kuia did not know of its use as a genuine Maori implement.

A koko or tikoko was shaped like a canoe baler, and was used to scoop up earth. It was however longer and narrower and had a shorter handle. My kuia used one when she whakaeke (banked up) the rows of potatoes after weeding them. She told me that the tikoko was also used for scooping up earth to place in baskets when soil had to be carried for some distance.

Tapu nature of plantations while growing

My old kuia Marara told me that the ara or paths which led up to a kumara plantation were made tapu by a Tohunga after the planting, and that no one ever attempted to walk over or go near the plantation. The tapu was indicated by a taura, a cord or rope plaited from flax fibre with several knots tied a few inches apart, and anyone seeing this would know that it was tapu there. Sometimes a bunch of grass would be tied to a tree. No one knowingly would venture near this, and anyone who did so would die. A Mara kumara was kept safe by the tapu laid upon it, and no outsider would ever dream of asking a man of a hapu how their crops were growing, nor would he dream of going to see how the cultivation was progressing. If he was caught trespassing, he was killed.

Gathering and storing

Great care was needed in the hauhakenga, lifting out of the ground, and storing in the rua kumara (pit), as bruised kumara would destroy the pitful. Te Ngahuru, the autumn, in April, was the time for taking up the kumara, when Whanui, the star Vega appeared as a morning star. When the Tohunga saw it, the news was sent round telling the people that Whanui had arrived. This was the tohu, the sign telling them to begin to take up the kumara crops, and it was hailed with joy.

First a karakia of thanksgiving was repeated to the gods by a Tohunga, giving them praise for the good crops which had been given, and then the ceremonial whaka noa followed, taking off the tapu from the cultivation. Next the puke tapu, te mauri o te rua kumara, the first mound planted with the kumara tuber which was the mauri[1] of the kumara pit, was taken up by the Tohunga, and these first fruits were carried by him to the tuahu, a place where all religious rites were performed, and presented to Rongo-marae-koa, and buried in the ground at the foot of the tuahu.

Taking off the tapu

First fruits

Lifting

After this the men proceeded with the hauhake, or lifting of the crops. A short kaheru in the form of a short paddle slightly scooped out was what I saw my koroua using at Parekarangi when I was a child. This was made of manuka or mairi (Olea). As in the planting, the work was performed by an ohu, a number of people, who were divided up to do certain things. If there were ten or twenty men, each would take his place at the beginning of a row of kumara, and sitting on his haunches would put his kaheru carefully into the ground at the base of the mound, working in from side to side and pressing down until he thought he was far enough under the roots. He would then lift up the mound with the tubers. The men who did this did nothing else, but moved on to the next mound, and each was followed by a man who collected the kumara and placed them in the shallow ditches between the rows. The work of sorting and gathering was done very carefully to prevent bruising the tubers. The least good were separated for immediate use in the kainga, and placed in a storage pit close by, where they could be got when needed.

Storage pits

The rua kumara or storage pit is an excavation in the ground, generally on a hillside or small rise, the entrance being cut at the face of it. A small entrance is cut for a door, and the earth is excavated from here, and taken away in baskets. From the top of the doorway to the bottom of the rua the distance would be anything from six feet or more, which would be the depth of a medium-sized one. Some would be much larger and some smaller, according to the size of a cultivation. One descended into it by means of a log with steps cut out for the feet. The floor was slightly raised at the end below the doorway, and the whole floor was covered with fine gravel to a depth marked by the first joint of the thumb. The rua was lined with kaponga, slabs, of the Mamaku tree fern. This tree has a large conical base of very hard matted root fibres, sometimes three or four feet across at the surface of the ground. This base was split into slabs two or three inches thick, and made a lining which apart from its extreme hardness, had a smell which kept the rats (kiore) away. "E ka mutu te ruru o te kirikiri ki te whenua." When the gravel had been sprinkled on the floor, something soft had to be placed over it. Sometimes soft decayed wood of the pukatea rimu or other trees was crumpled up in the hands and spread over the gravel. And again rarauhe (bracken), manuka bush, or kaponga fern were used. Then the kumara was carefully placed in rows overlapping each other, keeping the heads uppermost. The seed tubers were at the back, and those for eating on each side of the entrance. Those for eating were laid down first, and then a dividing line of manuka brush was placed to separate them from the place for the seed tubers, which were then attended to. The manuka brush was also placed along the entrance at the sides and front. Sometimes the front entrance was boarded up with rough timber, but more often it was covered with earth and grass. The earth taken from the interior was thrown either on the top or the sides of the rua. The doorway was lined with thick slabs, and the top was often ornamented with carving. A thick slab which fitted the opening was used as a door, and was kept in place by a stout log or two used as a strut. Sometimes a small pit shaped like a hangi would be made to hold a few kumara for immediate use. Big ones might be 10, 20, or more feet in length, according to the size of the cultivation.

Cooking

I think I failed to mention the fact that kumara was sometimes baked in hot ashes, and the dust taken off with a stick. It was very good to eat when so baked in its skin. The roots taken away from the kumara before it grew to full size were sometimes dried, and were then called kao. They were scraped and dried in the sun on a taka or tuwhara, being turned every day, and covered over every night to prevent their getting wet with dew. When dry, they were put into baskets and eaten as they were without cooking. They were very sweet, and were eaten at any time during the day, or on a journey.

Drying

Karakia after crop was lifted

After the crop of kumara was lifted, the following karakia[1] was repeated.

Whererei, whererei te puke i te iwi roa,

    Kia tu ahua iho, kia tu ahua ake, *to,*

    Whererei te puke i a Maui, kia tu ahua iho,

    Kia tu ahua aka to,

    Teua ra to tawau e kuiai, ka rere to tawaue kuia,

    Ka ti to tawau e kuia, hai,

    Takoto au iho, au ki raro ki to Matua,

    Kia papa,

    Ko papanui,

    Ko Paparoa

    Ko papa-i-tukia

    Ko papa-i-matoe,

    Ko papa-i-wawahia

    Wawahia e Tau,

    Wawahia e Rongo

    Teua te Kano

    Ko Rua-kaeke,

    Koi waho

    Koi te hapu nui.

I have explained earlier in this chapter why the karakia cannot be translated.

The karakia used by the Maori of old show how very seriously they took agriculture, and the account I have given of their labour in clearing and preparing the soil, and in bringing sand and gravel from long distances, their care in cultivating and lifting, and their work in making storage pits and food houses, and many other details, show what good agriculturalists they were. When you see their primitive tools in the Pitt-Rivers Museum, you realize how patient and industrious they were. Another thing which shows their ability and care is the trouble they took to choose new varieties which were needed. There were fifty or more varieties of kumara.

Extent of cultivations

Early voyagers have mentioned the cultivations of the Maori as scarce in some parts. Compare, for example, Cook's First Journal, cap. v. I have already shown how our cultivations were at some distance from our kainga. The voyagers probably expected to see the plantations close to the kainga where the people lived. In the following pages I will show how my own people had their kumara cultivations in the old days, and how they were worked by the hapu who were related to each other from my remote ancestors down to the time of my grandfather and the granduncle who brought me up. But first let me quote another early author.

Nicholas, 1814–5, says:

"We observed some plantations of kumara and potatoes

belonging to Bennu and his tribe; these were not contiguous to any village or habitation, and I consider it a great proof of the insecurity in which these people live that their grounds are rarely cultivated to any extent in the immediate vicinity of those places where they reside in congregated bodies. The plantations, although they very frequently surround the villages, are generally at some distance from them, and the latter are always constructed upon either the summit or at the foot of some high and almost inaccessible hill. This is most certainly occasioned by that state of disunited barbarism and feudal enmity in which the different tribes reside among each other; who, having no moral institutions, but resorting on all occasions to physical strength, are obliged to choose those places for their defence which are best calculated for that purpose, without any regard to the barrenness or fertility of the situation. Hence the plantations are commonly in detached places where the soil is favourable, and they have no idea of concentrating their industry. But this casual plan of cultivation is however disadvantageous to the regular improvement of their land, and could the tribes be brought to live in amity with each other, and build their villages on the fertile grounds, their respective districts would in a short time assume a much more civilized appearance. The lack of concentration in industry was owing to an objection on the part of the Maori to putting all his eggs in one basket, as illustrated in the popular saying 'Ka mate kainga tahi, ka ora kainga rua,' showing that single-homed people pinch, or are overtaken by disaster, when two-homed people survive."

Our cultivations of kumara

We had kumara cultivations at *Titiwhare* and *Te Houroa*, on the north side of Tarawera Lake, and at *Toroahunganui* near Ohorongo. At *Ohorongo*, these cultivations were continued from the time of Mahanga down to Katene's time. *Keina* was a cultivation close to Ohorongo, *Karamea* was a little further to the south-west, *Te Miro* was south-west of Ohorangi. *Te Whakaki* was east of Okareka, *Te Anapoupou* north of it. We had cultivations at *Omaruarere* near Anapoupou, at *Otaikaka* near Omaruarere, at *Otahu* on the north-west side of Okareka, at *Kotore Kotia* near Okareka, at *Te Kohatu* south of Okareka, and many others, from Mahenga's time down to Te Katene.

At Rotokakahi

At Rotokakahi we had the following kumara cultivations, at *Epeha, Pikitara, Te Waipuni, Te Rapa, Te Whakahoronga, Te Parepara, Otamakare, Kaiteriria, Te Huaki, Punaruku, Tauranganui, Te Kirikiri, Owhitiki, Te Ohu, Te Pureirei*, and at other places all worked by Tuhourangi from their ancestors down to my koroua's time.

At Te Wairoa

In the vicinity of Te Wairoa, we had the following kumara cultivations: at *Punaromia, Opekarangi, Waitoharuru,* and *Punarimia,* from the time of Tutea mutu down to Rangipuawhe's time. We also had cultivations at *Kerikaria, Putanaki, Kakanui, Te Oneroa* on the south side of Tarawera Lake, and *Rotokakahi* on the peninsula. These were also old cultivations down to the time of Te Mutukuri, Te Rangiheuea, Kapekape, Te Reu, Patara Ngungukai, Te Ringitanga, Himioia, Te Kura, Te Rangipuawhe, Te Ngahue, and others.

At Rotomahana

We also had kumara cultivations at *Rotomahana,* near Te Purakua, at *Matarumakina* on the peninsula, at *Puhehou* close by, at *Mairenki* close to Hakaipari, at *Otuapani* on the mouth of Wairoa stream, at *Te Kauhanga,* at *Tapate* as far as Piripoi, at *Te Karaka,* at *Te Ariki,* at *Tahumatorea* close to Te Ariki, at *Koraranui* close by, and at *Ohapu, Ngawhana,* and many other places, from ancient times down to the time of Rangihenea, Rangipuawhe, Tamarakau, and other chiefs.

On the Waikato River, we had cultivations of kumara at *Ngaawapurua* and *Te Waihuruhuru* close by, down to the time of Keremete and Irihei, also at *Waiwhakahihi, Waikiti,* and other places, from Tuohonoa to Pehia and Takeke. We had *no* kumara cultivations at Kapanga. *Ohakiwi* was a kumara plantation at *Te Tau* down to the time of Ihaia, my grandfather.

238

And there were many others.

Other cultivations were *Te Kotuku a Wahiao, Okahu Te Pukutawhero, Te Tara o te marama, Opawhero, Waewaetapahia, Rauporoa* at Tikitapu bush, *Te Hinahina* at Moerangi, *Puhinui, Te Kapiti, Te Mairi* close by Lake Piopio, *Te Pakira o Rangiheuea, Moerangi, Te Onepu, Te Taheke, Taopu, Te Waipuna, Otanemoia, Tuwiriwiri, Tikitapu, Takapu, Karangatarau* near by, *Te Kirikiri* near Punaruku Island, *Tauranganui* at the same place, *Kaihihi, Kapkapiko* close by, *Te Pourere* close by, *Te Ewe a pareao* close by, *Pareuru* on the Huarahi (track) ki Kaiteriria, *Waikorowhiti* near Te Hemo, *Kauwaka* near Te Puna, *Te Waihuahuakakahi* close by, *Ngahawahawai* between Parekarangi and Kaihiki on the huarahi (track) to Rotokakahi, *Parihati* near Parekarangi, *Korako* near by, *Ngahe* close to it, *Tuahuahu* near by, *Raketekohenga, Oteao, Te Ruakiore, Kauhunui, Te Reinga, Te Wharewera, Te Waipaepae, Parekarangi, Mangakara, Waimate, Te Herenga, Hamutinui, Te Taie, Wharerangi, Maringiawai* near Haparangi, *Te Uraponga* in the Totara country, *Motukiore* in the same place, and many others.

People who worked on these cultivations

The people who worked on these cultivations were all hapu of Tuhourangi, namely, Ngati Uruhina, N. Puta, N. Umukaria, N. Umararoa, N. Te Amo, N. Taoi, N. Huarere, N. Tukiterangi, N. Waihakari, N. Wharetokotoko, N. Wahiao,

N. Tuohonoa, N. Tutea, N. Taumeke, N. Te Anumatao, N. Te Apiti, N. Tawaki, N. Hinemihi, N. Te Ipu, and others of Tuhourangi. *Ngati* means "descendants of", and this list may be compared with the genealogies in the chapter on Social Organization. The genealogies will also contain the names of the other chiefs mentioned throughout the above account of the kumara plantations.

Kainga of these people

Kainga (villages) of the above hapu were Motutawa, Kaiteriria, Te Wairoa, Taumaihi, Okareka, Te Whakarewarewa, Parekarangi, and Te Motuwhauake on the Waikato River, and others.

Perhaps I have said enough about the cultivations worked down to the time of my koroua and kuia Maihi te Kakauparaoa and Marara to show that other writers have not known or have failed to note the extensive plantations of the Maori, and so have failed to give a just account of their economic organization.

Fern root

At the beginning of things after Rangi and Papa had produced their many children, Tane, the one who separated his parents, took as wives various females, so that many species of trees and plants could be produced. When aruhe, i.e. fern root, was wanted, he took as his wife Tutorowhenua, and from their union came aruhe. Te Aruhe (Pteris esculenta) was one of the principal foods of the Maori. To him, Aruhe came from Haumia, the god of the fern root, who was one of the many children of Rangi and Papa, the sky parent and earth mother. Again, it was always to be had, even when other roots failed him. The fern root which was eaten was always to be found wherever one saw bracken (Rarauhe, Pteris aquilina), and this grew wild all over New Zealand. Aruhe was cultivated, and there were many fern root grounds, some of them very ancient.

Preparation

The rhizome was roasted on embers, then the roots were laid on a wooden or stone block about eighteen by eight inches, and beaten with a wooden or stone pounder, patu aruhe. The roots were then peeled and eaten. They were full of a starchy substance which tasted somewhat like arrowroot. This substance was often made into small flat loaves. The aruhe roots were anything from a quarter to an inch thick, and the outside was brown to dark brown in colour. There was usually woody fibre mixed with the starch, but when a cultivation was near the edge of the bush and the soil was rich, there was a good deal of starchy substance and little or no fibre. A favourite relish eaten with it was inanga, a small fish found in many of the lakes.

Cultivations

Cultivations were not always close to the kainga, but might be anywhere from two to fifteen miles away. A few houses would be put up close to these cultivations for the people to occupy during the work of planting, harvesting, and so on, and on these lands would also be the flax swamps, and the rat and bird snaring grounds. The cultivations would be used only by the hapu which owned the land, and no outsider would dare to come on them. All of these cultivations, like those of kumara and other vegetables, would be under rahui, that is "an enclosed place which was made tapu", and even closely related hapu would ask permission of the owners if they wanted anything special in the way of harakeke, raupo, kakaho, or anything else which might grow on this land in quantities. I will now give the reader the names of the fern root grounds which belonged to my ancestors down to the time of my grandfather, to give some idea of how the Maori worked, and the distances which he had to travel to work on his cultivations, and to gather his fern root in the spring or early summer, when he dug it up with the ko. All this travelling was done on foot except when he could cross a lake or travel by a river in his canoe. There were very narrow tracks leading in all directions to the various grounds.

Kainga of hapu which worked these cultivations

The Pa Kainga of Tuhourangi in the time of my koroua

Maihi te Kakauparaoa were at Motuiti and Te Motunui close
to Oherongo, at Kaua, Waitangi, Toumahi Otatou, Kakapiko,
Parekarangi, Kakariki potiki, Te Motuwhanake, Ngaawapuma,
Te Kopiko, Tuhureo, and all along the lake from Pukekiore
to Tikawe, Morutawa, Kariri, Pukura, Puwai, and others,
such as Kaiteriria, Te Wairoa, Okareka, and Whakarewarewa.
Motutawa was an island in the green lake Rotokakahi, and
was reached by canoes, Kaiteriria was on the mainland about
a mile and a half from the island. Te Wairoa was about two
miles from Rotokakahi, Okareka was four to six miles away
from one end of the lake, and Parekarangi was eight to ten
miles from the other end. Whakarewarewa was about nine
miles from the lake and Motuwhanake was twelve or more
miles away from it.

Fern root grounds

These kainga had fern root grounds at *Titihore, Te Heuroa,*
Te Akakahia close to Tuaparo bush, *Te Anapoupou* on the north
side of Okareka, *Matapai* on the south-west of Pukepote,
Opawhero, Puketawhero, Kahotea near Moerangi, *Puhinui*
near Waipa, *Tutihinau* south-west of Kaihiki, *Kaweka* west
of Kaihiki, *Tukoroa, Ongakero, Pukehoa* near Parekarangi,
Omanga near Parekarangi, *Ngapouwhakatutu, Horohore,*
Haparangi near the lagoon Waipupu, *Te Uruponga, Motukiore*
south of Puaiti, *Te Hikumaru, Otute Kawhara* north of
Paeroa, *Tumunui, Opuhia* at Tumunui, *Te Whakaki* north of

Opuhia, *Te Waiaireoera* near the source of Te Mitimiti north of Tumunui, *Pakaraka, Te Kawakawa, Tutaeheka, Raturoa, Toetoewhitiki, Matakana, Pareheru, Wairia, Te Pupuaka* near Matakana, *Hakaipiri* near Tunoroa, *Te Renepure, Maireriki*, both near the same place, *Te Oneroa, Karekaria, Otupoto* south-west of Wairoa, *Whenuakite* on the south-east shore of Lake Rotokakahi, *Ngatamahine* close to the lake, *Hineata, Otamatoine, Te Whakahoronga* near by, *Te Maire, Raupo, Te Puna* on Rotokakahi, *Tauranganui* near here, *Te Heke* near Te Puna, *Te Kotukutuku* on the north-west shore of the lake, *Ngaparehu* towards Moerangi, *Otupahaka* and *Te Waipuna* on Tikitapu Lake, *Karanga tarau, Taopo* on Moerangi, *Punaromia* near Te Wairoa, *Te Wharangi* close by, *Te Anga* further to the north, and many others. These were ancient fern grounds used by our tupuna, and continued in use down to my koroua.

Para tawhiti

Para tawhiti, para reka, or para (Marratia fraxinea), the fern tree, was another important food of our people. It used to be plentiful in many parts of New Zealand. The Maori means this root, when he says that he always had potatoes in New Zealand. The rhizome was a rough shaped tuberous mass of fleshy roots which were cooked and eaten. This tuberous mass was separated into many parts and planted.

Tawa berries

Tawa berries (Beilschmidia tawa. Nesodaphne tawa) were an important food of the Maori. The fruit was about an inch long, and like a dark-coloured plum when picked fresh. When ripe, it was eaten as a fruit and was juicy and not unpleasant to taste. The kernel is very like the seed of the date, and very hard. These berries were collected in plenty in baskets, many being picked up from the ground where they had dropped. The kernels were cooked in a hangi for several hours, then dried in the sun, and stored for future use. If cooked well, they would keep for a long time. My own hapu of Wahiao gathered their tawa berries at Moerangi, Kakapiko, Parekarangi, and other places, and took them to cook in the boiling and steam holes of Whakarewarewa. The baskets of tawa were first cooked in the boiling water for a few hours, and then placed in a steam hole in the ground and left to steam for two or more days. They were then spread out on the papa hohatu, the silica formation beside a boiling hole, to dry. After this, they were put into a pataka (store-house) where they would keep for years. Berries which were needed for immediate use could be eaten as soon as they were cooked, but the dried and stored tawa had to be soaked in water and placed in a hangi for several hours until they were soft. They were dark brown, and the water in which they were soaked was quite thick when the tawa was ready to eat. We had plenty when I was a child, and I used to enjoy them. With a little sugar, they were very nice indeed. A woman who was mate wahine (menstruating) was not allowed to cook tawa berries, nor would she think of it. The belief was that if she did so the berries would be mata, and would not get cooked. Nga hapu of Tuhourangi gathered tawa berries at Pakareka, Tutaekeha, Tumunui, and other places, and took them in baskets to be cooked in the hot springs at Rotomahana and Whakarewarewa. A rahui, sign that the place was tapu and belonged only to those hapu, stood at Otamakari over these places. Some of the hapu of Tuhourangi who gathered tawa berries in the above-mentioned places were Ngati Taoi, N. Tuohonoa, N. Te Apiti, N. Tutea, and N. Umukaria. The reader is again referred to the opening pages of the chapter on Social Organization, and to the genealogies in that chapter for an explanation of the above names.

People who may not cook tawa berries

Various other foods

Tawhara was a favourite food of the people, and was eaten fresh. It was the large thick fleshy part of the climbing kiekie (Freycinetia banksii), and was white and sweet to taste. The bracts were collected in large taha, calabashes, during the summer. The fruit of the kiekie was called Ureure, and was not ripe until the winter, when it was collected and eaten fresh. Thus kiekie supplied the Maori with food in summer and winter. Kiekie also supplied the Maori with the material for their finest whariki, floor mats. The leaves were scraped and prepared like the flax, and became quite white when dry.

Kiekie

Nikau

Te korito, the blanched heart of the Nikau palm (Areca sapida) was also a favoured, though not a common food, as the Nikau died when the korito was taken. It was cooked in a hangi, and was also eaten raw.

Maikaika

Maikaika: (I) Orthoceras solandri, (2) Anthro-podium cirrhatum, (3) Thelymitra pulchella.

The root of the kawakawa was used for toothache.

Kotukutuku

Fruits were very plentiful in the old days. Among others was the kotukutuku or konini (Fuchsia exorticata). The shrubs were easily got at, and were gathered in baskets, each berry being picked off the shrub with the hand. The berry was deep purple, and very nice to eat.

Rohutu

The rohutu (Myrtus pedunculata) was a small orange-coloured berry, about the size of a red currant, with a large and very hard seed. When the berries were ripe, an old tuwhara, rough floor mat was placed under the tree which was then shaken hard so that the fruit fell in quantities on to the mat.

Poporo

The berries of the poporo (Solanum aviculare) were about the size of a small plum. They were gathered when ripe and eaten fresh.

Tutu of puhou

Tutu, the berries of the puho (Coraria ruscifolia), also called tupakihi or tutupakihi, were gathered when fully ripe and of a deep blue-black colour. These berries were borne in long racemes like the flowers of wistaria. They were squeezed in the hand, and the juice was caught in a calabash, making a drink known as wai puhou. Great care must be taken not to leave any of the berry in the liquid. Bad results would follow if the berry were swallowed whole as it is poisonous. The drink is a thick deep purple one, and is very sweet and refreshing in summer. Tutu juice was often mixed with other food such as aruhe (fern root), after the starchy substance has been pounded.

Karaka

The berries of the karaka tree (Corynocarpus laevigata) were a favourite food. The berries were never eaten when green as they are then poisonous. They are gathered when they are of a bright orange colour. The outside is a pulpy layer, and the berry looks like a small plum. Inside the pulp is a seed which is enclosed in a tough fibrous network. The berries are gathered in great abundance in the autumn, and placed in large baskets of flax. As soon as the baskets are filled, they are emptied into a large hangi, and baked and steamed for about twenty-four hours. They are then collected into rough flax baskets which are loosely plaited, and placed in running water, being shaken from time to time to get rid of the outside pulp and skin. The berries are then free inside their tough husk. When eaten, the tough husk was cut round the middle with a shell, and each half was pressed between the thumb and forefinger to get the soft substance out. I myself had plenty of karaka berries, tawa berries, and most of the fruits I have mentioned.

Tii

Tii, kouka, or whanake (Cordyline australis) was and is a favourite food. Te korito, the blanched heart shoot which formed the base of the youngest leaves of the tii after the outside had been stripped off, was cooked in a hangi and eaten. It was also eaten raw, or roasted on hot embers or ashes. It tasted like an artichoke to me, and is spoken of by English people as the cabbage tree.

Ti Para

Ti Para used to be highly thought of. The root was prepared like fern root, being pounded on a flat log or stone to break up the fibre in the pulpy mass. This was cooked in a hangi for several hours, and when cooked appeared as a gluey mass. It had a sweet taste. It was stored in a pataka (food house) and kept a long time. When one was travelling for long distances, or in time of war when there was nothing else, it was most satisfying.

Hinau

The fruit of the hinau tree (Elaeocarpus dentatus) was collected in great abundance from under the tree when ripe, but was not eaten in this raw state. The fruit was about the size of a sloe or small damson, and had a hard dry skin without much pulp. It was placed in a wooden trough and covered with water and left to soak. The mass was then rubbed between the hands and the skin and nut were strained out and the water carefully drained away, leaving a kind of coarse meal which was made into a large cake and cooked for several hours in a hangi. The old Maori considered it a great luxury.

Makomako

Makomako (Aristotelia racemosa). The fruit of the makomako was eaten in the old days. It is a small red berry which turns almost black when ripe. The fruit is eaten as it is, throwing away the seed inside. This fruit could also be squeezed in the hands or through a basket to get a thick fluid like the "tutu", which made a nice sweetish drink.

Moku and pikopiko

The very young fronds of the fern moku (Asplenium bulbiferum) were cooked and eaten as a vegetable, and also the very young fronds of the paretao (Asplenium obtusatum). The very young fronds of the pikopiko were gathered when they were four to six inches high, and cooked in a hangi on top of the kumara and eaten as a vegetable. It was as tender as asparagus, and not unlike it in taste, and very nice indeed to eat. These young fronds of pikopiko were sometimes cooked and left in water for about two weeks, when they acquired an acid taste. The taste was like that of tinned asparagus slightly acid, and it was considered a great luxury.

Mamaku

Mamaku or korau (Cyathea medullaris), known as the Black Tree Fern, is the largest of the tree ferns, often growing to a height of fifty, sixty, or more feet. The pitau (pith) is slimy but sweetish. It is cut into thin slices and cooked for a long time in a hangi, and the cooked slices are then threaded on flax string and hung up to dry in the sun. It is nice to eat. The fibrous cone at the base of the tree is split into slabs two or three inches thick and used for lining the kumara pits. This base is made of hard matted root fibres, and rats do not like gnawing through it.

Hakeke

Hakeke (Polyporus sp.) was an edible fungus which the Maori enjoyed eating, and also the harore (Agaricus adiposus). These were found in the bush on live and dead trees in plenty, and were gathered and eaten in the warm weather in summer. I have heard others mentioned, but have only tasted these two. The colour is a darkish brown.

Raupo

The pungapunga, the yellow pua, or pollen of the raupo (Typha angustifolia) was mixed into cakes with water and baked. The pungapunga was gathered in summer when the plant was in full flower, and was obtained by shaking the dense flowering spikes gently. Raupo grows in swamps by the edge of streams and rivers and lakes. It has a sweetish taste. The middle part of the white succulent roots of the raupo, called koreirei, was also favoured as a food. It was generally eaten raw during the summer season. I have often eaten it, and found it not unpleasant.

Puwha

Puwha (Sonchus oleraceus. var.) was a very favourite vegetable of the Maori. I myself gather the sow thistle here and cook it to eat, as it reminds me of our own puwha, of which I am very fond. Puwha was used only as a vegetable, and was gathered each day when needed. After thorough washing, it was placed wet on top of the kumara or other vegetable in the hangi to cook. It might even be placed on meat or fish, but never on the hot stones. Only the young leaves or the tops of the older plants were used. When the puwha was not picked young, it would grow into a plant two or three feet high, and the shoots would flower. The succulent stems contained a bitter milky juice which came to the surface when the flower tops were plucked off. This was left on a sunny day, for a few hours, then gathered between the thumb and first finger, adding the thick creamy mass of several plants together. This was used as a sort of chewing gum called pia or ngau, which tasted very bitter at first. But after a little chewing the bitterness disappeared, and this gum was much enjoyed, especially by the women, who vied with each other in seeing who could make her pia crack the loudest.

Pohue

The roots of the pohue (Convolvulus sepium) were dug up out of the ground, cooked in a hangi and eaten. The root was long and tough, and got after much trouble. It was quite good to eat.

Taro

Taro, like kumara, had many varieties, but unlike kumara,

it was not dug up out of the ground until ready for cooking. It was scraped and cooked in a hangi, and was very good to eat, being floury or mealy (mangaro). Taro played an important part in many ceremonial observances, such as a tangi for a tangata rangitira,[1] at a hakari (feast) given at the marae, after the tohi rite[1] had been performed over a tamaiti rangatira, at a Hahunga (exhumation), and at the visit of a distinguished rangatira visitor. All of these subjects are treated under their appropriate headings.

Hue

The hue, gourd, was cultivated largely by the old people from seeds. It was thought much of as it would bear all summer in plenty. The Maori used it when it was very young, a kotawa about four to eight inches long, and cooked it in a hangi with potatoes or kumara or any other food. It was also eaten cold. It was cooked whole or cut in two, without peeling, and the young seeds were left in, so that the whole was eaten. From the hue came the gourds or calabashes for holding water or oils, and the taha for holding preserved birds and animals. These latter are treated later in this chapter. The hue would be left until it was quite ripe and the skin hard. These gourds were dried carefully in the sun and by a fire. A hole was made close to the end where the stalk was, and from this small hole all the seeds and everything inside was carefully scooped out with a piece of wood. When the gourd is ripe, the inside shrivels up, and much of it can be shaken out through the hole. A large taha would hold many gallons of water, and the same one would be used by a family for several generations. In such a case, the family would give it a name. Small gourds (oko) were cut in two when ripe, and used for serving small fish and liquid food. When I was a child, inanga (a small fish) was generally served in these vessels, or in wooden ones of the same shape. Scented oils for the hair and body were often kept in these small gourds. The kakano, seeds, of hue were placed in fern fronds (Pteris esculenta) and put into a basket which was tied to a stake in running water and left there for two or three days, so as to help the seed to grow quickly.

Calabashes

Planting

Mingi or tumingi

The fruit of the tumingi (Cyathodes acerosa) was eaten fresh and was good. The fruit was white, pinkish, or red, and was about three-quarters of an inch in diameter.

Potatoes

The pakeha introduced the potato, and a large kind of reddish sweet potato which the Maori called waina, and both of these roots were very much easier to work than the kumara of the old days. This was why the large kumara cultivations were neglected, for the new foods took the place of the old. Some of the old varieties of kumara were the toromahoe, kokorangi, matakauri, moio, kirikaraka, kawakawa, papahaua, taratamata, pokerekahu, and very many others of which a few are still planted in many parts of the island in a small way. But for the most part they have disappeared.

The Maori liked the potato as much as any of the introduced plants in the very early days, although it was some time before he was used to it. It was supposed to have been introduced by Captain Cook at Queen Charlotte Sound in 1773, with many other seed plants and the pig. It was also planted by Crozet in the Bay of Islands in 1772. In the Journal of the Polynesian Society, vol. iii, p. 132, it appears to have been introduced by de Surville in 1769, when wheat, maize and the seeds of European fruits were planted, and it was first planted at the Bay of Islands on the north of the North Island. As the roots increased in after years, it was passed on to other people living on the coast, but it was many years before it was introduced for the first time to our parts by Te Whatiu, a man of Tuhourangi, and by Te Whiu, a man from Ngati Rangiwewehi at Puhinga. This was told me by my papa (uncle) Mita Taupopoki. The hapu of Tuhourangi made cultivations of potatoes from the time of their grandfathers down to the present time, according to my papa, and thus it appears that our potato cultivations in the inland parts were started in the early part of the nineteenth century. My papa also stated that the potato took the place of the fern root, aruhe, as it contained the same starchy substance. My old koroua and kuia told me the same thing. The potato was cooked in a hangi with the kumara, or was boiled in a "kohua", a pakeha iron pot on three legs. It is supposed to have got its name thus. When the first Maori made a bargain for an iron kettle, the man from whom he got it said "Go ashore". The Maori called it "Kohua" ever afterwards, and all saucepans have the same name, a corruption of the words "Go ashore".

Cultivations

Tuhourangi made large cultivations of potatoes, and these were at Titikore, Tikitapu, Orangipurea, Te Horoa, Te Piripiri, Te Manuka, Te Puna, and other places between Ohorango and Maungarawhiri. Our grandfathers worked them down to our time. There were also cultivations at Te Manukapiko, Kaua, Ngotengote, Waitangi as far as Te Whakaki, Te Areapoupou, Omaruare north of Okareka, Akakahia on the edge of Okareka bush, Matapaia on the boundary of the same bush, Te Huruhu, Otahu on the west side of Okareka, Te Kohatu on the south shore, and at many other places, all belonging to Ngati Uruhina, a hapu of Tuhourangi, and these were worked from our grandfathers' down to our time, i.e. from the early nineteenth century until the eighties.

Fish from the sea

Fish was a very important food of the old Maori, who was an expert fisherman with the seine or with the hook and line, and there was plenty of fish in the sea. He thought nothing of going a long way from shore in his frail canoe, for was it not under the protection of Tangaroa, the god of the ocean? Tangaroa was one of the offspring of Rangi, the heavens, and Papa-tuanuku the earth mother, and he represented all fish which live at Rangiriri, where all fish come in from the sea.

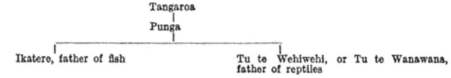

Fishing expedition

When a fishing expedition was arranged, several canoes, each manned by several men, were placed under strict tapu. If a man was married, he kept away from his wife until all fishing operations were over. Both men and canoes were under tapu, and each canoe would carry a mauri, such as was explained in the section on kumara, in a hidden part to maintain the tapu, and add mana to move the gods when an appeal was made asking protection for the ropu (company) from the many dangers at sea, and from the many beings who lived in the deep waters of Moana-nui-a Kiwa, the great ocean of Kiwa. [Here a karakia is omitted.]

Kiwa and Tangaroa

Kiwa was an atua under whose care the ocean was, and was looked on by the old Maori as a very important atua in the seafaring days when they traversed the ocean exploring the great expanse beyond. With this belief no fear came into their hearts, for were not their karakia heard by Tangaroa, who had taken them under his care while they were on the sea?

First fruits

The first fish caught on an expedition was offered to Tangaroa as a thanksgiving, and it was done with the ceremony of karakia. The fish was then placed in the sea again, and this karakia was repeated asking that abundance of fish might be sent to fill their nets or bite on their hooks. [Here a karakia is omitted.]

Tapu

As I said, tapu was connected with almost everything pertaining to fishing, the people who went being tapu, and their canoes, and the making of their nets. The men who went on fishing expeditions had no food before they went, and none until after their return, when the tapu was taken off by a Tohunga. Tapu entered into all that they did, as atua were watching over them close at hand in all their work at fishing, and the success of their venture depended on their observing strict rules of tapu. Even when fish was caught, and pulled up into the waka (canoe), it must not touch the top of the gunwale. If it did, it was considered to be an evil omen, aitua. When fish was placed in the canoe, it was laid in the way of the canoe, and not across it. If the fish were placed across and a man stepped over them, it was thought that some aitua (bad luck) would happen to him.

Property in fishing grounds

The tribes or hapu who owned land down to the sea would own the fishing rights for some distance out to sea. A stake would be put in at each end to mark the boundary line on each side, and these might be a few miles, or many miles apart. The stakes prevented any outsider from fishing in the waters. Only the members of the hapu, or of the several sub-hapu, who owned the land would have any right here. A mauri (talisman) would generally be buried on the land near the coast. This was often a stone. This mauri of sea fish had great mana from the gods, and so represented their mana, and was supposed to have the power to bring the fish from other parts of the sea to those parts. The Maori had names for each fishing rock, ground, or bank which belonged to a hapu, and called them all by name. Some of them were eight or ten miles out in the deep water. The Maori knew all the signs of a good fishing ground.

Mauri

Of course no Maori went out fishing alone. Fishing, like nearly everything else, was done by a ropu or company of men, and a fishing expedition would be talked over and arranged several days beforehand. Two or three canoes, or a fleet would go out manned by men who were members of a hapu, or of two or three hapu which were related to each other. Their fishing grounds were sometimes five, eight, or more miles away.

Nets

When a new net was to be made, an expert would go to the place where the harakeke, flax, grew and would pull out two young leaves from the root part in the middle. If a tioro, i.e. screeching sound was made, that was a good omen for the new kupenga (net). He would take these to rito harakeke (leaf-buds of the flax) to the tuahu, the sacred place of the kainga, and place and leave them there. Not until this was done would the men go out to cut the flax for preparing to make their net. The mata (mesh) in the centre was smaller than that at the two ends. Many men made it over their fingers, but sometimes a papa kupenga, a wooden mesh-gauge, was used. A gauge for a small mesh is papa kutikuti, and one for a large mesh is papa matahaere. Te rangatahi is a small form of kupenga eight or ten fathoms long.

All of the parts of the seine net are mentioned in the

following account[1] of the net belonging to Te Pokiha, who lived at Maketu in the Bay of Plenty.

The great net of Te Pokiha

Te Pokiha, a chief of Ngati Pikiao of Te Arawa tribe had a kupenga made by the members of his hapu in 1885. At the beginning of the winter, each family group began to make one of the sections, and while doing the work, the men were all under tapu. It took eight or nine months to make, and three hundred or more men worked on it. One family group made te konae or ngake, the middle part of the net, others made the two matakeke parts on either side of the konae, while other family groups made the taura-matakeke or two sections outside the two matakeke parts, and still others made the two end sections. Some other men went to Motiti Island (Flat Island) to gather smooth oval stones on the beach there, each stone weighing about a pound. These stones were put into woven pouches and used as sinkers. The floats, korewa, karewa, or poito, were made of whau wood (Entelea aborescens), one of the lightest of New Zealand woods. Then there was the kaharunga, the rope which was strongly plaited from the leaves of the whanake (Cordyline), and also the kahararo, the same kind of rope which ran along the bottom of the seine. The pae-runga and paeraro were the ropes used to haul in the seine.

When everything was ready, the net was taken to Otumakaro

flat just below Maketu kainga, and here the toronga or setting up occurred with high ritual by the Tohunga. As all this was a very tapu ceremony, the men took no food until after each day's work, when the tapu was taken off by the Tohunga. At Otumakaro the net was tightly drawn to many rows of strong posts. The sinkers, karihi, were placed inside the akopua or pouches of mesh, and tied strongly to the kahararo, that is the lower rope, about a foot apart from each other. The floats were secured to the kaharunga or upper rope, and a taketake or rod was put at the end to keep the seine stretched. When the net was completed, it was measured, and the length of it was ninety-five chains, and the weight of it was about two tons. On its completion, the net was spread north and south, and the Tohunga cut off the loose ends and took them to the tapu place and left them there. He then repeated a karakia so that the first wetting and hauling of the net might be waemaria, i.e. lucky. He then returned to the net which was still spread out at full length on the ground, and had to be carried by numbers of men in this same position to the canoe. Then came a great difficulty. There was no canoe at Maketu large enough to carry this heavy net. Men were sent to Te Awa te Atua several miles further down the coast to Ngati Rangitihi who had two large war canoes, and on the following day they paddled them to Maketu, steering them straight into the Maketu River. The net was then carried by a great number of men. These took their stand on the west side of the net, about ten feet apart, waiting for the signal from the Tohunga. At the word "Hapainga!" (Lift it) each man gathered the net together, and threw it up so that it lay on his left shoulder, and at another signal from the Tohunga, they all moved forward as one man with the Tohunga leading the line.

The rauawa, the beautiful carved topside, was removed from each canoe, for with these carvings, they were war canoes and could not be used for fishing, and the canoes were placed twelve feet apart and a strong platform was nailed across the two to make a stage on which to place the seine. On New Year's Day of 1886 then, the great seine was taken and placed on this smooth stage, and thirty to forty men paddled the double canoe out of the river into the sea, going some distance along the coast in a westerly direction under the directions of Tohe te Whanarere, who managed operations from the top of a telegraph tower on shore, a tower nearly a hundred feet high. The men on the canoe could not move or let the net down until instructions were given, even though they saw many shoals of fish as they steered their canoe. When the old man Karanga shouted "Haukotai mai!" (Surround it), the canoe passed quickly beyond the shoal while half a dozen men put out the net. They steered north then west, and lastly brought the canoe to shore with much of the net not let out, some little distance from the mouth of the Maketu River. The seine was so full of fish and so heavy that even the thousand or so spectators who tried to haul it in failed. Te Whanarere now took off his clothes and rubbed his body with kokowai or takou, i.e. red ochre which has been mixed with fish oil, and went into the sea. The many fish were struggling about in the net, some being sharks and sting-rays, but he did not heed them, as he said that they would not notice anything as they were only seeking a way out. He swam out to the canoe, and asked the men to lift the konae, the middle part which had now turned and formed the corner part, clear of the bottom, and they did so twice, emptying out many fish to try to lighten the net. After much labour and time, the incoming tide helped to bring the net a little way up the beach, where it was staked. Then there was a long wait until the tide receded, and the fish were left on the sand, and were carried up on shore above the high water mark.

All this time none of the men had partaken of food. Then Te Pokiha arranged thirty-seven spaces, and placed a man at each of them. Five hundred fish were placed in each of these spaces, and then two hundred and fifty on each again, and so on until each tahua or mound contained a thousand fish. These tahua were then presented to the various hapu of Te Arawa who were present, and a tahua was presented to Captain Mair and the pakeha people who were there. These tahua were made up of schnapper, traveller, kahawai, gurnand, parore, tarakihi, kingfish, mangopare, pepeke, kapeta, tutahuna, mangotara, many kinds of small shark, koheriri (horse mackerel), kutorotoro (sand fish), and many other small fish.

Division of catch

Offering of fish to Tangaroa

When the catch is collected and taken out of the net, the Tohunga takes two of the fish from the catch, and takes them to the tuahu, sacred place. He first places two sticks in the ground, one on the western and the other on the eastern side of the wahi tapu. He hangs a fish on each of these sticks, offering them to Tangaroa, after which he repeats another karakia lifting off the tapu. After this a feast of fish is prepared to celebrate the occasion, and the tapu is lifted by the Tohunga from the people, and from the land and sea which is around them. Then two sacred fires are kindled, at one of which food is cooked for the more important tapu men and the influential women, and after this the people can eat.

Taking off tapu

Watching for fish

There were expert men who understood all the movements of a school of fish. These men generally took up a position on the top of a hill near the sea, and looked out for any signs of a school of fish, and then passed on the sign to a party of men who were fishing in a canoe. The seas which surrounded New Zealand were teeming with fish. A number have already been mentioned in the Maketu account. The mango (shark) was taken, not only to eat, but for the teeth. The teeth of the mako shark, or some of its species, were used as ornaments and as cutting implements. The flesh of the dried shark was considered a great delicacy. It had a very strong smell. There were also hapuku (groper), tamure (schnapper), kanae (mullet), warehou (sea bream), moki, kahawai, kumukumu (gurnand), and other fish.

The shark

Preservation of nets

Large nets were hung up to dry on high tarawa, rails, and when dry were put away on a whata (elevated platform), and a roof was made over it to preserve them from the weather.

Seine fishing

Two large canoes 40–50 feet long were used for taking out a large fishing net, and in the case of an extra large net like that of Te Pokiha, two large canoes from 60–80 feet long would be used. In the old days when the seine was placed on the canoes, the Tohunga repeated a karakia directed to Tangaroa. During such performances very heavy tapu lay on the land and sea. Then the prow of the waka (canoe) is turned towards the sea, and the Tohunga steps into it, followed by each of the men in turn, who are careful to step into it with the left foot first.

Its tapu nature

5. Prow of Fishing Canoe.

They then take their hoe, paddles, and paddle as one man towards the place where they intend fishing. When they get there they begin to pass the seine over the side of the canoe, and as it touches the water and gets wet, the Tohunga stands up and repeats another karakia. While the canoes go ahead, the net is let out, and when the centre passes out, another karakia is repeated. When the net is drawn, the Tohunga takes a fish out with his left hand, but holds it so that its head is still in the water, and says, "Go under the great ocean, and gather in the multitudes, and bring them here." If the catch is a heavy one, the Tohunga repeats a karakia to prevent the net from breaking.

Making a net

I have already described the way in which a large net was made in sections in the account of Te Pokiha's net, and have shown how each section was the work of several men in a family group. Each man netted a line of meshes, and they worked so as to follow each other. The work was done from left to right, and when starting to make a net, te ngakau, a strongly plaited rope, was doubled and tied securely to a peg which was firmly driven into the ground. The first line of meshes was made on this rope which was looped, the meshes working loosely and freely on the looped rope. Te kaita, the man who makes the meshes, gets on with his work, and pushes what he finishes along the rope to his left, so bunching the meshes together. When making a mesh, he passes the strip of flax he is working with over the gauge, and hitches it on to the row above. When the section is ready, the ngakau is drawn out. The worker often has to tie on another strip of phormium as he works along. These nets are owned by the community.

Small nets were made of dressed muka (fibre) string, which was rolled into a ball that was held and passed through the upper mesh. The ngakau was stretched between two pegs. As I have seen it, the worker had a bundle of strips of dressed flax beside him. He doubled the end of the flax to pass it through the mesh, and when he came to the end of the strip, he tied on another strip with a knot. The mesh was exactly the same as that used by Europeans.

How the Maori got the net

When I was a small child, I never got tired of hearing the many stories of te patupaiarehe. One of our old stories says that the fishing net was not always known to the Maori, but that they acquired the art of making it from the Turehu or patupaiarehe people who were fair skinned people with light reddish hair. An ancestor called Kahukura happened to find some of these Turehu people while they were hauling in their nets one night. They never used their nets by day but only by night, and he thought this very strange indeed. One night he helped them to haul in their nets, and as it was dark, they did not see that he was a stranger. He was much pleased to find out about the net which was then unknown to the Maori, and thought of a way by which he could procure one of these nets. He thought that if he worked slowly, he would delay the work, knowing that the Turehu could not stand the light of day. After a catch of fish, they put the fish on a string to hang them up. While they were busy doing this, he thought of his plan, and instead of tying the cord to the first fish, he left it loose, so that as fast as they threaded the fish at one end of the cord, they slipped off the line at the lower end. Thus morning appeared before the work was finished. The Turehu all ran away frightened of the light, and flew into the forest, leaving the net on the beach. This is how we came to know and to use the fishing net and learned how to make it. The story came with our people from Polynesia.

Various early authors

In *Cook's First Voyage*, Cook writes: "The seine, the large net which has already been noticed, is produced by their united labour, and is probably the joint property of the whole town. Their fishing hooks are of shell or bone, and they have baskets of wicker work to hold the fish." On, he writes: "Early in the morning, the Indians (meaning Maori) brought in their canoes a prodigious quantity of mackerel, of which one sort were exactly the same with those caught in England. These canoes were succeeded by other canoes equally loaded with the same sort of fish, and the cargoes purchased were so great that everyone of the ship's company who could get salt cured as many as would serve him for a month's provision. These people frequently resort to the bay in parties to gather shell-fish, of which it affords an incredible plenty. Indeed, wherever we went, whether on the hills or through the vales, in the woods or on the plains, we saw many wagon loads of shells in heaps, some of which appeared fresh, others very old."

Crozet in his *Voyage*, writes also of the abundance of many kinds of fish caught by the Maori, and of the art of the Maori in all that concerns fishing, and goes on to say: "Their fishing lines, as well as their nets of every description, are knotted with the same adroitness as those of the cleverest fishermen of our seaports. They manufacture seines five hundred feet long, and for want of corks to hold up the nets, they make use of a very light white wood, and for lead to weigh it down, they make use of very heavy round pebbles enclosed in a network sheath which runs along the bottom of the seine, etc."

Koura

The taruke is a lobster pot which the Maori used in taking the sea crayfish (koura), and some of these pots were very large. The bait, and some stones for sinkers were put inside. A plaited rope was fastened to the taruke, and the end was fixed securely to a float. Karakia were repeated when these large pots were set. Crayfish were also taken by diving. Men and women were clever at the work of ruku koura, that is diving for crayfish among the rocks of the sea.

Trawling

Kahawai (Arripis salar) was caught by trawling. A fleet of small canoes went out, with one or two men to paddle each. Then a man would throw out his line and hook when they reached a good fishing ground or shoal of fish, and the canoe would be paddled swiftly through the water. The Pa fish hook was generally used when trawling for kahawai, and no bait was required, as the coloured paua (haliotis) shell in the water was just like a small fish, and was sufficient to lure the kahawai.

Hapuku (groper), another favourite fish, was also caught by trawling. This was good eating, especially the head, the part I always liked to have. Kanae (mullet) was another favourite, which to me tasted like the mackerel I have eaten in England.

All the fish were steamed in a hangi, though some were dried and put away in a whata for future use.

Usages in connexion with line fishing

When men went fishing, and one of them had a new line, none of the others would throw out his line till after the new line had been wetted. When placing his bait on the hook or hooks, he would tuwha, spit on it, and after gathering up his line, he would pass it under his left kuwha (thigh). After this he would turn his face to the bow of his canoe, and throw his line over the left side of it, and as the line went out and got wet, he held it in his left hand, and picking up some sea water in the cup of his right hand, sprinkled this on the line. The first fish he caught would not be eaten, but kept to be given as an offering to the gods. This offering would be cooked on a fire which was specially kindled on his return to land, and the fish, which was divided into two parts, was offered to the spirits of his male ancestors, and to the spirits of his female ancestors.

Lines

Te aho hi ika, the lines used for fishing, were made from the finely dressed muka (fibre) of the flax. They were very strong, and often carried hooks to catch very large fish, such as the manga (barracuda), or the hapuku (groper).

Hooks

Hooks were made from wood, shell, or bone, and often from human bone. They were very cleverly made from many different designs, according to the mind of the man making them. Those of wood were often lined with paua, i.e. haliotis shell, the surface of the wood being gouged so as to fit the rough back of the haliotis exactly, and then the barb was fixed on at the end. These were called pohau manga. Some hooks were made of shell only, and when they were drawn through the water, they looked very like fishes.

Some details of making

A lecture of Mr. Balfour's reminded me of certain hooks which were fashioned by nature, and needed little finishing by the human hand. In my district manuka grew near Lakes Rotoiti and Rotorua, and this became quite famous for making hooks. People came from the coast on purpose to get these manuka sticks, which the prevailing winds had blown almost into the shape of fish hooks. The illustration shows the manuka bush growing, and the slight alterations needed to make it into a strong hook.

Natural hooks

Use of haliotis

Wood of the tawhai was often used for making hooks.

When the strip of haliotis shell was cut to line a hook, the back had to be left in its original lumpy state, as the removal of the lumps would break the shell. As I suggested before, the wooden back of the hook was gouged so as to receive these lumps, and thus the strip of haliotis was made to fit the wooden back closely.

Various fish

Hapuku the groper was caught with a hook and line. Whai or sting-ray was taken with a wooden spear. Wheke or octopus if small were taken by hand from among the rocks. Should the wheke twine its many legs round the arm of the catcher, he puts his other hand underneath the body. Kahawai was taken with a hook and line, the hook being a wooden one lined with haliotis which served as a lure.

Shell-fish

Shell-fish was an important food, and many species were found in the sand of the beach when the tide was out. The varieties are too numerous to mention, but the shell middens found all over the country, not only by the coast, but far inland in the middle of the islands, will show how important shell-fish was as a food. All shell-fish were collected by women and not by men. An old belief was that they are all descendants of Hine-moana the Ocean Maid. Tuangi or cockles originated from Te Arawaru and Kaumaihi. Kuku or mussels originated from a relative of Hine-moana, from whom also sprang all the different kinds of seaweed which were to form a shelter for her descendants.

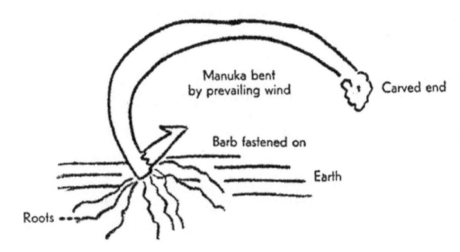

6. Manuka hook fashioned by nature.

Seaweed

Karengo (Laminaria sp.) was a seaweed which grew on flat clayey tidal rocks. It grew in plenty on the east coast of New Zealand, and great quantities were gathered round the East Cape. The plant was very slippery to touch, and anyone treading on it would slip immediately. It was collected and left in the sun to dry, and then put into baskets and stored for future use. Rimurehia or rehia was an edible seaweed, gathered in the sea close to the shore, or on the beach, and cooked in a hangi and eaten. Rimiparo was another seaweed gathered and cooked and eaten in the same way. In the summer it was sometimes eaten cold.

Use in sacrifice

Rimurimu or rimu (seaweed) was used as a sacrifice by a Tohunga in a religious ceremony when giving thanks for a successful ocean voyage Ki nga atua o te moana, i.e. to the sea deities. It was also offered Hai whaka noa i te waka hou, to take the tapu off a canoe nearly finished, and for taking the tapu off persons or places which had been connected with the dead.

These children, that is to say the seaweeds, were taken to Rakahore, the personified form of rock, who has charge over them and looks after them.

Various shell-fish

Shell-fish were eaten raw, or cooked for a very short time on hot coals. They might be placed in a heap, and a fire built round them. Or they might be dried and threaded on takiaho, a string of prepared fibre.

Kuku, mussels, were taken from the rocks by hand and collected in baskets. Ngupara is described by Tregear as a fresh-water mussel, but the only ngupara I know were found on the rocks on the east coast. It is a very small mussel, perhaps one to two inches long, and grows in bunches. It is shaped like the large mussels and tastes rather like them, only perhaps not so strong in flavour. It is either cooked or eaten raw. Paua, haliotis, generally called mutton fish, has a univalve shell. It is taken from the rocks by hand, and the inside is taken out and beaten to soften it before it is cooked on hot coals or in a hangi. The inside of the shell has many beautiful rainbow colours, due to the outer layer being covered with many tiny grooves which decompose the rays of light as they reflect them. This shell was as I have said used for fish hooks, and was also used for ornamenting wood carving. In making the eye on the figure on a slab, the whole paua shell was used, and held in place by a small wooden peg which formed the pupil of the eye. Kina (Echinus) commonly called the sea egg, has a prickly shell, and the inside is generally eaten raw. It is usually collected at the same time as the paua. Tio, oysters of two kinds, were found on the coast. One kind is rather small and has a rough and crinkled shell, and is found on rocks. The other is much larger, and has a comparatively smooth shell, and lives in mud. The Maori did not care a great deal for oysters, as he did for other shell-fish.

Pipi

Pipi is a small bivalve, $1\frac{1}{2}$ to 3 inches long, with a smooth white shell nearly oval, and faint marks that follow the lines of the shell. It grows all over New Zealand, generally in sand banks or in sandy mud, and was a favourite food. The shell-fish itself was of a creamy white or yellow colour, and was eaten raw, dried, or cooked either on hot coals, or by steaming for a very short time. The shell was used for shaving. The old Maori did not like hair on his face because it covered up the beautiful lines of his moko (tattoo). The hairs on his face were pulled out by means of an empty pipi or kakahi shell. The operator would hold the two pieces in his right hand, and with his left hand on the back of the neck of the man who was to be shaved, would catch the hair between the two shells and pull it out. Although this was a painful operation, no sound was ever made by the patient.

Shaving

Fresh-water fish

The old Maori was an expert in taking fresh-water fish, and the people who lived inland had an enormous supply of the kinds which will be described, until the Europeans introduced the trout and other fish. Now our fresh-water fish have almost entirely disappeared. Fishing grounds belonged to the hapu which owned the land going down to a lake or along a river, and were marked by posts as described in the account of sea fishing. In Lake Rotorua about half-way between Owhata on the mainland and Mokoia Island was such a post, called Hinewhata. My ancestors Wahiao and his father Umukaria who lived at Owhata used this post for tying their fishing nets on when they were getting inanga, and they also tied on bunches of fern for catching koura, or crayfish. In my chapter on Marriage I mentioned this post as the one on which my ancestress Hinemoa, the sister of Wahiao, rested when she swam across the lake from Owhata to Mokoia to her lover Tutanekai.

Property in fishing grounds

Koura

Koura (crayfish) were found in great quantities in the lakes and rivers. My people in the Lakes district, at Rotorua, Rotoiti, Okataiua, Tarawera, Rotokakahi, and other lakes, took the koura in many ways. They used the paepae, a dredge net, and also whakaweku, bunches of fronds of raurahe (bracken) sunk to the bottom of the lake, or tau, bunches of fern tied to a post. These bunches were left for some time before going to gather the koura which were found in great numbers on the fern. The bunches were drawn up into a canoe and shaken to loosen the hold of the koura, and the rest were taken off by hand.

My old koroua Te Pahau who lived at Motutawa Island was a great adept at getting koura, kakahi, and inanga in Lake Rotokakahi (Green Lake). He was a most industrious man, and went off in his canoe very early in the morning to set his ferns or to gather koura. He welcomed those who wished to go with him in his canoe, but they must be punctual. If they were late, he never waited, even though he saw them coming in the distance. So came the saying (whakatauki), "Ko Te Pahau kahaki waka," Te Pahau who would not wait, but went off in his canoe.

Our people also ruku koura, that is, dived for crayfish, going to the bottom of the lake and bringing them up between both hands.

Inanga

Inanga (Retropinna), a small fish, was a favourite food of the Maori, and was eaten either fresh or dried. It was the relish eaten with the fern root. The inanga was taken in great quantities in most of our lakes with the kupenga, or seine net. They were also taken in an oval hoop net with a long wooden handle which went right across the net, and also in a small conical scoop net. The fishers who used these small nets waded near the shore. But the big net was generally used in the old days in Lake Taupo and Lake Rotorua, Lake Rotokakahi, and other lakes. The first inanga caught in the season were always offered to the gods, and the rest of that first catch was used at a ceremonial feast, karakia being repeated by the Tohunga. In the old days inanga was taken by the hapu of Tuhourangi from Otamakari on the north of Tarawera Lake, Owhaia and Te Puna north of Tarawera, Te Manuka at the same place, Waitangi to the north-west, Parahamutu, Rahuiroa, Terapatiki, Matakana, all near by, from Kariri and

Punaromia, from Waitoharuru (Wairoa Falls), and Karikaria close by, from Hawaiki on the south-west of Tarawera Lake, from Taneroa, from Whangaruru on the peninsula, from Te Ariki, from Tutaiinanga on Paeroa block, from Motutawa, and from all round Rotokakahi Lake at Okareka, on the west side of Otaku. All these were ancient fishing grounds, and were continued down to the time of my koroua Te Pahau, and down to Maihi Te Kakauparaoa and my mother.

Toitoi and other small fish

Toitoi (Gobiomorphus gobioides) is a small fish caught in the lakes, and like inanga was taken in nets. Both it and the inanga were also taken in a taruke. Toitoi was also called titarakura and other names. Pahore was another small fish found in the lakes like the toitoi.

Koeaea

Koeaea or whitebait was much thought of, and it is one of the nicest of all small fish. I have seen these taken by a haokoeaea, an oval hoop net made of the wiwi rush. But these are not used now, the scrim net having taken their place. The whitebait went up the river like a company of soldiers in great numbers, keeping a column two or three feet wide. The old haokoeaea was made of wiwi rush bound together with fibre in the same style as the hinaki, eel basket, which is described a little later. The rim round the top was of kakareao or supplejack, or young manuka could be used. In one bottom corner was a hole two or three inches round. This was stuffed with grass or fibre while in use. When there were enough fish in it, the net was taken up and the stuffing taken out so as to let the fish drop into a basket. In the old days the koeaea was only eaten fresh. It was caught in July, August, and early September.

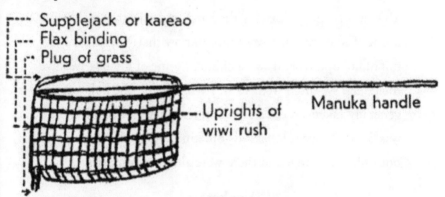

7. Net for whitebait.

Kokopu

Kokopu (Galaxias) was an important food among the people who lived inland. Lake Taupo was a noted place for it in the days of old before trout were introduced. It was caught with pouraku nets at night, also by bobbing, and in the smaller streams a hao or oval net was placed in the water ahead of it as it went upstream. A lighted torch was used so that the worker could see as he waded into the stream, and see the kokopu when he caught it. It was placed in tauremu fish basket slung round the waist. I have known it to be caught by the hands in small streams. Two people will go into the water about 12 feet from each other, near the banks, while another stands halfway across. The two on each side stir the muddy bottom with their feet and make the water dirty. The kokopu finding it dark and hard to breathe comes up and puts its nose above the water. Then it is caught by placing the hand underneath it and lifting it out. There are other ways too. I know that Taupo Lake was full of kokopu when I was a child, as some of my relatives live there, and we often went to stay with them. The kokopu was generally taken on dark nights in summer and autumn, and was 5 to 12 inches long and sometimes more. Its flavour was not unlike whiting, and there were about six varieties.

Upokororo

The upokororo or grayling, of which there were the tirango, kutikuti, and rehe, were caught in traps when they were going up rivers after a flood while the water was still dirty. The upokororo was also taken in nets and by other means.

Patiki

The Maori sometimes caught the patiki or flounder with a spear. The spear was made with a point at the end which was barbed. It was not unlike the spear used for catching birds.

Kakahi

Kakahi, the fresh-water mussel, was a food liked by the old Maori, but I did not care for it myself, as I missed the tang of the salt-water mussels. It was the only fresh-water fish I did not like. I have seen my people diving for them, or pushing them up with their toes in shallow muddy water. The kapu was a long-handled scoop used for taking them from the bed of a lagoon or shallow lake. The Rou kakahi was a dredge rake used for taking kakahi. It was worked by means of a long pole used as a handle, and a bag net was fixed on to the dredge.

Rou kakahi

Eels

The old Maori was very clever at getting freshwater fish, but at taking eels he was an expert. Eels were taken in a hinaki, eel trap, set at a pa tuna (eel weir), and with a bob, spear, or even with the hand. The spear was a short-hafted one with many prongs.

Eel weirs

Eel weirs (pa tuna, pa tauremu, pa rauwiri) were built across rivers, generally in a zigzag way. In small streams, two wing fences were built tending towards each other in a sort of V open at the point, with the opening at the downstream end. The hinaki were set with the opening upstream, a few feet apart at the open end of the V. The eels are caught as they come down the river to the sea, keeping in the middle of the stream.

Each hapu had its own fishing ground. For example Ngati Rangitihi owned the fishing rights on the Rangitaiki River which passed through Te Awa te Atua, their land. Here I saw some wonderfully constructed eel weirs of the zigzag kind, when I was quite a small child. When my mind goes back to those pa tuna, I realize how clever and industrious the old Maori were. I remember the fence which must have been 8 to 10 feet high, with the posts of matai or rata, made of long poles of the sharpened manuka (Leptospermum ericoides), lashed with split kareao (supplejack) to two series of manuka rails about 3 or 4 inches thick. The eel weir zigzagged right across the river, and the two posts on each side of the openings were braced with very strong poles used as struts on the downstream side. The wide spaces at the top of the weir were called waka, i.e. mouth, the part in the middle tuki, and the narrow opening was called the ngutu, the lips, for it is through the lips that anything passes. In the space between the fences from the mouth to the ngutu, matting of manuka brush is tied together, and pegged down to the bottom of the river. This matting goes a little beyond the ngutu, and prevents scouring of the river bed.

Important weirs were generally given a name, and in the very old days, the permanent maui posts had carved grotesque figures or a head on the upper part. No outsider would think of poaching. Death would be the penalty for trespassing on any place which was a rahui belonging to another.

The completed weir was a very strong affair indeed. But can the reader imagine the very hard work which it cost, when there were no English implements? There was much work in going to the forest where the thick tall manuka is to be found, and in cutting and sharpening each pole, and in preparing the heavy posts of matai or raka, and driving them in with a wooden maul. In many cases the material had to be carried several miles, and as they had no nails, the whole had to be bound with supplejack. Building and repairing were done in the dry summers when the river was not as high as usual, or when the tide was out if the weirs were near the mouth of a river.

The Maori studied the ways of the fresh-water fish, and knew that eels come down the rivers to the sea in autumn. He also knew that they travelled in the middle of the stream, and made the openings in the pa tuna, and set the eel baskets accordingly. Nets were also used for taking eels at these weirs when they were whakahekeheke, i.e. migrating or moving.

Eels were taken on dark nights with a spear, or by hand in muddy water, or by bobbing with a maunu, bait, of earthworms threaded on a string of flax fibre which was tied to a stick. This was done a great deal, and is still done. When eels were caught, they were placed in a hole made in the ground called a parua. Some people put them into a hinaki (eel basket or trap) which was tied to a post in the water near the shore. Eels were never taken with a line and hook.

Mauri

A mauri was placed in the vicinity of an important pa tuna. It was usually a stone, which brought luck to the weir, so that the eels would not desert that part.

Hinaki

There were many kinds of hinaki (eel traps), some of which were made from the aerial roots of the kiekie (Freycinetia banksii), and I have often seen them, and others from the mangemange (Lygodium articulatum), a climbing plant. Both materials were very carefully split down the middle. I have also seen these hinaki at Taupo, and was so impressed that I had a small one made, and have it in my collection. It was made by Te Waaka, a chief of Opepe, and Waitahanui, the husband of my mother's sister Rakera, thirty years ago. It is made from the wiwi rush, neatly plaited with strips of flax. The rough drawing will perhaps give some idea of its construction.

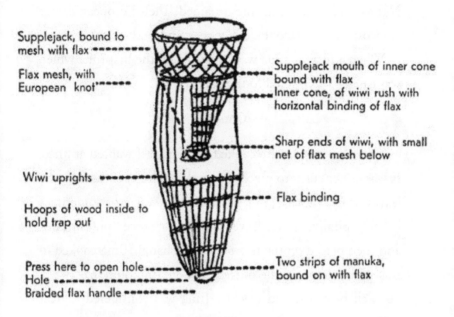

Supplejack, bound to mesh with flax

Flax mesh, with European knot

Supplejack mouth of inner cone bound with flax

Inner cone, of wiwi rush with horizontal binding of flax

Sharp ends of wiwi, with small net of flax mesh below

Wiwi uprights

Hoops of wood inside to hold trap out

Flax binding

Press here to open hole

Hole

Braided flax handle

Two strips of manuka, bound on with flax

8. Eel Trap.

The entrance to a hinaki had many names, one of them being puarero. The toherere or inner cone is bound to the outer basket very neatly with flax. This cone prevents the eels from getting out once they have entered. The mouth which is made of manuka or of supplejack, may be anything from a foot to three feet wide.

Origin of the Tuna

It was the Maori belief that Whaitiri married Kaitangata and from them came Puanga, Karihi, and Hema. From Puanga came Mango the shark, and from Karihi came Para, Manga,

Ngoro, and Tuna, in the order named. Their European names are frost fish, barracouta, conger eel, and fresh-water eel.

When a new pa tuna was constructed, the first tuna which was caught was offered to the gods.

Cooking

The eel was generally cooked in a hangi if wanted at once. It was either cut into pieces, or cooked whole, encased in the leaves of the puwha (Sonchus oleraceus, var.), or sometimes bound spirally in the leaves of the harakeke (phormium), and then placed on the hot stones of a hangi. Tuna cooked in this way was lovely, the outside skin getting quite pakawera, i.e. well browned and crackly. Tuna was considered a great delicacy.

Drying

During the season many hundreds of eels are taken in a weir, anywhere from a pound to twenty pounds each in weight, or even more. Many are dried and put away for future use, or for taking to relatives for some special gathering. The people prepare te ahi rara tuna, the fire for drying eels. The eels are laid on a frame made of green rods over the fire. If small, they are put on just as they are, but if large, they are opened out and kept open with small pieces of wood before they are laid on the fire (ka pawhara tia). They are then hung up (whaka tirewa) on a whata, which is a raised storehouse in which food is kept, such food generally being dried fish of all kinds.

Lampreys

The eel is taken as it comes downstream in the middle of the river, while the lamprey is taken as it migrates up the river, keeping close to the bank to avoid the strong current. The lamprey weir was built in summer when the water was very low, so as to have the advantage of the dry river bed. The Utu Piharau (weir) consisted of short straight fences built out at right angles to the bank, with rectangular openings in the wattlework. The one on the Whanganui river which I showed in my lecture at Oxford was about thirty-five feet long, and had five openings. The current of the Whanganui river is very strong, and to prevent scouring, a layer of manuka brush was pegged down to a distance of twenty-five feet upstream from the fence, and six or seven feet downstream below it. A small hinaki about thirty inches long is used as a trap, and is set with the mouth *upstream*. Two stout stakes are driven into the river bed just below an entrance to the weir through which the water rushes. They are set at a little distance below the fence so as to allow the fish to pass between them and the fence. To these stakes is secured a funnel-shaped net, and the smaller end of this net is inserted in the mouth of the trap. As the lampreys encounter the strong rush of water through the gap in the wattlework fence, they are swept back downstream into the pot.

Animals Kuri

The kuri (dog) was the only domesticated animal which the old Maori had, and this he brought with him when he migrated to New Zealand about six hundred years ago. It is now extinct, and has been since early in the last century when the pakeha dog was introduced. Or it may have been extinct by the end of the century before judging by all the accounts I have heard of it. The kuri is mentioned in the Tasmanian Journal of Natural Science, vol. ii, and in Annals of Natural History, London, vol. xiv. The kuri was a small animal with a long body and low in the legs, and had a head somewhat like that of a fox, with straight pointed ears, and a flowing bushy tail. The colour was either all black or all white. It lived on fish, vegetables, or any food eaten by its owner. The hair was long, straight, and fine, and the skin was used in making the special and rare cloaks for chiefs. There is one of these in the Pitt-Rivers Museum at Oxford. The hair was also used in adorning the chief's weapons. Cloaks too were decorated with the bushy hair of the tail (whiore or waero).

The flesh of this kuri was eaten, and was considered a great delicacy, as it was in other parts of Polynesia. In his Journal, Cook says, when he first saw the native dog at Tologa Bay, "No tame animals were seen among the natives except dogs, which were very small and ugly." Again when leaving Tologa Bay, he says, "We saw no four-footed animals nor the appearance of any either tame or wild, except dogs and rats, and these were very scarce. The people eat the dogs, like our friends at Tahiti."

The old New Zealand dog was supposed to be rather stupid and dull. The Maori used him when hunting the kiwi (apteryx) and other birds which moved about at night, and also for hunting parera (ducks) during the moulting season. It was not useful for anything else so far as I know, so that when the European kuri, a larger and more intelligent animal, came along, the few native dogs disappeared.

The kuri pakeha was big and strong and useful in hunting the pig which Captain Cook left behind in New Zealand. The pig increased quickly, and the Maori found it a good substitute for the kuri and kiore (Mus esculens) as a relish. The Maori liked the new large dogs. I remember the one which my koroua Maihi owned. It was a large dog, not unlike an Alsatian, of a dark cream colour. He named it Ngaumu, and it was a very good dog for hunting the pig.

Kiore

The kiore (Mus esculens) was an important food of the old Maori. Many members of a hapu would take part in the business of catching it, and everything was done with ceremonial. Before a company of men went out to take the rat, the Tohunga would repeat a karakia so that the expedition might have luck.

The old kiore of the Maori was much smaller than the

imported European rat. It was very plentiful in a forest on high land, where the tawhairauriki (Fagus cliffortioides) grew in plenty. It lived in the hollows of trees and in holes in the ground during the day, and came out at night to get its food. It lived mostly on the berries of trees, its favourite being the berries of the tawa-rau-riki. The kiore was said to be particular about what he ate, and to be a clean feeder.

Ara kiora, rat runs or paths, were made between his home and where he got his food, by the scraping of his feet as he journeyed backwards and forwards each year. Some of these runs were many miles long. My hapu Ngati Wahiao had several ara kiore at various places, but the one at Parekarangi went from a place called Tuahuahu to Te Tara o te Marama, a distance of a few miles, and was used down to the time of my koroua Maihi te Kakauparaoa, and to the following generation in their early days. Each rat run of importance was called by a name, and on these runs the tawhiti (traps) were set. There were many ways of taking the rat, but I know only the tawhiti. When the first rat was taken, a karakia was repeated, and a sacrifice made of it to the atua, by putting it on a small platform or at a tapu place. Many rats were caught during the winter season, and women often helped in the taking of them.

Sacrifice

Traps

Different ways of taking the rat were tawhiti, pokipoki, tawhiti makamake, and torea, kopiha, and paepae, the last three being names for a pit trap. To make a tawhiti kiore, first stick a double hoop of supplejack into the ground, with its ends on either side of the run. Then through this double hoop stick a number of turuturu (straight sticks), pressing their points firmly into the ground, leaving a space in the middle of the structure just big enough for the rat to pass through. Next, beside the path fix a spring stick of supplejack. This spring stick is called whana. To the free end attach a short piece of stick by a fibre cord. This vertical stick is called taratara. Also attach a tohe or cord loop to the free end of the spring stick, not a slip noose.

To set the trap, bend down the spring stick, and pass the loop through the double hoop until the end nearly touches the ground, and put the taratara in a vertical position at one side of the opening so that the top end is on one side of the hoop, while the cord attached to it is on the other side between the entwined supplejack hoop. Then let the spring stick go a little so that the pull comes on the taratara, and put a short piece of stick between the uprights, and the lower end of the taratara prevents it from being pulled upwards. The trap is now ready.

The kiore coming down his path finds only a small opening over this short stick (kurupae), and as soon as he steps on it, the vertical taratara is released, its lower end flies upwards, and its top end slips out from under the hoop. The looped string flies up between the entwined supplejack hoop, and pulls the kiore violently up against it. This process was repeated until many were killed.

Pit trap

There were other ways of taking the rat with us, and other ways practised by different tribes, some of which I have mentioned. The rua kiore was another way. A hole about 4 feet deep would be dug, wider at the bottom than at the top, in a place frequented by the rats. At the beginning of the berry season some would be gathered and thrown on the ground inside the hole. A slanting pole would be placed in the pit so that the rat would get used to going down and coming up again. After two or three nights the long pole would be removed, and several shorter sticks would be stuck into the sides of the pit to stick straight out horizontally over the opening, and berries would be tied to the ends. The rat was only too willing to get and eat them, but when he finished and wanted to go back, he could not turn. So the poor kiore fell into the pit.

Rat snaring grounds

We had rat snaring grounds at Moerangi, one being called Te Tihi-Whakairo-to-Taope. Ngati Umukaria used to hunt these. Te Kohika was the chief and there were other snaring places, and bird snares as well. At Parekarangi was the one I have mentioned. Te Paipai was the chief, his descendant was Takina. There was also a rat track at Kaihihi from Ka Kapiko to Te Ewe-o-pareao, belonging to Tukiterangi and Ngati Tuohonoa. There were bird snares as well. The chief was Kamana. No other people would attempt to snare rats at any of these places, or birds, nor would they cut any flax or raupo from the swamps without first asking permission from the owners.

Pigs

Captain Cook is credited with having been the first to introduce the pig, and often when going on a wild pig hunt, people say, "We are going to hunt for Captain Cook." As the pig increased in the forest, the Maori hunted for it with the large dogs which he got from the early whalers. The little young pigs were generally taken home to the kainga and reared, and from them came the domesticated pig, which was quite different from the wild one, though both were good in their different ways. The Maori has then enjoyed the pig for about a hundred and fifty years.

Pig hunting

As usual, the Maori did not hunt alone, but several men went and camped in the forest many miles away from the kainga. In later years the journey was on horseback. At night they had a large fire made, not only to keep away the atua which might be in those parts, but also to keep them warm, as they carried no blankets in those old days. The dog was used to hold the pig, while the Maori stuck it in the throat with a long sharp pointed knife. A fire was lit, and ka hunuhunu tia, the hair was singed off with burning branches. The pig was hung up by the hind feet, and the puku opened and cleaned. In the old days when there were no horses, after getting several pigs, the Maori tied their two front and two back feet together, and passed a pole under them. The domesticated pig was not singed, but the hair was taken off with boiling water.

Cooking

The pig was cooked in a hangi, or roasted on a stick in front of a fire. But the nicest way I know of cooking a pig is to roast it in fat in an omo, camp oven, which stands on three legs and has a lid, and is placed on hot coals to cook.

Huahua poaka

The Maori preserved pig by roasting it in its own fat. As each small piece was cooked it was placed in a taha (calabash), and when the calabash was full, the boiling pig fat was poured over the top, and the calabash was fitted with a tuki (stopper) which was sometimes ornamented with carving. Huahua poaka will keep for two or three years or more.

The Pig as a nuisance

Although the pig was regarded as a blessing, it was a nuisance in some ways. After his coming, the Maori had to fence his cultivations. There were two kinds of fences, one like the fence for a pa (fortification) only much lighter. It was made of split manuka or small straight poles sharpened to a point and thrust into the earth in a straight up position. The upper ends were then lashed to a horizontal rail. I might mention the fact that every picket of a Maori fence was sharpened and driven into the ground, just as the big supporting posts of the fence were. This is the takitaki. The other kind of taiepa (or taiapa) is the Pakororo, in which two upright stakes a few inches apart were driven into the ground every four or five feet. Then between the uprights, poles or split sticks were laid, the ends overlapping. The pairs of uprights would be lashed together to prevent their opening.

Birds

In the old days, birds were very numerous in New Zealand, and one could see them quite close to the kainga, just as I used to see them in my childhood days at Parekarangi. I could almost say that I lived with the birds, for they were in the forest all round me singing and talking to each other, and I used sometimes to think they spoke to me. Our kainga at Parekarangi was close to the forest and the only sound we heard was the singing of birds which was a wonderful sound, and the Mangakara stream flowing over its pebbly bed. My koroua Maihi te Kakauparaoa was the only member of our family of three who ventured into the forest either to get birds or to cut logs. I had always been warned not to venture into the forest of Tane (Te Wao tapu nui a Tane), being told that it was full of atua, so I never ventured further than a few yards on the border when my kuia gathered sticks for firewood, and I helped in my small way with my kawenga (bundle) which I tried to carry as my kuia carried hers. I have already spoken in my account of the building of houses of the way in which the Maori looked upon the forest of Tane as possessing a mauri, or tapu life principle, just like a man. Thus he looked upon the forest with great respect. He saw the trees as living beings like himself, only from an elder branch of the family. It is difficult to express the feeling that grew up with one, as it did with me, for I was brought up in the belief of all these things, so that when I sat on the edge of the forest I could almost imagine what the rustling of the leaves meant. Although many weeks and months were spent at Parekarangi with no other children to play with, I never knew what it was to be lonely, for I had the belief that I was never alone. The feelings I had as a child have never left me, and I still hear the voices of unseen beings in the sound of rushing water, in whispering wings, and in rustling branches. I know and feel that with all the education I have received, for which I am most grateful, I am at heart just the same as when I spent all those happy years of childhood with my kuia and koroua.

The tapu of the forest

There was always much tapu pertaining to the forest, and to all the things in the forest. During the fowling season, the forest was very tapu indeed, and people were careful not to pollute that tapu. If a ropu (company) of people went into the forest to snare birds, they must not take any cooked food with them. If they had a temporary home in the forest for the purpose of snaring birds, they must cook and eat whatever food they needed at the camp before leaving, and not carry food about with them. This was to prevent any insult to the gods, and desecrating the tapu. If they did such a thing, the birds were supposed to leave the place and go to another part of the forest. A mauri (talisman) was always placed in the forest, and this was sometimes a stone placed in the ground. This was supposed to hold the mana of the gods who had charge over all the forest.

Kereru

One of the many birds in the forest was the kereru (pigeon, Hemiphaga novae zealandiae). The time for taking it began in the late autumn. Some time before this, the adepts would go through the forest to see where the trees were which had plenty of fruit for the birds to eat. The miro was a favourite fruit of the kereru, and he got very fat on it. Tawa was also a favourite in midsummer. A kereru which had to live on the leaves of the kowhai was very poor, and was not generally eaten, as the inside had a nasty smell.

Snares

There was a certain amount of tapu connected with the making of snares (mahanga) and other things which the Maori used for catching birds. Everything of this sort was made in a whare takaha, the storehouse where all the implements for catching birds were kept. It was also called whare mata. Women were not allowed in a place like this for fear of desecrating the tapu.

The ahere-mahanga were fastened to a bough in the manner shown in the drawing which follows, high up in a tree. The cord was made from strips of whanake (Cordyline), its fibre being stronger and more lasting than that of the harakeke (Phormium tenax). These rauhuha, strips of whanake, were held over the smoke of a fire to make them strong; the smoking also took away the new appearance. When the cord is fixed on the mahanga, it is called a tari. The snare is usually spoken of as a mahanga, but I have always heard my old koroua speak of it as ahere-mahanga when the whole thing was complete.

Other names for the snare are tahere, taeke, kaha, pihere, and so on. A spear for taking birds is also called tahere.

Snaring grounds

Our hapu had snaring places at Moerangi, at Parekarangi, and at Kakapiko, which were used by Ngati Umukaria, Ngati Wahiao, N. Tukiterangi, and N. Tuohonoa, who lived round about Motutawa Island, Kaiteriria, Te Whakarewarewa, Parekarangi, and other places. These grounds were used down to the time of my mother's early days. At Moerangi, in Chief Te Kohika's time, he and our people hunted rats and snared birds too. Horohoro, a high range with a flat top, was a famous place for taking birds, and our clans had snaring places here too. Some of the places here were at Kakariki-potiki, and close by was Te Wharaurangi, and near that was Te Kawengaari. These were places for snaring the kaka or red parrot. We also snared him at Pahiko on the ridge, and at Pouteko. These are *very old* snaring places used by my ancestors down to the time of my papa (uncles), aunts, and mother. We also had snaring places at Ironui on the same ridge, and at Te Iranga-o-hine, Te Wheka, Te Kiriki, Te Tawhero, Te Rimu, Te Matai, Tauwharepuakau, and many other places, and these were used by Tuhourangi down to the time of my pāpā[1] Mita Taupopoki and others. The Horo-horo was six or seven miles beyond Parekarangi on the way to Taupo.

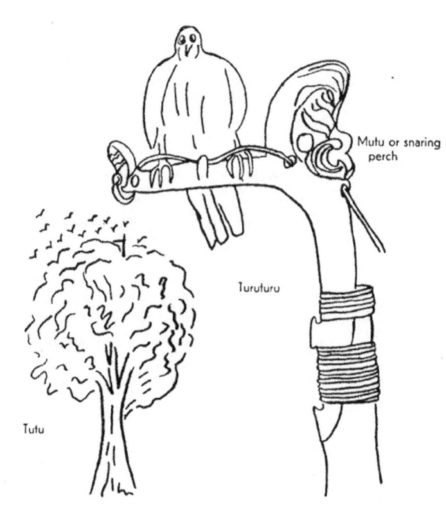

Mutu or snaring perch

Turuturu

Tutu

9. Bird Snare.

Kereru

The kereru (pigeon) lived only on the forest berries, so that when cooked for immediate use, it was cooked whole, either by baking it in clay, feathers and all, or by steaming it whole in a hangi after the feathers had been removed. In the hot lake district, we put the birds whole into some utensil, cover with water, and put into a steam hole for an hour. Whichever way kereru is cooked, its flavour is better than that of any other bird I ever tasted. When I went to New Zealand a few years ago after being away a number of years, relatives took much trouble to procure various luxuries for me. I enjoyed them all, but none better than the kereru, which I was able to have just before leaving, although they gave me huahua kereru from the time of my arrival.

Preserved pigeons

The recipe for huahua kereru, a great luxury, is as follows. Pluck the bird and clean it, cut the body in half through the lumbar region, leaving the legs and tail separated from the rest, and remove all the bones. Roast the flesh on sticks in front of a fire, basting from time to time with the fat which drips from it into a wooden trough or part of a calabash. As each part is cooked, place it in a calabash, and pour melted fat from the birds over it, and leave to cool. Finally a carved wooden funnel is inserted into the hole in the calabash, and melted fat from the birds poured in, and the calabash is closed with a wooden stopper. No further cooking is needed when the huahua is to be eaten. It is served cold as a rule. Pigeons preserved in this way will keep for two, three or more years.

Huahua kereru was considered a great luxury, and was only used on great occasions.

I myself preserved partridges in England by the same method, and three years later, they were as good as when I first put them down. One lot I boned as we do kereru, but had to use lard as there is not enough fat on partridges. About thirty were boned and cooked in an open pan on the fire with boiling fat. I then put the partridges in jars, and poured the boiling fat over to cover them. Stoppers were placed on the opening to keep the air out. About thirty more were done differently. The inside, head and legs were removed, and the partridges cooked in beef gravy. Then three were placed in each large preserving bottle, and the gravy poured over them, and the tops clipped down. This was done during the food shortage of the first years of the war. We had some of each lot before the season opened for three years, and one bottle of the first lot was quite good in the fourth year after it was put down.

Other birds

As there were more than two hundred species of birds, it would take too long to discuss them all. Birds formed one of the most important foods of the old Maori. There were many in the Wao-nui-a-Tane, the forest of Tane, many on the mania (plains), many on nga maunga (the mountains), many in the lakes, and on the seashore and on the sea. Some were wingless like the moa which is now extinct, and the kiwi, the apteryx.

Kiwi

The kiwi was highly thought of, mainly because of its prized feathers, used for cloaks. He and the moa were unlike all the other birds in New Zealand. They slept all day and came out at night to get their food.

Kakapo

The kakapo is another bird which does not fly, although he has quite large wings. His muscles seem too weak to work them. He lives generally in holes under the roots of trees. He was often kept as a pet by the old Maori, who found him playful and affectionate. The kakapo always looked to the future, laying in his store of food against bad weather. The Maori thought the bird had almost human knowledge, and spoke of the chief kakapo sending out invitations once every winter to all the other kakapo to gather together and hold a meeting. They met once a year in large numbers to discuss all their affairs, and very interesting it was. After the meeting, the kakapo all went back where they came from in small companies. What they talked about the Maori does not say.

Kakariki

The kakariki or parakeet was a beautiful coloured bird, mainly bright green, and red, yellow, or orange on his forehead.

He was generally very tame, and a clever mimic. Parakeets were taken in great numbers by the koputa, tanga or striking method, and by the puaka trap.

Tirairaka

The tirairaka or fan-tail was a very beautiful little bird. These birds hopped among the twigs and branches inside and outside the forest, opening and shutting their pretty tails which looked like fans every few seconds. These lovely little birds came quite close to me when I was a child, as they had no fear of us at all.

Pihipihi

The pihipihi or blight bird was a small bird found in the forest in great numbers. It was taken by the tanga or striking method, and it needed a great number to serve as kinaki (relish) for a large family. After plucking, a piece of wood was passed through six or eight, and stuck in the ground by the fire to roast the birds, which were turned round and round until they were cooked. This is the way my kuia cooked the pihipihi at Parekarangi when I was small; she cooked other birds larger or smaller, such as the tui, in the same way. A person who goes to get the pihipihi makes himself a hiding place of leaves and branches of fern trees, etc., and so partially covers himself. He has already fixed a pae (perch) for the bird to stand on. When everything is ready, he attracts the bird by blowing on a pepe, that is a call-leaf, and so making a whistling sound. When the bird comes, he strikes it with a hauhau (rod) which he keeps against the end of the pae close to his hiding place. This was also a way of getting the tui.

Tui

The tui or koko was often called a parson bird because of the tuft of white feathers on his throat. He was a great bird for singing, and had a beautiful note, especially in the early morning. The Maori kept tame tui, and taught them to talk. The birds were great mimics. The tui was very good eating, either freshly cooked or made into huahua (preserve). When preserved or cooked, it was usually called koko. When I was a child there were hundreds to be seen in the bush and on the edge outside. They did not seem to be afraid of anything, and one woke up in the morning to the sound of their beautiful tunes, and to the lovely sound of the bell bird, and many others, not forgetting my little friends the pihipihi and the tirairaka, the little birds I loved as a child.

Te pukeho

The pukeho or the swamp hen was a favoured food and much sought after. The legs and beak were red, and the plumage was very bright, the neck being indigo blue. The feathers were used in the making of cloaks, and the body was cooked in a hangi or roasted before the fire on a stick.

Ducks

Ducks were hunted with dogs at Rotomahana after the snaring season in the month of February. Tuhourangi people were the only ones who were allowed to hunt. Only the principal men had the privilege of snaring.

Bell birds

Te korimako, or the bell bird was one of the most beautiful songsters. Some of its notes sounded like the tolling of bells at a distance. It has now almost disappeared. Captain Cook mentions them in his first voyage. While they lay at anchor in Queen Charlotte's Sound, they were awakened one morning by the singing of the bell birds. "The number was incredible, and they seemed to strain their throats in emulation of each other. This wild melody was infinitely superior to any that we had ever heard of the same kind; it seemed to be like small bells most exquisitely tuned."

Weka

The weka or wood hen is another bird that has lost the use of its wings. These birds had no need to fly from danger or go off the ground, as there were no beasts of prey in New Zealand before the pakeha introduced their animals. The weka was a great thief, robbing nests and eating eggs and young birds at night. Its feathers were used in cloaks, but it was not a favourite food.

Kea

The kea, a parrot, is mostly found in the snow regions of Te Waipounamu (the South Island) on the mountains of Otakou, known to the European as Otago and Southland, and also round about the beautiful lakes and fiords in Milford and other sounds. Since the pakeha came with his sheep farms, the kea, so report says, will sit on the back of a live sheep and peck out its kidneys. I cannot vouch for this story, as it was repeated to me, and it must only happen in a certain part if it is so, as in many places the kea is not at all destructive.

Kaka

The kaka had a bright reddish plumage which was prized for making cloaks, and the body was eaten. It was supposed to be very noisy and active. It was useful for eating up the many insects which were so harmful to the plants. It was snared like the kereru. I did not mention before several things about snares. Sometimes several of these perching rods (paerangi, pae, rongohua, mutu) were placed in one tree, and after setting, the snares might be left for some time and only occasionally visited, for fear of disturbing the birds. Some of the snares were set on very high trees, such as the matai, rimu, and mairo, but the most favoured were the miro and the kahikatea (White Pine). Snares for the smaller birds were set on the kotukutuku (fuschia) and porporo. Snares for the kereru would not be set on a rata (Metrosideros) as the kereru does not eat honey, but the tui and kaka are taken on this tree. Snares are also set on the ti (Cordyline), and many were set by water. When the kereru is eating miro, it gets very fat, and after a heavy feed will go straight for water. Thus many snares are placed near water.

Snares

Huia

The huia (Plate XIX) is well known by all people who know anything of the Maori. He is black, and his tail feathers are white at the tips, and these tail feathers are worn by rangatira people as a sign of distinction. The male and female huia have different kinds of bills. The female has a long curved one, and the male a short sharp one. I was always told by my old people that a pair of huia lived on most affectionate terms. The female dug the ground for worms, but it was the male bird who picked up the worms to feed her, as she was unable to do it because of the formation of her bill. If the male bird died first, the female died soon after of grief. The writer has a beautiful pair of huia mounted in a case in her collection, and they have been photographed for this book.

The body of the huia was considered tapu and was not eaten.

Mauri

If there was a scarcity of birds in a forest, it was thought that there was something wrong with the mauri, probably because someone had done wrong. A Tohunga would karakia over it, appealing to the gods to bestow its protection on it again, when it would have its mana restored. The mauri is supposed to have the mana to attract birds to that part of the forest where it is.

Origin of birds

In our old belief, Tane, one of the offspring of Rangi and Papa, was the origin of birds, and was spoken of as Tane-mataahi, but the birds are under the care of Parauri and Tuihaia, who have charge of them in the forest. One old story says that Tane took Parauri for a wife.

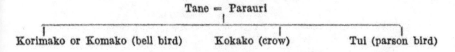

Tane = Parauri

Korimako or Komako (bell bird) Kokako (crow) Tui (parson bird)

The food which these birds ate did not make them fat, and they were very poor indeed, so they were fed on the vermin which grew on the heads of their relatives, the trees of the forest, which were also produced by Tane, but as Tane-mahuta. These trees were the miro, make, mairo, and others from which the birds eat the berries. The birds then began to get fat, and there was plenty of food for them. The atua which

313

Tane arranged to take charge of the forest were Parauri, and Punaweko, and Tuihaia. There were other beliefs about the birds, and it was also believed that Punareko represented all the birds in the forest, and that all those at sea were under the care of Hurumanu, and the kaeaea (sparrow-hawk) was represented by Tane-i-te-hokahoka. Rehua was spoken of as the origin of the tui, but Rehua was also a word used in Polynesia for the forest.

[1] See chapter on Social Organization.

[1] Figured in Elsdon Best, "Maori Agriculture" *Dominion Museum Bull* 9, c.

[1] See Grey, Sir George. *Ko nga Moteatea, me nga Hakirara o nga Maori*, Wellington, 1853.

[1] Grey, *op. cit.*

[1] Tapu life principle.

[1] Grey, *op. cit.*

[1] Mourning for a man of rank.

[1] See chapter on Children ff.

[1] Cf. Gilbert Mair, *Reminiscences and Maori Stories*, Brett, Auckland, 1923.

V

FIRE

How Maori made his fire

THE MAORI MADE his fire by friction, and used te hika ahi, the fire plough, to get his fire. Two pieces of wood which had been thoroughly dried were used. One, the kauahi, or lower stick, a piece of Mahoe (Melicytus ramiflorus), was generally 14 to 18 inches long, 2 or 3 inches wide, and 1 to 2 inches thick. This was very soft wood, and the stick could be used on both sides. Pate (Schefflera digitata) was sometimes used as a kauahi, but Mahoe was much preferred. The other piece of wood used was te hika, the rubbing stick, made from the Kaikomako (Pennantia corymbosa), a very hard, compact, and durable wood. The stick was scraped down with tuhua (obsidian) or shell to a rounded point at the end.

Man and woman together generate fire

Te hika also means "generating stick", and a man and woman would both take part in generating fire, as both took part in the generation of children. The kauahi or lower stick was kept in position by the woman, while the man worked in hika, or the generating stick. A small log is placed on the ground, with the lower stick against it. The lower end of the kauahi is held firmly in position by the woman, who stands with her foot on it, and the man kneels at the other end, which is raised up 5 or 6 inches from the ground. He holds te hika firmly, with his thumbs underneath, and his fingers placed flat on the outer part, with his right hand passing over his left. He begins rubbing the lower stick until a groove is formed about 5 inches long. The rubbing is slow at first, then a little quicker, with heavier pressure, until a hollow, a $\frac{1}{4}$ to $\frac{1}{2}$ inch deep, is formed, and a minute heap of dust begins to collect at the lower end of the groove. When plenty of dust has been made, the man uses te hika again, working it backwards and forwards more vigorously and with greater pressure, and the hollow gets hotter. He knows by the smell when the fire will come. The hollow gets darker, and from the heap of dust comes a little smoke, then a little bright speck in the middle. "A kua ka te ahi," the fire has come to life!

The burning dust is turned out of the hollow on to some dry kindling material of dry leaves or layers of bark and sticks which are already prepared. Some of the dry leaves are put on the dust, and this is blown gently with the mouth until flames come. Sometimes this burning dust is placed within a dry branch of the Manuka (Leptospermum ericoides), and waved gently from side to side so that the fire soon burns up.

Firewood

Wood was the only fuel, and there was plenty of it. Rata (Metrosideros robusta), Tawa (Beilschmiedia tawa), Manuka (Leptospermum ericoides), Whau (Plagianthus lyallii), and many other trees made excellent firewood.

Keeping and carrying fire

Burning logs were left in a hollowed out place in a wharau (cooking shed) with ashes thrown over them to keep the fire in, so as to start the cooking fires on the next day, or slaves kept them alight. Fires were not allowed to burn out except in the hangi, i.e. the cooking ovens. Slaves attended to fires for warming a wharepuni or wharewhakairo (large meeting house), and kept them going from a fire outside which was always burning. Only the embers were brought into a house, and placed in the hollow prepared for holding them. These embers would be replenished from time to time all through the night if there was a ceremonial gathering. The process of generating fire was so tedious and slow that care was taken not to let a fire out, either a fire for cooking purposes or one for heating the houses. A fire used for cooking would not be used for heating a house. Burning or smouldering logs were carried from place to place by slaves. A man would carry such a log a day's journey.

Cooking fires not used for heating houses

Care in use of fire

The old Maori was careful where he made his fires. If the hangi were outside, he would study the way the wind was blowing, and so place a shelter accordingly. If the hangi were in a cooking shed, he would be careful about the length and quantity of wood he used. I have never known a fire to occur in a Kainga Maori (home and village), nor a house to be burnt accidentally. A house would be burnt if a person died in it, or a woman gave birth to a child in it.

Tapu

Heating

Sometimes a fire was lighted in a korua (hollow) made in the ground in the centre passage of a whare, between te roro (front) and the pou-toko-manawa (centre pole which supports the ridgepole), but nearer the latter. This fire would be made some time before the people entered the whare, and by then only embers would remain in the hollow. But the embers were usually taken in by slaves from a fire outside, carried between two flat pieces of wood. If the house was a large one, the hollow would be lined with flat stones, laid in a square or rectangular shape. Of ventilation there was very little, and only through a koro pihanga, the small opening with a sliding

318

shutter which was used as a window.

Lighting

The lighting of a whare was by oil with a flax-fibre wick. Oil from birds, or fish oil was placed in a hollow stone, about 4 or 5 inches in diameter and the same in depth, and in this the wick floated. If the house was a very large one, two wicks would be floated. Even this did not give a very bright light, but the Maori did not mind, and was quite happy with his dim light. Generally he had only the light from his fire.

If a fire occurred, neighbours would co-operate to extinguish it.

How fire came into this world

When a comet is seen above, a Maori will say, "Ko Auahi-turoa tera, nana i kare mai te ahi," That is Auahi-turoa, who brought us fire. The old Maori belief is that Tama-nui-te-ra (honorific name of the Sun), the father of Auahi-turoa, thought that he would like to do some great thing for the people who lived in the world below. He tried to think of something that would be of great use to them, and would bring them comfort. He thought and thought, and decided that fire was the very thing which they needed, for it was not only useful in cooking, but also gave warmth and light. Tama-nui-te-ra spoke his thoughts to his son Auahi-turoa (personified form of comets) and said, "I want to send something very important to the people below on the earth, and I want this gift of fire to go through you." And his son consented. Auahi-turoa then took the fire with him, and presented his father's gift to the people on earth, who thus became possessed of this wonderful thing, ahi.

While Auahi-turoa was on earth, he took as his wife Mahuika, the goddess of fire. They had five children, and they were named after the five fingers of the human hand, Takonui, Takoroa, Mapere, Manawa, and Toiti. They are known as the five fire children.

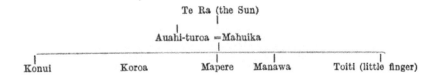

Te Ra (the Sun)
Auahi-turoa = Mahuika
Konui | Koroa | Mapere | Manawa | Toiti (little finger)

Maui's visit to Mahuika, the fire goddess

Maui wanted an excuse to go to see his grandmother Mahuika and to find out how she produced fire. One night he put out all the fires in the wharau or cooking house of each family in the kainga (village and home). Early next morning, he called out, "Kua hemo au i te kai," I feel faint for want of food. The slaves went to prepare him some food, but found that the fire had gone out, not only in their cooking house, but in all the other cooking houses.

Taranga, the mother of Maui, then said to the slaves, "Tikina he ahi ia Mahuika," Go and get some fire from Mahuika. Tell her that all the fires have gone out on this earth, and ask her to give us some. But the slaves were too frightened to move, for Mahuika was an atua, a goddess.

So Maui said, "I will go and get some fire, if you will show me the way which leads to the place where my grandmother Mahuika lives."

His parents, who knew the country well, said, "Follow that path which lies before you, and when you reach the place where your grandmother lives, you will find her sitting in front of her home. If she should ask you what your name is, tell her, for then she will know you. But we want to warn you, and we ask you not to play any tricks on your grandmother. You are noted for doing this, and we ask you not to do it to her."

Maui replied, "No, I only want to get some fire, and I will return again to-day."

So he went on his way, till he reached the place where Mahuika lived. He marvelled at the wonderful things he saw, for bright light seemed to shoot from all directions. He stood in awe for a long time, then spoke: "E kui e? Maranga ki runga, kai whea te ahi?" O Dame, will you rise up? Where is your fire? "He tiki ahi mai taku," I have come to get some fire.

The aged Mahuika rose and said, "Aue kowai ra tenei tangata?" Who can this mortal be?

He answered, "It is I."

She asked, "Where do you belong to?"

He replied, "To these parts."

She said, "You do not belong to these parts, nor do you look like the people who live in this country. Do you come from the north-east?"

He answered, "No."

"Do you come from the south-east?"

He answered, "No."

"Do you come from the westward?"

"No."

She said, "Well then, you must have come from the direction of the wind which blows right upon my body."

He replied, "Yes."

"Then you must be my grandchild. What is it that you want?"

He said, "I have come to get some fire from you."

She said, "Welcome, welcome: here is fire for you."

The aged grandmother then pulled off the nail from her little finger, and when she did so, he was amazed at what he saw, for fire flashed out of the fingernail. And she handed this to him.

Maui turned as if to go away, but he only went a short distance and put the nail into water and so extinguished the fire.

He returned to Mahuika and asked her to give him another light, as the other one had gone out. She pulled off another finger-nail and handed the fire to him. He went away as before, and again put out the light.

This happened several times until all the nails from her two hands had been pulled off, and also the nails from her feet, except the konui (large toenail). She then realized that Maui had been playing a trick upon her.

Mahuika was full of anger at what Maui had done to her. So she pulled off the remaining nail from her konui, threw it on the ground, and said, "There you are!" Fire sprang up at once, and set fire to the ground.

Maui was greatly alarmed, and ran away as fast as he could from the flames which seemed to be following him and catching him up. So he turned himself into a bird and flew into the water, hoping to find a cool place. But he found that the water was getting hot from the heat of the fire. The flames spread over the forest, the land, and the ocean, and it seemed certain death for Maui.

He then appealed to his ancestors Tawhiri-matea, the god of wind, and Whatitiri-matakataka, asking them to send him help in the way of water to put out the fire which was following him. They immediately sent Te Apuhau (squalls), Te Apu-matangi (gales), Uanui (heavy rain), and Ua-roa (lasting rain), which put out the great fire of Mahuika.

Mahuika was nearly drowned by the great quantity of water which fell. She ran from it, as Maui ran from the flames of her fire, and only reached her home just in time to save some sparks of fire which she placed for shelter within Hine-kaikomako (the personified form of the Kaikomako tree, Pennantia corymbosa), and into a few other trees such as Mahoe, Pate, etc. This is the reason why the Maori uses pieces of these woods for generating fire by friction. It also explains how the fires of Mahuika died out.

A sister of Mahuika called Hine-i-tapeka has the fires of the underworld under her care. These fires sometimes break out in volcanic eruptions.

Sacred fires

A special sacred fire, ahi tapu, was kindled in connexion with all litual performances. This was a very old custom of the Maori, who firmly believed that fire was of divine origin. All of the Tohunga (priestly experts) had knowledge of generating fire by friction. This was taught in the Whare-kura, the Tapu school of learning, where they were taught. All ahi tapu, and all tapu ceremonial fires were generated by friction. It was most important that a new fire should be generated for each ceremonial by a Tohunga, while another one intoned a tapu chant suitable for the occasion. The karakia (chant) made the fire tapu, so that the Tohunga might place nga atua, the gods, in it. In the ahi tapu (sacred fire) would then be the beings to whom the Tohunga would make certain appeal.

Ahi tapu was used by the Tohunga for many things in his ritual performances, and some of the ritual functions were called "Ahi", fires.

Various rites with fire

When there was war, the rites performed were Ahi marae, Ahi korakora, and Ahi takoha, but when the first enemy was killed, the rite performed was Ahi manawa. The rite performed over the bones of the dead was Ahi pure. Ahi taitai was a fire at which were performed rites suitable for the home, the birds, and the forest. Ahi toronga was a rite performed to kill the anuhe (caterpillar) which settles on the leaves of the kumara (sweet potato), and does great damage to the crops. The karakia used in connexion with first fruits was Ahi amoamohanga. Ahi purakau and Ahi tumu whenua were rites used in connexion with tree felling.

Hissing fires

When a fire makes a hissing sound ending with a whistling sound, a Maori will say, "He atua, kai te tiki ahi mai ma ratau," The gods have come to get fire for themselves. If it is just a soft hissing sound caused by the escape of gas, it is nga patupaiarehe, the fairies, taking some fire for themselves.

Fire and witchcraft

When people intended visiting another tribe in another part of the country, Ahi tapu (sacred fire) was used when performing the rite named Whakau to protect them from the evil influence of makutu (witchcraft). Several years ago, my mother and I with other relatives had occasion to visit another tribe many miles away from our home, because of the death of one of their members who had died in our part of the country. We accompanied the body back to her home. Before we left, one of my relatives visited a Tohunga, telling him about the journey which we were going, and saying that we needed protection from makutu for a certain period. Ahi tapu was used by the Tohunga, and the rite performed by him placed us under the protection of nga atua, the gods, for a time. He cooked some potato, of which each of us was given a piece. This we carried on our person at the waist. The cooked food was to drive away all evil influences which might be floating in the air, or which moved in space. The very air in a strange tribe's kainga was full of danger, and one had to take great care to prevent makutu taking effect. On our return a few days afterwards, the Tohunga removed the tapu which had protected us. This happened twice with me personally, but I know of other occasions when it took place among my relatives.

Fire and evil spirits

Evil spirits will not come near a fire. A man or men sleeping in the bush would light a fire as a protection from evil spirits. Ordinary fire was used for this.

Human hair

Human hair must not be put into a fire. Should this be done, the person to whom the hair belongs will die. The fire must be extinguished at once.

Fire as protection from frost

Sometimes crops suffered from frost, and if a frost was expected, a piece of lighted wood would be carried by a man ki te wahi miinga (to the urinal). He waved the burning stick over it, while he repeated a karakia called "tatai whetu" (star recital), and as he repeated the words, he moved the forefinger of his right hand, as though counting the stars. This protected the crops.

VI

HOUSES

Caves

CAVES WERE USED in former times, but not as permanent dwelling places, by people who travelled great distances and had to spend a night or two on the way, or by people who went bird-snaring or to gather berries and fruit at some distance from the kainga. They were also used as temporary refuges or hiding places from enemies. Near my home is Te Hinau, a cave where an old chief called Te Tukutuku lived in hiding from his enemies for three years. Traditions also speak of small whare (houses) built on platforms in the forest. These also were used by people when hiding from their enemies.

Houses not rebuilt nor site changed

When once te whare o te Maori (the Maori house) is erected, it is not taken down and re-erected. To do this to an important house is asking for trouble, as nga atua (the gods) would send punishment in some form or other to the owners and builders. Moreover, when a site has been prepared for a new and important house, it is considered a wrong thing to leave it and prepare another one. Something bad is sure to happen, for the site chosen has been made tapu, and already the body of Papa-tu-a-nuku the Earth Mother has been prepared by digging the holes for the four corner pegs to mark it.

General plan of a house

There is a uniform plan for building a whare, whether large or small. It is always rectangular, and has a porch and one room. The timbers and the roof are morticed, and lashed with flax fibre ropes, the windows and doors slide back, and there are no locks or bolts, nor raised floors. The only light comes through the door, which is about 4 feet by 1 foot 6 inches, and a window 1 foot 6 inches by 1 foot, or somewhere about that size. Small hollowed out stone lamps are used at night if required.

For warming the house, a hole might be dug in the centre, and a fire lighted, or glowing embers from a fire outside might be brought in and placed on a stone hearth about 1 foot to 1 foot 6 inches square, chipped out from soft rock by a stone adze. Or again, a fire might be lighted on the ground in the centre. Smoke escaped through the window, and through a small opening in the gable at the front end of the house, just below the place where the poutauhu (one of the two main supports of the house) joined the ridgepole.

Cooking was not done in houses, but in specially built sheds called wharau or kauta, or in the open. Food was generally eaten in the open, or in a wharau. Distinguished visitors, if sleeping in the large important meeting house, might be served with food in the house, but the food must be placed in the narrow space left in the centre as you enter the door. On no account whatsoever must food be put on a sleeping place.

Inhabitants slept round the sides with heads to the wall, the place of honour being nearest the pihanga (window). This place would be occupied by the chief guest and his wife, people of high rank. The floor would be covered with rarauhe (fern) or raupo (bulrush) or both, and on these would be placed whariki (floor-mats) plaited from flax, paopao, and kiekie. So that rushes and fern spread for the sleepers should not be scattered from the two sides, pauruhanga (lengths of timber) were pegged to the floor, leaving a narrow clear aisle down the centre. There was no furniture of any kind used.

A whare whakairo (carved house) or wharepuni (meeting house) had each a name, generally that of an ancestor, the name being given at the kawa o te whare, the opening ceremony for a house.

Te Kainga Maori, the home and village of the Maori

Before describing the building of the houses in detail, it will be best to describe Te Kainga Maori, the home or village of the Maori, for to the Maori, the village was his home, and I prefer to translate the word Kainga as Home. In the days that are gone, the Maori built his kainga on high land, for a good look out, and for protection. He also chose a place where there was a spring, either in or near by the place, or a stream or river. Such a choice of site made the Maori a healthy people, for the air was pure, and the kainga easy to keep clean. In this the Maori was particular. Captain Cook was greatly surprised at their progress, and speaks of it in his Journal, to the detriment of European cities of that period.

The kainga would be close to a ngaherehere (bush) where wood could be procured, although the Maori never cut wood or anything else just by a kainga, but always at a little distance or some distance away.

Whare

A kainga would be occupied by a hapu made up of several family groups. No outsider would come and settle in a kainga; he would only come as a guest. Each family group had its own piece of ground which would be fenced off, and within this they would have their houses, two, three, or more. These houses would be used for sleeping, and would be anywhere from 12 feet long by 6 or 8 feet wide to 20 or 25 feet long by 10 or 12 feet wide, the head of the family using the largest one. There would be space for more houses if necessary. The houses would all face the rising sun, and also face the marae (plaza) of the village. A family group would have a wharau or kauta built close by, to use for cooking in the bad weather.

Many things would be stored in the wharau, such as dry wood stacked in a corner, and various necessary things such as baskets for carrying potatoes and floor-mats would hang up on the wall. In fine weather, all the cooking was done outside, and all meals eaten in the open. Near the wharau would stand a whata, a wide slab across two posts on which food was stored, and beside this would be two poles standing up from the ground to a height of 15 or 20 feet, on which fish was hung for drying, or strings of pipi or other shell-fish ready for winter use. Each whanau (family group) had a paepae (latrine) in a secluded place behind the sleeping whare. The Maori was very particular as to cleanliness in this. Near to the outer part of the kainga in the direction of the wharau there was a small rua (pit) in which kumara was kept for everyday use, the rua kai, or food pits, being some distance away from the kainga. All of the buildings or places connected with the storing or cooking of food are described in the chapter on Food.

Wharepuni

At the head of the marae, and facing it and the rising sun, stood the wharepuni, the meeting house of the kainga, which was generally used by the chief, who sometimes had a smaller wharepuni standing close by. The wharepuni would be used for entertaining and receiving visitors, for holding meetings, and for laying out the dead during a tangi (mourning), or anything else which might affect the hapu. Near the large wharepuni would stand a pataka, a food house raised on posts, and close to that a whata.

Wharekura

In one corner of the pa at the end facing east was the Tohunga's house. He was the priestly expert, a most important person in a community, and his influence was far reaching. The wharekura or sacred school of learning in which the Tohunga lived will be described later in this chapter.

Movement from village to village

In my chapter on Social Organization, I have given the names of all the people who were living at Whakarewarewa about 1880, so that the reader can get an idea of the size of a typical village. But the Maori did not live in one kainga all the year round. If nothing of importance was taking place, many whanau would leave the kainga, and go several miles away to another kainga which belonged to them, perhaps at the edge of a ngaherehere (forest) where they had waerenga (plantations) of kumara and taro, or gathered berries to eat or store for winter use. Or they might go to a small kainga near a lake to get inanga, koura (crayfish), or kakahi (freshwater mussels). The Maori had many kainga a few miles apart which he occupied at different times, but he would have one special kainga where he had well-built houses. At these other kainga, he might have rougher houses, with perhaps one small wharepuni built like a better-class whare. My old Koroua, Maihi te Kakauparaoa, had a whare where he lived at Whakarewarewa in the thermal district, and six miles away at Parekarangi he had another whare, and ten or twelve miles away at Motutawa Island in Rotokakahi Lake, he had another kainga, with temporary whare in other parts. One often reads in European books that a kainga was found deserted. The writers did not realize that the Maori moves about from kainga to kainga, and probably what they came upon was one of these kainga which were used for a certain period and for a certain purpose, such as gathering food, or cutting down trees, preparing the ground and cultivating food, snaring rats, snaring birds, or collecting fern root. Most of these things were got at some distance away from the kainga. In my chapter on Food, I have spoken at length about our different kainga and plantations and places where we collected food.

Now that a brief description of the kainga in which these houses stood has been given, I will describe the houses themselves, the method of building them, and the ceremonies which accompanied the building.

Common whare

The commoner whare which were generally used for sleeping in had little or no carving, except the tekoteko, the figurehead which was called after some ancestor of the owner. These very small whare would not be lined with kakaho (pampas reed) like the larger, but only with raupo (bulrush). But all would have a tekoteko, unless they were very small, and when the Maori spoke of any particular whare, he would call it by its name. (See Plate XIII).

Whare whakairo

All houses were whare, but a large house would be a wharepuni, and if it were a meeting house fully carved, it would be a whare whakairo (Plate XX), or a whare kura, this last being the name for the house where the Tohunga taught ancient lore and religious rites. The whare whakairo had all the wooden slabs inside and out adorned with carvings, and between the carvings there would be panels called tukutuku, made of platwork in beautiful designs. The rafters would be painted with scroll work and coloured white, black, and red, and the whole house would be finished with the most artistic taste both inside and outside.

Wharepuni

The wharepuni was also a large house, though not as large as the whare whakairo, and its interior was not elaborately carved throughout. The poupou or slabs at the sides, and the epa, the slabs at the front and back, might be plain slabs, but the poutauhu at the tungaroa, that is the post which supports the ridgepole at the back, and the poutauhu at te roro, the post which supports the ridgepole at the front, would be either carved, or decorated with scroll work. The rafters would be decorated with scroll work, and the roof lined with kakaho. The space between the poupou would be lined with kakaho, bound and laid either horizontally or diagonally, or the spaces might be filled with platwork like those of the whare whakairo. The maihi and amo maihi outside, that is the gables of the porch, and the posts which supported them, would generally be carved wholly or partially, and the tekoteko would be carved. Every kainga had a wharepuni, a large house which was the property of the community, although the chief had the privilege of occupying it if he so wished. This house would be from 30 to 50 feet long, and 15 to 20 feet wide. A large kainga might have both a wharepuni and a whare whakairo; anyway, if it was a large kainga, a whare whakairo would be erected. This would be anything from 50 to 80 feet in length, and from 20 to 30 feet wide.

Tapu connected with building

There was always tapu connected with the building of a whare hou (new house), but when it was a whare whakairo, it was very tapu indeed, and great care had to be taken not to pollute that tapu, as the house was under the care of the gods. Preparations for such a building would begin four to eight years, and sometimes more, before the actual building was commenced.

Choice of trees

Certain totara trees (Podocarpus totara) had to be chosen and marked for cutting. The cutting was done early so as to get the wood seasoned. This was the wood preferred for all the interior carved slabs, and also for those which adorned the front part, because it was a wood easy to split and work, and lasted well, enduring wind and weather. The Maori had stone tools, so was careful to choose a wood that was easy to work, for the carving was hard and tedious and took a long time.

The forest of Tane

The Maori of old believed that the forest, especially the trees, were as living beings like himself, who possessed a mauri (life principle). He lived very close to Nature, and the life he led made him understand the beings which his mind created, and who lived in the forest. Te wao tapu nui a Tane, the great sacred domain of Tane, was the offspring of Tane the Fertilizer, just as he himself was, and he treated the forest with great respect. This was the reason why, before cutting down a tree in the forest for building a house, a Tohunga would chant a rite to pacify nga atua before he began cutting and killing one of the children of Tane with human hands.

Tapu

The men who accompanied the Tohunga to cut the tree would all be under tapu. They would leave the kainga at dawn before partaking of any food, and when they reached the tree which was to be cut, they laid all their toki (axes) at the foot of it, while the Tohunga karakia.

Karakia

The karakia was an appeal to Io, the supreme being high up in the heavens, asking him to look down upon them and hear their appeal, and to listen also to the name to be given to the new house which was to be built. Nga toki tapu, the tapu axes which possessed the power of cutting, they presented to him, and appealed to have them made noa, to lay their tapu aside, and so make them fit for use.

The Karakia, before Toki cut the Tree, while it is still standing

E Io i runga ia Rangi, titiro iho, whakarongo iho,
O Io above in the heavens, look down upon us, listen to us,
Ka huaina te ingoa o te whare nei ko mea.
A name is given to this house: it is So and So (mentioning name).
Tenei nga tapu, nga mana, nga ihi o nga toki nei,
Here are the sacred, the powerful, the sharp edges of these axes,

Ka hoatu kia koe, kia whaka noa ia,

We present them to you, so that you will make them noa,

Kia whaka tahia i koe.

And put away the tapu from them.

Waerea, waerea, waereai runga ia Rangi e tu nei,

Make a clearing by chopping down timber, with Rangi
standing above,

Waerea i raro ia Papa e takoto nei,

Make a clearing and cut, with Papa the Earth beneath us,

Waerea, i nga Maru, wehi kia tu tangatanga ua tika,

Make a clearing of Maru the feared, who is powerful,
and who has authority, and whom we fear. Stand up,
straighten your back!

Tane pepeke, Pupuke o te wao a Tane.

Tane the quickener, Tane the enlarger of the forest.

Sung in a chorus, while beginning to cut down the tree

Whano, whano, haramai te toki,

Proceed, proceed, thither with the axes,

Haumi e, Hui e, Taiki e.

And join in, in the cutting of the rib.

The word *waerea* was used when clearing or cutting away
any small branches round the base of the tree, or the shrubs
round it, so that the place is clear for the tree to be cut and

to fall. *Waerea* is also used when appealing for tapu to be removed.

When they returned to the kainga in the late afternoon, the Tohunga removed the tapu from the men, and not till then did they eat any food.

Totara

Totara (Podocarpus totara) wood is of a deep red colour, and old slabs which are not carved in a whare give the appearance of mahogany well polished with age. It grows to a height of 80 or 100 or more feet, and the trunks are from 2 to 8 feet in diameter. The outside is covered with a thick fibrous brown bark. Massive symmetrical trunks from 60 to 80 feet long are found in many parts of New Zealand. The wood is clean, straight in the grain, compact, and of great durability. It does not warp or twist, is easily worked, and does not rot. Totara was the wood preferred for ornamental carving, especially for the slabs for the interiors of houses, and for the outside in the front.

Carving

When the wood was seasoned, the Tohunga whakairo rakau, an expert in the art of wood carving, prepared nga poupou (the slabs) in the lengths required, and began the carving. He was generally a skilled worker, and very few men acquired the knowledge. A carver began his work with his stone adzes and chisels at one end of the slab, with no drawing to guide him. His scheme was carried in his mind, and each figure or part of a figure was carved from memory, as he worked the length of the slab until the whole was covered with the grotesque figures of his imagination. Te ngarara, the lizard, was the only thing he carved to nature. A design much liked by the Maori carver is the spiral, and this appeared in decorated carving on houses, canoes, implements, etc., as well as the double spiral that the Maori knew so well how to carve with exactness. Manaia is another figure, with a long slim body, a bird-like head, and a number of legs. In some cases, only half the body is shown, in others a manaia head merges into the arms of a human figure. Marakihau are figures partially human, with the lower part resembling the tail of a fish. A long tongue protrudes from the mouth. Paua, that is Haliotis shell, was used for the eyes in carved figures. Figures were carved with three fingers only.

The art of carving was known to certain families, and the knowledge was handed down from generation to generation. Nearly all of the carving was of grotesques, whether it was on the slabs of houses, on food houses, gateways, or posts for palisading. The very fine work on weapons, treasure boxes such as kumete and waka huia, and the spiral decorations on waka taua (war canoes), was most beautiful. The Tohunga whakairo would carve all the slabs for a house near the site chosen for it to stand. The building of the whare did not begin until all the material was ready for it, and the preparation and the building together took anything from four to ten years.

Tapu of site of a house desecrated by presence of women

No woman was allowed to go near the place where the men were working on a house. She must not set foot on the site chosen for the whare to stand, as it was all under tapu, just as all the men were whether they were working on the carvings or on the building. Should a woman desecrate this tapu the whare would never be finished, and a woman was careful never to go near the place until after the whai kawa (opening ceremony), when the tapu was removed. During this ceremony the whare was made noa by a woman who entered the building through the pihanga (window) with cooked food, and ate some of it inside the whare before coming out of the kuaha (door).

Woman removes tapu

Decision to build

The building of a wharepuni or a whare whakairo was not generally suggested by the chief, but by the chiefs of his hapu, who were closely related to him. The suggestion might come up at a meeting or gathering of the people. All important matters were discussed publicly at meetings, and never done on the quiet by one or two individuals. When it had been decided to build the house, then meetings took place to arrange for the site. Such a house had to occupy a central position in the kainga facing the marae, the open space where visitors were welcomed and their food served, and the front must face the rising sun. All these things were decided by the principal men of the kainga, including the chief and the Tohunga.

Preliminary measurements

When the site of the house was chosen, the length was marked by placing a peg in the centre, and then measuring the distance to each end peg. The width was then measured. The maro (stretch) was used when measuring, and was done by a man with both arms stretched out to their full extent, that is, about 6 feet. The four corners were marked with wooden pegs driven in by a wooden mallet.

Foundations and places for uprights

The kaupapa (foundations) were dug about I foot to $1\frac{1}{2}$ feet below the level of the ground. A taura (rope made of flax fibre) was tied to one of the centre pegs, then passed round the outside of the four corner pegs, and stretched tightly. This line was used to mark the place where each poupou (side slab) was to be placed in the ground. Pegs at each end marked the place for the poutauhu i te tungaroa, the large slab which supported the ridgepole at the back, and for the poutauhu i te roro, the one which supported the ridgepole at the front end of the house. The two poutauhu slabs were generally 15, 18, or more feet in height, 2 to 3 feet wide, and 4, 6, or 9 or more inches thick. A trunk of a tree was often used for a poutauhu, left rounded on the inside. As the two poutauhu supported the ridgepole which was the mainstay of the whole house, it was important that they should be strong and well sunk into the ground.

Poutauhu

Tauhu

The tauhu or ridgepole was a whole tree trunk which went the whole length of the roof, and might be 50, 60, 80 or more feet long. It was triangular in section. This tauhu was lifted and placed in position in the rangi tapu way.

Rangi tapu way of placing ridgepole

Two fairly thick tree trunks were set firmly in the ground 6 or 8 feet apart, and another tree trunk was set into the forks left at the top of each. There was one of these contrivances at each end of the house, each 1 to 3 feet higher than the poutauhu. The beam set in the forks at the top was the trunk of te parapara or puwha-ure-roa (Pisonia brunoniana), a tree which has a very sticky surface, so that a rope put on it slips round or up and down very easily. A stout rope made from flax fibre was tied to one end of the tauhu, and passed over the beam to the other side where several men were standing in a row to pull it up. A rope was also tied to the other end of the tauhu, and similarly passed over the beam to another row of men. At a given time, the hauling was done by many men in unison, and the tauhu was quickly lifted to the height required, and placed in position on the poutauhu at each end of the whare. The tauhu fitted exactly.

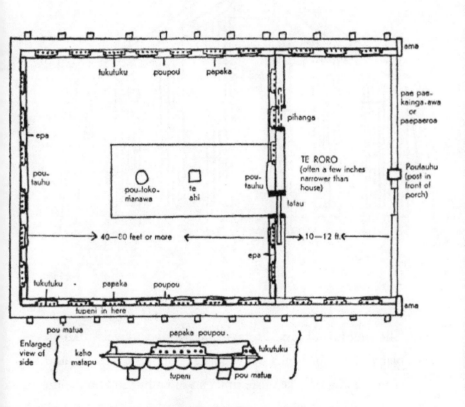

10. Ground Plan of Whare Whakario.

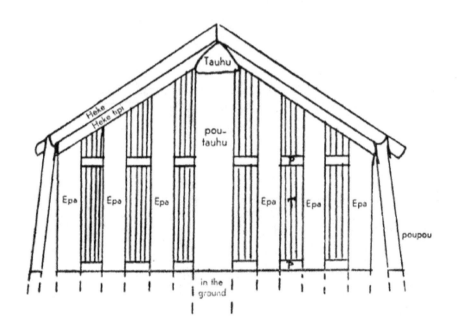

11. Tungaroa, Interior back of house.

Shewing Epa of carved totara, alternating with tukutuku of
platwork (T) bordered with papaka (P) of carved totara, also
corner poupou, heke, heke tipi, end of tauhu, and poutauhu
i te tungaroa.

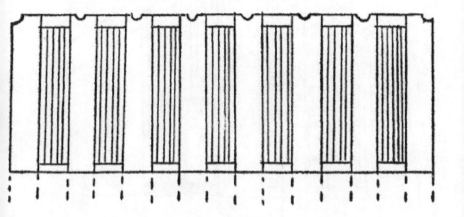

12. Te Tara o te Whare, Side of house, interior.

Shewing poupou of carved totara wood with whakarua whetu (rounded cavities), alternating with tukutuku (platwork panels) bordered at top and bottom with papaka of carved totara wood. Dotted lines represent the extension of the poupou below ground.

For a whare whakairo (a large meeting house) all of the poupou and papaka would be carved by a Tohunga whakairo (adept in the art of carving). For a wharepuni (a meeting house of fair size) the interior slabs would not always be carved.

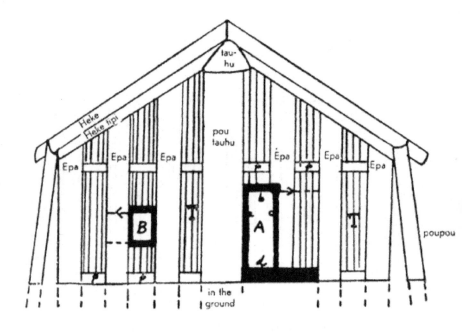

13. Interior front.

T—Tukutuku; pp., etc.—papaka.

A—sliding door (b—korupe, c—whaka-wai, d—pacpac). Arrow and dotted line shew direction and length of slide.

B—sliding window. Arrow and dotted line shew direction and length of slide.

The window and door slid behind the epa into a recess in the double wall, lined with battens. The epa must be cut for the door and window frames.

348

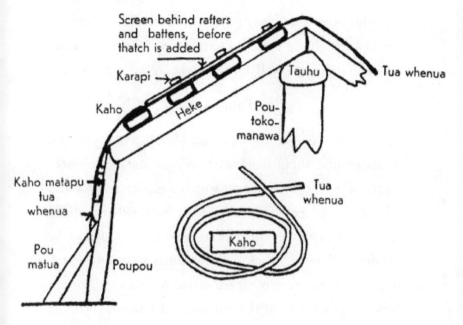

14. Partial section at pou-toko-manawa before thatch is put on.

Poutoko-mana

If the whare was a very large one, a pou-toko-manawa (centre pole) was placed in the centre of the interior to support the ridgepole, and another pole was placed at the front from the tekoteko (figure-head) to the paepae (threshold). Thick slabs like the poutauhu and pou-toko-mana and other heavy slabs would be placed in position close to the deep holes dug for them. They would be tied only at one end, and then lifted in the rangi tapu way, while the bottom ends would be made

349

to slip into the holes ready to receive them. When the slabs were in a straight-up position, several men filled in the holes with earth, beating it well down with heavy wooden posts.

Poupou

The poupou or side slabs were also firmly and deeply put into the ground, about 2 feet apart, an equal and even number on each side. They were placed with a slight leaning inward, with a cavity gouged out at the top of each, either rounded (whakarua whetu), or squared (waha paepae), so as to take the rafters, whose ends were cut into tongues (teremu) which fitted the cavities exactly. There would be six, eight, or ten poupou on each side of the interior, and four, six, or more in the porch, each slab being 2 to 3 feet wide and about 4 inches thick or even more. The upper ends were held firm by a kaho matapu, a batten of the full length of the side of the whare, tied on the outer side, and fastened securely to holes in the corners of the inner side of each poupou. Outside each poupou was a pou matua, a strut which was firmly set in the ground, and served to push it inward against the weight of the roof. The four corner poupou were tapu.

Heke

The heke or rafters were made of long and strong timber, and were of the same number as the poupou, as each rafter fitted into the cavity on the top end of the poupou, while the top ends of each two rafters met each other on the top of the ridgepole, where they were tied together, or kept in place with the rope which passed over the outer side of each pair of rafters, holding in the battens on the way down to the poupou, where it was tied tightly to the pou matua. The rope used for this was called tua whenua, and was made from leaves of the ti kouka (Cordy-line australis). It was very strong, as great strength was needed. The rafters were 15, 18, or more feet in length, and 4 to 6 inches thick, and were either of straight timber, or rounded at the lower end to fit into the whakarua whetu (rounded cavity). They were trimmed with toki (stone axes), whose edge could trim four heke before requiring to be re-sharpened. The top ends of the rafters were sometimes bound tightly together in pairs above the tauhu with strong ties of aka (vines), and were also tied at the lower ends where they passed through the cavity on the top of the poupou.

Kaho

The kaho or battens, 2, 3, or 4 inches by $\frac{3}{4}$ to 1 inch, were laid across the rafters from end to end, about $1\frac{1}{2}$ to 3 feet apart, and about 1 foot from the poupou, and about 1 foot from the ridgepole. There was an even number on either side. They were put on to support the thatching of reeds and raupo. These kaho were held in place by a stout rope on the upper side of the rafter, as I have already said. A double turn was made round each batten before passing the rope over the ridgepole down the other side of the slanting roof, where the double turns were repeated. When the rope reached the outside wall, it was secured tightly by a process called mimiro. A strong tree trunk was dug in straight-up at the base of the strut (pou matua) on the outside wall. A short piece of rope was tied to the tua whenua described on the previous page, while the other end was tied to the tree trunk to be used as a lever. The use of this lever placed a great strain on the rope, and this strain locked the timbers of the house. The two poupou opposite each other took the strain, and the rafters were held together on wall and ridgepole. The creaking of timbers was heard under the strain. The end of the tightened rope was tied to the outer strut, and then the lever and short rope were taken away. So each pair of poupou and rafters were jammed together. The rope end which was tied to the strut was covered with the thatch, which saved it from the bad weather. Great care was taken in lashing the kaho, as it was an omen of evil import if the kaho next to the tauhu were insecurely fastened.

Thatching

Over the curved heke of dark coloured totara ornamented with their paintings of red, black, and white (the tapering hook-ended puhoro, or many branched koiri), and crossed by their firmly lashed battens (kaho), the first roof covering was laid. When the heke were hewn from light coloured timbers such as the whau or tawa, this covering might consist of the pennate leaf of the many ringed nikau, neatly plaited. To show against the dark heke, screens of the ever dropping toetoe, of a size to fit in the kaho already in place, were closely laced. To the kaho they were bound with bands of flax, the split blade of the honeyed harakeke. Over the reeds were then strewn the dry blades of the raupo (bulrush), each layer being held in place by strips passing over it, and under the laths (karapi) of the toetoe screen. Upon these layers (tuahuri) were again placed bundles of raupo, then of toetoe, then of raupo, and so on until the desired thickness was obtained. Over all this was a thatching of toetoe (ara-whiu-whiu) made, not of the plant which grew by the open streams, but of the forest plant, the toe-toerakau, as this was the most durable. To hold it in position, light rods of manuka were cut from a clump where many shaggy-coated trees thickly clustered, and these were fixed lattice-wise over the now completed roof.

Epa

The slabs of upright totara at the back and at the front of the interior are called epa. They were set in the ground deeply and firmly, upright and not leaning inward, and formed the framework of the tungaroa (back) and te roro (front), and numbered three or five on each side of the poutauhu.

Heke tipi

The top ends of the epa were cut slantwise, so as to allow

the heke tipi to rest on them. The heke tipi were boards 4 to 6 inches wide and $\frac{3}{4}$ to I inch in thickness, which extended from the ridgepole along the tops of the epa down to the corner poupou. The heke tipi were lashed to the epa, and were close up against the rafters above them. Some whare had no heke tipi, and in these, the end rafters lay against the tops of the epa, and fitted into cavities on the sides of the poupou.

Pou-toko-manawa

The pou-toko-manawa, generally a totara tree trunk, was, as I have said, placed in the centre of the interior in a line with the two pou-tauhu at each end, and helped to support the roof. It was either left round and plain, or chipped with an adze to form four flat sides and carved. At the base would be the carved figure of an ancestor, after whom the house would be named. Pou-toko-manawa means the post which supports the heart. Before this figure, and midway between it and the poutauhu at the front was the hearth (taku ahi), its position being marked and kept enclosed by four stones. Here the fire was kindled at sundown, and when the smoke from the burning wood had cleared, red embers only remaining, the occupants would enter, close both door and window, and sleep soundly through the night. So that rushes and raupo spread for the sleepers should not be scattered from the two sides, pauruhanga or paepae (lengths of timber) were pegged to the floor.

Papaka

Between each pair of carved slabs there were small slabs of totara wood called papaka, each $1\frac{1}{2}$ to 2 feet wide, 8 inches to I foot deep, and 2 to 3 inches thick. These small slabs were placed along the lower end of the wall, and also along the top, all the way round the interior of the house, with plat-work panels or reed lining between each pair of papaka and poupou or epa.

Tukutuku

Some of the whare were lined with kakaho reeds, either plain, or bound with harakeke and smoked so as to make a pattern on each reed of alternate narrow bands of dark and light colour. The kakaho would be cut into proper lengths so as to allow about 2 inches behind the poupou on either side, and these lengths would be tied one below the other, the slabs covering the tied ends. The reeds might be arranged either horizontally or diagonally. But for a wharepuni or whare whakairo, being specially built, panels called tukutuku, harapeke, or pukiore, were made. The long toetoe reeds (kakaho) were arranged vertically, and horizontal wooden laths (kaho-tarai), black, white, and red, each of a finger's breadth, and each about 2 feet long, were tied all the way up the vertical reeds. Each lath was laced to each reed with strips of leaves of the kiekie, dyed black, or left in its natural colour, and the single stitches of the lacing made the pattern called poutama. The tuitui worker would begin making the pattern with narrow strips of undressed leaves of phormium, some of which would be dyed black or yellow, while other was left in its natural colour, which is cream or dark cream. If it could be obtained, kiekie (Freycinetia) was the favoured material for tuitui, as it is very white, and when some of it is dyed black or yellow, the three colours are beautiful together. Sometimes only the black and white were used. Pingao (Scirpus frondosus), which is orange in colour, was sometimes employed. The tuitui work in the tukutuku is most effective, and the patterns with colour help to show up the carvings on both sides. These carvings are generally very dark, as most of them are painted a dark red, with only the paua (ahliotis) shell eyes of the grotesque figures to relieve them. Sometimes, but not always, a round rod, tuma-taka-huki, is cross-laced up the middle of each panel. The tukutuku were made by two people, as in the picture, with one on each side to pass the kiekie or harakeke strips through. This was done by means of a piece of wood, generally green manuka, doubled over. Sometimes the worker simply doubled the piece of kiekie or flax, which is quite stiff. Workers had to be careful that there was no mistake in the tuitui lacing, as it would throw the whole pattern out of place. The panels were fitted into rebates cut for the purpose in each poupou, the whole being kept in position by horizontal battens fixed at the back. Behind these panels, and lashed to the battens, were bundles of raupo (mparu) reaching from the ground to the eaves, their closeness and thickness excluding all cold air from the interior of the whare. (See Plate XXI.)

Banking

As a further precaution against the cold, the earth was heaped up against the tuparu to a cubit (whiti-anga) or more in height. The back and front walls were finished in the same way, except that the packing in the mahau (open porch) was of a more ornamental nature.

Tatau

The epa slabs in te roro, the front interior, were cut for the doorway, and for the shuttered opening used as a window. The tatau (kuaha, or whatitoka) was generally $1\frac{1}{2}$ to 2 feet wide, and 3 to 5 feet high, and was a single slab of wood 2 or 3 inches thick. It was opened by sliding it to your left on entering the house, and to the right on coming out. The door was close up against the poutauhu, and was slid into a recess in the wall by means of a cord of twisted fibre with a knot at the end. To fasten the door, the cord was secured by a peg. The frame was begun by laying the threshold, a piece of timber about twice as long as the door was wide.

Paepae

The threshold, paepae, was a piece of wood 4 to 6 feet

long, and about 12 by 12 inches. There was a groove along the upper surface to carry the door, hai toanga i te tatau. The left jamb (whaka-wai), looking from the inside, rested on the paepae, and stood close against the poutauhu, while the right jamb was in two pieces, to allow the door to slide into it. This recess was lined with horizontal battens, to prevent injury to the packing of the walls.

Pare

The lintel (pare, korupe, kororupe) over the doorway was generally most elaborately and finely carved. So also were the pieces at the sides, and the paepae.

Pihanga

There was only one window, called pihanga, mataaho, or matapihi, about 2 by $1\frac{1}{2}$ feet. It slid, like the door, but to your right as you enter, and to your left as you came out. It was used more for the escape of smoke than to look out of, and was $2\frac{1}{2}$ to 3 feet above the ground, being so placed that a person sitting on the floor would have the bottom of the window just below the level of his eyes.

Te roro, or front

The front wall of a whare was set back so as to leave a porch in the front, which would be from 8 to 12 feet deep in a meeting house. As a rule the roro or porch was narrower by a few inches than the rest of the building, though sometimes it was the same size or wider. Its rafters and side slabs were like those in the interior, and there were also papaka between the carved poupou. Reaching from side to side at the ends of the two walls forming the mahau or open porch before the whare, and resting on its edge on the ground, was placed the paepaeroa, a whitianga (cubit) in height. This "long threshold" of the porch is shown in the picture of the meeting house of Wahiao, with a part cut away in front of the door to make entrance to the porch easier.

Amo

Covering the ends of the walls and framing the porch on either side were two broad pieces of timber, the amo, carved with figures fiercely eyed with paua. The amo supported the lower parts of the broad barge-boards (maihi), whose ends, however, carved and perforated with intertwisting spirals, projected downwards beyond the amo. The maihi fitted into a place cut for them at the back of the amo. The angle at the upper ends of the carved maihi was covered by the flat grimacing koruru, above which stood the defiant tekoteko.

Tekoteko

The tekoteko or figurehead was decorated in times' of rejoicing with red feathers from the kaka. When the koruru and tekoteko ornamented the gable, the end of the ridgepole was left uncarved, the tekoteko glaring with terrifying features from the gable bringing the many-producing sea-gods to mind. It is said that a long time since, Tangaroa seeing the son of Rua-pupuke bathing with other boys in the shallow waters of the shore, shouting when the breaking surf was pouring over their heads and down their gleaming bodies, seized that son, and bore him away below the waves, and set him as a tekoteko upon the gable of his sea-ridden whare. Rua, learning the fate of his son, in the shape of a fish dived deeply into the realms of the sea-god, and beholding him thus degraded, he destroyed the people with sunlight and the whare with fire, saving only the carved amo and maihi, the tauhu, and the frames of the door and window. These carvings he took with him, and leaving the watery realms, brought them as patterns for the use of the sons of Tiki. Of these sons, Hinga-nga-Roa built the first carved whare and Take Take first used carving for such building.

Whare kura Whare wananga

There are many names known of the famous old-time whare kura, the Tohunga's house and sacred school of learning. The second whare kura or whare wananga was the first known in the world. The form of semblance of this building was obtained from Rangi-ta-muku, the second of the twelve heavens, counting upwards. This knowledge was gained by Tane, Paia, and Rongo-marae-roa, three of the offspring of the primal parents, Rangi and Papa. Whare kura was built after the pattern of that in Hawaiki. The building itself faced the east, and was divided into three parts, the most western part being that of the chief priest, the most eastern the open mahau, and the centre the part where instruction was given. The people procured the material for this edifice, but the Tohunga erected it, and whilst engaged in this labour, they abstained from food until the close of each day. The chief Tohunga performed ceremonies over the pou-toko-manawa or centre post, and when the kakaho reeds forming the patterned walls were laced in position, karakia were repeated. On the completion of the building, the ta-te-kawa or dedication was performed. A sacrifice of a dog, man, woman, child, or slave, was made, and the blood only presented to Mua. The victim was killed in front of the whare, the body afterwards being buried in the wahi tapu (sacred burial place). A sacred fire and umu (sacred oven) were lighted in the whare and kept burning while the victim was being killed. At the close of day, another fire was lighted in the marae, and kumara and eel were cooked and eaten by the Tohunga and sacred men. In each instance a fresh fire was made, produced by friction.

Communal works on houses

I have spoken before of the fact that a wharepuni would not be finished for some years after it had been decided to build it. When the decision had been made, all the members of the hapu immediately began to get together the things required for building. Some went with the Tohunga to fell the trees in the forest, as I have already described. Others went great distances to gather bundles of raupo (bulrush) which they carried on their backs to the kainga. The raupo had to be cut at a certain time of year, and a great number of bundles were needed to thatch the inside walls to make the house warm. The raupo had to be dried before the bundles were put away to keep until they were needed. Then a great deal of kakaho, reeds of the toetoe (Arundo conspicua) was needed for lining the roof and walls between the carvings, and the roro (front porch). This also had to be cut at a certain season, and much time and trouble were spent in finding kakaho of a light instead of a deep yellow colour, and in getting long lengths of the same thickness. The kakaho preferred grew in the forest. It was made up into bundles, tied at each end and in the middle, with green flax, then put into the thick plaited flax-fibre kawe and carried on the back. The kakaho was dried and hung up in bundles in a wharau until it was needed. To gather all the material took many seasons. Wiwi (rush) or toetoe was gathered for the outside covering of the roof, flax fibre for tying; kiekie had to be found in the forest for tuitui nga tukutuku, to thread the plaitwork between the carvings on the walls. Flax and kiekie had to be gathered for making the whariki (floor-mats).

Food had to be provided for the workers, and extra crops

were planted. Everyone in the kainga would be busy doing various things, and it was a great pleasure to them, for were they not helping to build their own whare whakairo, the meeting place for the whole hapu? Although it was the chief who wanted to erect the whare and use it, still it was for the whole hapu to use on all their ceremonial occasions.

If they had a pa tuna (eel wier), they would renew it at the right season, and get quantities of eels, some of which they would open (pawhara), though the smaller would be left as they were. The eels were cooked in a hangi and hung out to dry for a day or two, then stacked away in a cool dry place in baskets, or hung up in a wharau or kauta for a time.

Hapu who were related to the hapu which were building the whare would all help in some way by collecting material, sending expert men for carving, scroll-work, or building, or food for the workers; many also were engaged in gathering or growing food for the hui at the opening. The news would be spread far and near, and all of the various hapu helped with everything, so that there was little expense for the hapu who were building the whare.

All this time, many relatives from other hapu would stay in the kainga and help in the various work, and food was being sent from all directions to feed the workers. Some of the people would gather the small fish inanga in the lakes and dry them, others would get koura (small crayfish), and cook and thread them on long strings and hang them up to dry, while still others would gather berries from the forest and cook and dry them. Then, the year of the hui, great quantities of kumara and taro would be planted by many of the clans, who would send the food to the marae where the hui was taking place. Aruhe, fern root, would be gathered and stored in the various whata, and there would be large rua kumara (sweet potato pits) to hold the kumara and taro so that there would be no shortage of anything. The women would be busy plaiting whariki from flax and kiekie, and rougher mats to go under the finer. Then rough tuwhara, flax floor-mats, would be made for the wharau, and for holding the cooked food on the marae, and kete (baskets) would be plaited for holding the various foods. Wood was collected and stored in great heaps for the hangi, so that when the clans arrived for the opening ceremony, they brought loads of wood and other necessary things for the hui, which lightened the burden for the tangata whenau. Thus there was plenty to eat for the many hundreds of visitors who generally assembled for such a great function.

VII

WEAPONS

TRAINING IN THE use of arms was a thing important to the Maori of old, from youth until he was too old to use them. The old people taught the young, and from the very first, one of the most important things to learn was to keep the eyes from moving when facing an opponent, and to keep them fixed on one of two points, the big toe, or the point of the shoulder. Looking at the advanced foot of his opponent, the fighter will see his big toe clinch downwards a fraction of time before he delivers his blow. This warns him of what is coming, and he is prepared to karo (parry) or avoid it. Another thing to do is to look at your opponent's shoulder. If you notice the slightest movement of its muscles, you reckon that a blow is going to be delivered at once.

Training is use of weapons

A man had to be very quick in the use of his weapons, whether long or short, and always ready for an opponent, however he might wield his weapons. For this reason, a great thing to remember was to keep always on the move in single combat, never to stand still, and always to be light and agile on the feet. The old Maori always said that the legs were the means of parrying and avoidance, and never tired of telling how he would avoid a thrust from a spear, or how he got the better of his opponent.

Choice of weapons

When a Maori was going to fight, he usually took two weapons, one a short striking weapon, generally carried in the waist of his marotaua (war apron), and the other a long two-handed weapon. A man might carry a greenstone patu and a taiaha, or a pou tangata and a taiaha, or a patu pounamu and a kotaha; or he might carry a tewhatewha, and as a short weapon a kotiate, a patu paraoa, a wahaika, etc. He would carry the weapons which he liked best and always use them.

Taiaha

The taiaha (Plate XXII, figures 2–5) was the most important of the two-handed weapons of the old Maori. It is generally made of hard wood of great strength, such as manuka (Leptospermum scoparium) or puriri (Vitex littoralis, a kind of iron wood, very heavy, that will turn the edge of an axe), and is 5 to 7 feet long. The manuka is very tough and fibrous, and if it broke, would never snap off, because of its fibrous consistency. It was slightly burnt, then cut and polished, so that the edges were almost like tempered steel, very hard and sharp. The rau, or blade end, is flattened, and gradually merges into the oval or cylindrical shaft. The arero, or tongue, at the other end is adorned with fine carvings in curvilinear designs, and where it joins the shaft, there is a grotesque carved face, chinless, with elongated eyes of haliotis shell, out of whose mouth the tongue-like blade comes. Though the whole weapon is slim, there is no fear of its breaking, and the Maori felt quite safe, and faced the enemy with confidence if he carried a taiaha.

The taiaha is essentially a chief's staff or weapon. It is beautifully adorned with a band of bright red feathers from beneath the wing of the kaka (red parrot), fastened on to a woven strip of material, and then bound round the shaft just below the carved head. This band is called a tauri kura. Just below this band, small tufts of long white dog's hair are bound to adorn it further, as in figure 4.

Use in combat

In combat, the taiaha is generally held with the tongue or arero downward, as in Plate XXIII. The left hand gripped the shaft just above the carved head, and the right held the shaft at a comfortable distance further up. The fighter might give his opponent the point of the tongue in the pit of the stomach, or pretend to do so, thus causing him to drop his guard, and bend forward or duck. The fighter then swung the heavy blade end over and hit his enemy's head with the edge of it.

The three pictures in Plate XXIII will show some of the uses of the taiaha, as shown by Te Rangi, who was a past master in the art of whakatu (war dancing), as in many other things.

1. Popotahi, before engagement, or at the beginning of a dance. In this guard, the taiaha is held almost vertically, the tongue downward, and a little below the waist, the shaft a little to the front of the point where the right shoulder joins the arm, and sloping a little to the right. The left foot is forward. The left hand, back outward, grasps the weapon just above the carved head, the arm being bent at a right angle across the body, and the elbow being close to the body. The right hand, back outward holds the shaft at about the level of the cheek.

2. Whakarehu, the point from the guard just described. The arero or tongue is swiftly raised and thrust at the opponent, the shaft sliding quickly through the left hand of the wielder. If the thrust gets home, or destroys the guard of the opponent, the fighter can swing the blade end over and hit his opponent's head a crack with its edge.

3. Huanui, a guard. In this guard, the taiaha is held diagonally across the body, the arero on the left at about the level of the knee, the left leg being forward. Point and blow may be delivered from this guard, as the reader will see if he experiments with a wooden rod. These guards, points, and blows, are not unlike those described by Mr. T. A. McCarthy in his book on "The Quarterstaff", published in London in 1883.

When making speeches at a ceremonial gathering, a chief would use a taiaha just as a baton is used. Such a baton might be made of softer wood, such as kahikatea (white pine). The shafts of old taiaha were very highly polished, and these old specimens have a slight rippled appearance on the surface. This was the result of scraping the surface with sharp-edged shells or stone flakes.

Pouwhenua

The pouwhenua (Plate XXII, figure 1) is not unlike a taiaha in appearance, having the same spatulate blade merging into the shaft at one end. But the other end has no tongue, that part being brought to a thick point. It was as commonly used as the taiaha, and was used like it. It had no decoration except a grotesque head, which was generally carved just below half-way down, a little nearer the point than the other end. There were stone specimens used years ago which were about 4 feet long, but very few are now to be seen. There are two of these stone pouwhenua in the Auckland Museum.

Tewhatewha

The tewhatewha (Plate XXII, figure 6) is generally 4 to 5 feet long, and is not unlike an axe in shape. One of the names for this weapon is paiaka (a root), as it is made mostly of the root of the maire tree, a very hard wood. The small end was used in delivering a point, but the common thing to do was to strike a blow, not with the edge of the blade, but with the thick back of it. There was a small hole in the lower part of the blade, and from this was fastened a bunch of feathers of the kahu (hawk) or kereru (pigeon). This bunch hung loosely from a fibre cord, and was used to attract or disconcert the enemy, the fighter drawing it swiftly across his opponent's eyes with a very quick movement of the weapon. In combat the tewhatewha was held with the point downward. Sometimes the tewhatewha had no adornment in the way of carving, and was all quite plain, though highly polished. Sometimes, however, a grotesque head was carved about 18 inches from the end point, and sometimes the axe part was carved and about a third of the shaft below it.

Kotaha and Kopere

The kopere, known also as pere, whiuwhiu, tarerarera, and makoi, is a dart about 3 feet 6 inches to 4 feet long, made of the very hardest wood, with the point hardened in the fire. It was propelled by means of the kotaha, a stout piece of manuka wood a little over 1 inch thick, and about 4 feet long, whose lower end was carved, with a hole in it. The upper end was sometimes carved with a figure which looked like a human hand. To the hole at the lower end was attached a very strong piece of flax cord, which ended in a round, flat-looking knot.

The dart is stuck loosely in the ground at an angle and direction calculated to strike the object aimed at. The thong is wrapped once round the dart just below a small ridge, the knot passing under the thong so as to hold it loosely. The fighter then seizes the wooden part of kotaha in both hands, and propels it as shown in the diagram; the string frees itself as the dart flies forward.

It was often told me as a child that Ngati Whakaue (the descendants of Whakaue), who lived at Ohine-mutu, Rotorua, were very famous for their skill in using the Kotaha. When they attacked Puhirua pa, over a hundred years ago, one of the warriors, named Te Umanui, hurled his kopere with such true aim that it would go right through the heart of a chief who was inside the pa. The place where the dart was thrown was anywhere from 70–80 yards distant.

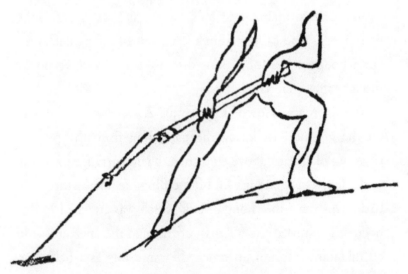

15. Use of Kotaha and Kopere.

The kotaha was also made in a much heavier form, and then it was worked by two people, as clusters of darts were thrown at a time. This had a great effect on open land against a whole body of charging men, as the enemy could not parry the darts with any success, and their solid front was broken up.

Hoeroa

The hoeroa was a very rare weapon, and the Pitt-Rivers Museum at Oxford is very fortunate in possessing one. It was made from whalebone, and was generally 4–6 feet long, 2 inches wide, and a $\frac{1}{4}$ inch thick, or a little more. It was a weapon thrown by the hand, and a very important one. It was not commonly used like the taiaha and other two-handed weapons. Its principal and most deadly use was for dealing with people who came within a few yards of the pa defences, and who, being out of striking distance from hand weapons, thought they were safe.

The hoeroa was used in this way. A warrior went down on the ground just inside the palisading from the puhara (fighting platform) above, and then, having arranged a space in the fence wide enough for him to fling the hoeroa through, tied to his waist the thong of hair which was attached to the hoeroa. He hurled the hoeroa out through the aperture with an underarm motion, in much the same way as a fielder at third man throws down the wicket at cricket. Having struck his victim, he hauled in his line and withdrew the hoeroa. The hoeroa was very much feared, because there was no guard or parry to it.

Mere or patu pounamu

The short striking weapons of the old Maori were all used with one hand, and termed patu, and those made from stone were mere or patu pounamu, patu onewa, okewa, uiti, and toki hohoupu or pou tangata. In some places the word "mere" was applied only to those made from the pounamu. Greenstone weapons were called mere pounamu or patu pounamu. The other names, such as onewa, etc., depended on the material from which the weapons were made, while the toki hoheupu or pou tangata, to be described later, was a weapon hafted like an adze.

The greenstone used for making a patu pounamu was very carefully chosen, as the stone must not have a flaw, and the colour had to be good.

Kinds of greenstone

The kinds of greenstone were as follows: 1, Commonest of all, a very dark green. 2, Kawakawa, dark green. 3, Kahurangi, light green. 4, Inanga, blue-grey. 5, Tangiwai, translucent. 6, Inanga kawakawa, 2 and 4 on same stone. 7, Tangiwai inanga, 4 and 5 on same stone. The Inanga and Tangiwai were the most prized.

Uses of greenstone other than in war

All greenstones, whether weapons or ornaments, are a source of wealth, and may be given in utu, which is payment for insult, in dowry, or as kopaki for the dead. If a stranger dies away from home, his body is returned to his village with flax and feather cloaks and greenstones befitting his rank. Eventually, a present of equal value at least is returned to the people who so honoured the dead.

As heirlooms

The mere were very highly prized by our old people, and many of them were of great historical interest and were handed down from generation to generation as heirlooms. The one most prized of those I have here and of those at home, is Riwai, in my sister's possession, and a fine old heirloom.

Plate XXIV, figure 2, shows one of my mere pounamu, 14 inches long and $4\frac{3}{4}$ inches wide at the widest part 3 inches from the end. The handgrip is about half an inch thick. This is of kawakawa greenstone.

Figure 4 on the same plate shows a mere made of inanga greenstone $12\frac{1}{2}$ inches long and a little over $3\frac{3}{4}$ inches wide at its widest part, which is about 3 inches from the end.

Figure 6 is a small mere which has been through fire. It is just under 11 inches long, and is $3\frac{1}{4}$ inches wide at the widest part 2 inches from the end.

Making a mere

The mere or patu pounamu was much thinner than those made from ordinary stone, because the nephrite was very tough, and it took a great deal to break it. The. blade was brought to a fine thin edge all round the sides and bottom, and the butt end of the hand grip is marked by two, three, or more grooves, with a hole just below for the wrist cord. The weapon was made by grinding or rubbing on sandstone, and was very slow and laborious work. In days gone by, a mere was not always finished during a man's life-time, and the next generation was left to complete it.

A block of nephrite was first cut into a rough outline with pieces of quartzite used with hard sand and water. Greenstone does not chip easily. The last process was a dressing of the surface with fine sandstone and then a piece of very hard smooth stone.

Use in war

The old Maori used the mere both for patu and tipi, i.e. both for striking and thrusting. A favourite use of the mere was to drive the sharp thin edge of the blade into the thin part of the skull by the tipi or end-wise thrust. It was said that experts were able to wrench the skull open by a certain turn of the wrist after this thrust.

When a tangata rangatira was captured and was about to be slain, he often passed his own patu pounamu to his captor, asking that he might be killed with it. If his captor was also a tangata rangatira, the request would be granted, for a chief of high rank would do this. The Maori warrior did not mind dying, and loved to die in battle, especially if he was killed with a greenstone mere, a rangatira weapon. It was said by our old people that a man who was armed with a short patu often defeated a man who was armed with a long two-handed weapon, such as the taiaha or spear. A man using a short patu often had a whakapuru, a form of pad, in his hand, or on his left arm. This received the impact of a thrusting weapon.

The short weapons were generally carried in the tatua or belt, suspended from the wrist by a thong, sometimes on the left wrist, so that it will be hidden by the cloak. A highly valued mere will often be hidden when not in use, and some of these hiding places are not in the kainga, but in a secret place in the forest. For example, the mere may be buried at the foot of a tree well-known to the owner.

Spears and other long weapons were generally kept in the owner's house, where they were handy when he was called to fight without warning. They were usually hung up on the left side of the whare, as you enter it. If an alarm were given, the man ran straight for the door, taking his spear with his right hand from its supports as he ran. The Maori always kept implements ready for use.

Patu onewa

The patu onewa was very like the patu pounamu in shape, but much thicker, as the material onewa, a kind of greywacke of dark colour, would break easily if it were too thin. The material lends itself to smoothing and polishing, and also to chipping. Some of the specimens in the Pitt-Rivers Museum at Oxford are fine examples of the old Maori workmanship, and prove the keen true eye of the worker. Stone found under water was much preferred. If the stone was got from a boulder on the land, the outer parts were broken away. The surface of the rock mass was shattered by a fire which was made to heat the rock; then cold water was thrown on to the heated surface. Patu onewa, also known as patu kurutai, were of various sizes and lengths, from about 13 inches to a little over 16 inches long. Generally the large ones were 4 inches wide at the widest part, and about $1\frac{3}{8}$ inches at the handgrip. They would be about $1\frac{1}{3}$ inches thick at the handgrip, and decrease evenly in thickness towards the outer part of the blade, where the edge is very thin. They have a fine smooth polished surface. The patu onewa is not illustrated in the Plate showing patu.

Patu paraoa

The patu paraoa (Plate XXIV, figure 3) was a weapon made of whalebone in the shape of a patu onewa. This weapon was thought much of by the old Maori, and was generally anything from 12 to 13 up to about 16 inches in length. The one in my collection is 15 inches long and $4\frac{1}{4}$ inches wide at the widest part about $2\frac{1}{2}$ inches from the end of the blade. The butt end is like that of the greenstone patu in form and adornment, and like all the patu, has a hole for the wrist cord. Like the other patu, it was used in three ways, for a downward blow, and upward blow, and a tipi, or endwise thrust.

Kotiate

The kotiate (Plate XXIV, figure 5) was also known as meremere, kokoti, kokotiate, kakati, mere kati, patu kakati, etc. This weapon was made of whalebone and of wood. The whalebone kotiate which I have is 13 inches long and $5\frac{1}{4}$ inches wide at the widest part, which is 3 inches from the end of the blade. The handgrip is about $\frac{3}{4}$ of an inch thick, and the butt end is carved into a grotesque head with the tongue protruding. Just below this head is a hole for the wrist cord. A kotiate made of wood, about 12 inches long, was generally used as a baton by leaders in the dances. These were sometimes carved all over with fine scroll-work, except the part where the hand grips the kotiate.

It has been stated by writers that the two openings, one on each side of the kotiate, have no meaning, and are a mere decoration. This is not the case. It was explained to me many years ago by my old people that a kotiate was not only a weapon, but was used to punish herehere, prisoners taken in battle. These would be men of high standing, fine looking men, who were treated well by the chief and his people who took them. If one of these men happened to forget himself and fell in love with the wife of the chief, or one of the chiefs, and did things which he should not do, the punishment was severe, and the kotiate was used for it. This punishment I have described in my chapter on Marriage under the account of herehere. The modern kotiate of course were not made like the old ones, and all kotiate were not used in this way, but the very old ones were so used.

Wahaika

Wahaika (Plate XXIV, figure 1) is a weapon which looks very like the old bill-hook. The one in my collection is 13 inches long, and $4\frac{1}{2}$ inches wide at the widest part, which is about $3\frac{1}{2}$ inches from the blade end. The butt end is carved, and on the back, forward of the handgrip, is a carved grotesque human figure. The handgrip is about $2\frac{1}{2}$ inches long or more. This one is made of whalebone. Wahaika and other short weapons were sometimes made of hard wood, such as akerautangi (Dodonea viscosa), but as I have already said, these wooden weapons were only used as batons in dancing and ceremonial.

Toki

The Toki poutangata or toki hohoupu was a one-handed

weapon. The blade was generally of pounamu (nephrite) cut in the form of an adze with a very sharp edge and polished, and might be 4, 8, 10 or more inches long. The handle is usually 11 or 12 inches long, and the "shoe" or part to which the blade is bound is generally carved and decorated with dog's hair or red parrot's (kaka) feathers. The butt of the handle is often carved as well. The toki was used as a weapon for finishing off an enemy who had been tripped with the taiaha or other long-handled weapon, and was also used by a chief in a ceremonial manner like a mere or other weapon. The usual carving represented a grotesque man sitting on the butt end of the stone blade. The kakau, or butt end of the handle had a knob, generally adorned with carving, which the wielder found very useful. A hole was made in the butt through which a string was passed and put round the thumb. The wrist cord was also used.

Tapu of warriors

The old Maori warrior thought nothing of death in a battle, and would rather die fighting than from an ordinary illness. All male children were taught the art of war from their earliest years, and the child was placed under the mana of Tu the war god by the Tua or Tohi rite, and when he grew up and went to battle, a karakia was repeated over him. The Tua rite appealed to Tu to make the boy strong to fight, to overcome his enemies to be able to storm a pa, to hold his stone patu, to wield a taiaha, etc. A Tohunga repeated the karakia over him before he went to battle, and he would be placed under Maru and Uenuku as well. The tapu of a man going to battle was very great, and when the fight was over, he could not return to the kainga until the tapu had been taken off him by the Tohunga. This was generally done in water in a lake where a certain part was reserved entirely for this purpose.

Kohuru and causes of war

Kohuru, the murder of a person in a treacherous manner rather than in an open fight, was very bitterly avenged. When an avenging expedition went out and encountered anyone in its path, he was killed whether he was an enemy or a friend. No one would knowingly be on the ara (path) when a war party was coming that way, and people generally knew. Another cause of bitter fighting was the making of the bones of a chief into implements, such as bird spears, or fish hooks, or the placing of skulls on the posts of fences.

When the Maori went to war, he was naked except for a maro taua[1] or war apron round his waist, so as to leave his arms and legs free for fighting. Even when he had to wear a thick and closely woven cloak to protect his body from spear-thrusts, this would be tied at the front and not at the side, so as to leave his arms free. As will be seen in the pages o nga whawhawi (of the fights) of my own people, most of the wars were a series of raids, though there were of course great battles when storming the fortified pa of another tribe, which generally ended in a great slaughter when the pa was taken.

Rangitihi

A war party was generally led by a chief of high standing, who would have many chiefs to accompany him. Fighting was the work of tangata rangatira (men of rank) and not of slaves. The influence and mana of trusted chiefs was remarkable in war time as at all other times. Many a panic or flight has been stopped by these chiefs. Our ancestor Rangitihi, father of Tuhourangi, when leading a war party in battle had his head split open with an axe. His people seeing this retreated, and the fight might have been lost. But Rangitihi asked for some akatea (Metrosideros albiflora), (a climbing plant used for tying the palisading of fences) to be brought to bind up his split head. Then, rallying his people round him once more, he led them to victory. This incident is famous in history and in song, and there is a proverb (whakatauki) about him; "Rangitihi upoko whaka-hirahira, no Rangitihi te upoko i takaia ki te akatea. Ehara ma te aitanga a Tiki," which means, Rangitihi the arrogant, proud, and haughty-headed one, the akatea bound his head. Well! he should be able to do it. He is a descendant of Tiki. The last two sentences are of a form generally applied to a tangata rangatira who does great things, and express pride.

Omens

When Tuhourangi were going on a war party, they always looked for omens. One of the principal signs came on a hill called Pukeri. Whenever lightning played on Pukeri Hill, it was a bad omen for the Tuhourangi people, and even to this · day it is believed. There are other hills of this sort.

Whakatu waewae

Whakatu waewae was a dance which the old Maori performed before going to fight, and it filled all the warriors with enthusiasm. It also gave the people the chance to see whether the warriors were fit and able to carry out the art of war. The war dance had to be performed without a mistake. Every man had to move as one in all the different movements. If it came to the part where they all jumped off the ground, those who were looking on must see a perfectly even space between all of the dancers and the ground, that is, all of the dancers must be the same height from the ground. Should any mistake be made, it was a sign of aitua (bad omen). This war dance, the last before starting off, was done at the kainga, or just a little distance off, while the old people, women and children who are remaining, look on. Often one or more women who were well up in all these dances would jump up and dance in front of the column, and when they did this, it was a good sign, for they saw and found the performance true. This encouraged the warriors, and they went forth ke ti whawhai (to fight) with the thought of conquering the enemy. To the Maori, both the men and the women were brave warriors, and the whakatauki (proverb) is, "He puta taua ki te tane, he whanau tama ki te wahine," which is to say, The battlefield with man, childbirth with woman.

Peace

When peace was made between two hapu or tribes after war, and the defeated chief gives his daughter to the victorious chief in marriage, either for himself or one of his children, there was always great ceremonial. There was a hui (gathering) where speeches were made by leading chiefs on both sides, each speech ending with a waiata (chant), generally a song of peace. Dances were held, and all the other Maori entertainments, and the hapu or tribes competed. All did their best, and in the old days it was very good. The serving of cooked food (te whiu kai) was always an interesting ceremony, but this was done as at all hui, tangi (mourning for the dead), marriage ceremonies, etc., and I have described it elsewhere.

Ambuscades, Signalling, etc.

When a war party wanted to take a fortified pa, they generally sent a hunuhunu, a small body of men, to show itself in front of the pa, hoping thus to lure the people inside the pa into a kokoti moe roa, an ambuscade. A false retreat is called takiri, and the term hurahura kokoti is used when an ambush is unmasked.

A sign of friendship, and often of protection, is to double the forefinger of the right hand and place the projecting second joint on the tip of the nose, thus signifying the hongi or pressing of noses. Many a person's life has been saved by this sign. If a man meets a party of an enemy tribe, and the principal man of the party makes this sign, then the man is to be treated as a friend and not killed. A person of influence could save any enemy in the midst of a fight by placing his cape over him.

Te whakarewha, or sideways glance, is a sign suggestive of a secret attack on a third person, or something similar.

To shut both eyes and nod the head downward is a sign whose significance depends on circumstances. I have seen it used to induce a person to drop a particular subject of conversation.

Signalling is called rotarota, smoke-signalling, whakapua. In olden days signalling to a distance was performed by fire, smoke, human semaphore, and by sound, the sound being made by two forms of trumpet. To raise the arm and wave it twice outward from the body signifies that the person so signalling is about to go somewhere. To strike the buttocks twice denotes that he is staying where he is. To raise the arm and place the hand on top of the head means that the other person is to join the signaller. To hold the arm outstretched with the hand open is a sign of dissent, while the kamu, or closing of the hand, is a sign of assent. These are east coast usages.

Return of a war party

When a taua (war party) started off to fight, the Tohunga repeated karakia and the ope (company) was under the mana of Tu. This meant that the company was under heavy tapu. Should any or all return safely, they must not dream of going to the kainga till all this tapu was taken off by the Tohunga. The Tohunga who met them was naked like the warriors, that is, except for the marotaua or war girdle made of very fine muka fibre, te maro kai taua ko te maro o Tu, the war girdle of Tu. Mr. Balfour has the finest marotaua I have ever seen in the Pitt-Rivers Museum in Oxford.

A war party made its return known to the kainga by the whakatu waewae (war dance). The earth would shake with the stamping of feet and the air resound with the words shouted to accompany the dance as the warriors advanced in rows. One or two leaders in front pukana (roll their eyes), as do many in the front line, and with arero whetero (tongue out), and long weapons, taiaha, koikoi, tewatewha, waved in the air at the right time, and as one man, they advance, the leaders with the patu pounamu or toki poutangata in their right hands quivering so that they appear like quivering leaves being blown by the wind. The warriors repeat the ceremonial reply to the question addressed to them in a ceremonial manner by the Tohunga who met them. (The account is unfinished.)

Tu

War was looked on by the old Maori as one of the most important things in his life, and every man was born to it and brought up to it. There was no asking, or making a man go to fight. Every Maori man was a warrior. The god who represented war was Tu, one of the offspring of Rangi, the heavens, and Papa-tu-akuku, the mother earth, and the tapu laid on a war party before leaving the kainga by the Tohunga came from Tu, the most important of all the gods connected with war.

Causes of war

The saying of the people of old was "He wahine, he whenua, e ngaro ai te tangata," By women and land are men lost, these being the most important of the reasons for nga whawai o mua, the wars of the past. There were other reasons, such as kanga (curse), kohuru (murder), and puremu o te wahine maronui (committing adultery with a married woman), especially if she were a wahine rangatira. The husband would raise a war party and kill the man and anyone who might be with him at the time. Ridicule was a cause of war, for the Maori was easily offended. The wars of the old Maori must not be mixed up with the wars of the civilized pakeha of a supposed higher culture. The Maori wars were generally small raids of a few chiefs from a hapu, and perhaps relatives, chiefs of another clan, would join them.

Some examples

We will take the murder of my ancestor Umukaria, a great chief who lived about ten generations ago at Owhata. Umukaria lived at Owhata on the mainland of Lake Rotorua. He was murdered on the beautiful island of Motutawa situated in Lake Rotokakahi, the Green Lake, the home of my ancestors, and where hundreds of them lie buried. This is where my mother was born. Of Motutawa I should like to write more another time. Umukaria, father of Wahiao and Hinemoa, was murdered at Motutawa pa on Motutawa Island, by Ngati Apumoana, Ngati Pikiao, Ngati Tuteata, and other small hapu. They came to Motutawa and murdered Umukaria and others who were living there. Very few escaped, but among those who did were the two children of Umukaria called Whareaiti and Raeroa. These two escaped and walked to Rotorua, a distance of nine miles, where Wahiao was living, and told him that their father was murdered. Wahiao was grieved to hear the sad news. He then assembled together the chiefs of Tuhourangi who were living in those parts. At this time Wahiao lived also at Te Pukeroa, a hill overlooking Lake Rotorua, on which now stands King George V's Hospital. All this most valuable land was presented as a gift by Ngati Whakaue, Ngati Uenukukopako, and their clans for this purpose of building a hospital which bore the name of our noble King George V.

The chiefs of Tuhourangi assembled on Pukeroa, and it was from there that this war party started for Rotokakahi, the Green Lake, under the leadership of the chief Wahiao, and other chiefs called Patutarutaru, Tutea, Uewa, Rangiwewehi who was a brother of Wahiao, Tawakeheimoa son of the chief Whakaue who was married to the sister of Umukaria, and Tutanekai, brother of Tawakeheimoa, and husband of Hinemoa, the sister of Wahiao, and daughter of Umukaria. There were also other chiefs who were of the party.

This war party went first to Whakarewarewa, and from there marched to Rotokakahi. When they arrived there, they met and destroyed many of Ngati Tuteata at Te Whakahoronga. They then paddled over to Motutawa Island in their canoes, where they found the headless body of Umukaria with the other dead. Those of Ngati Tuteata who were killed at Whakahoronga were Puraho, Inanga, and many other chiefs. The rest of Ngati Tuteata fled. Then the war party of Wahiao went on to a place called Whareroa on Tarawera Lake, where they found the head of Umukaria hidden in a cave. This cave was afterwards called Te Rua-a-Umukaria.

The war party found this place deserted, and went on to another kainga called Ohorongo, and found this also deserted, the people having collected at a place called Moura. The war party then returned, going the same way as they came, but made a circuitous way round the south-west part of the lake, and, in the evening of the same day, arrived at a place called Tutaehioi where they stayed. Very early the next morning, the pa at Titika was attacked, and Ngati Apumoana were captured and killed. The chiefs killed were Tunoke, Tutoa, Mokai, Tuwhakura, and others, and some escaped. The victors observed a wooden bowl called a kumete floating about in the lake. This bowl was followed by Taupopoki, son of Wahiao, and when he got to it, found there was a man underneath it, whose name was Tarainoke, and he was taken ashore and kept there.

Te Apiti, a great chief of Ngati Apumoana, was away during all this murder and avengement of the murder of Umukaria. Te Apiti heard of the fight from those of the people who escaped from Titika. Te Apiti made peace with Wahiao. In commemoration of this peace, Pareheru, the daughter of Te Apiti, was given by her father in marriage to Tukiterangi, son of Wahiao. Tarainoke who was found floating under the kumete, was taken with some other prisoners to Motutawa, and he was handed over by Wahiao to his sister Hinemoa to be her slave. The other prisoners he kept for himself. After this, Tutanekai returned to Rotorua with his wife Hinemoa, Tawakeheimoa returned to Mokoia Island, and Wahiao, Uero, Rangiwewehi, Tutaepatutarutaru, and the Tuhourangi people remained at Motutawa, and their descendants have lived there till the pakeha came.

Wahiao and Taupopoki his son lived for a number of years at Pukeroa at Roturua. While living here, Uruhina, one of the wives of Wahiao, puremu (committed adultery) with Te Whatumairangi, son of Hinemoa, Wahiao's sister. Wahiao was grieved at this, and he went with a war party over to Okataina, a place nine miles or more distant on the shore of Lake Okataina, not far from Lake Tarawera on the side nearer Rotorua. He went to Okataina to see the chief Te Rangitakaroro who lived there, and mentioned the matter to him. They then went to Makititi on the north side of Tarawera Lake, and related the account of the puremu to Te Apiti, and Te Apiti advised Wahiao to return to Rotorua, and he did so, Te Apiti accompanying him with other warriors. When he reached Te Ngae on the shore of Lake Rotorua, he was met by Te Whatumairangi and his war party. They had crossed over from Mokoia Island where they lived to meet him. A battle took place here at Te Ngae, and Te Whatumairangi was killed by Te Apiti. Then Wahiao and Te Apiti went to Uenga, a fishing place belonging to Wahiao, and Te Apiti returned to his own home. When Ngati Whakaue heard that Te Apiti had left, they crossed over. . . .

Here ends the manuscript as Makereti handed it to me on April the 15th, 1930.

[1] My great-grandfather was named Marotaua

APPENDIX TO THE CHAPTER ON CHILDREN

He Tua pana mo nga tamariki tane. Tua pana for male children; Karakia used by the Tohunga to banish tapu, repeated while standing in the water as one with Para-whenua, the personified form of water.

Tena te pukepuke ka tu,

Ka tu ki uta,

Ka tu ki te wai

Ka tu ki ahungai mai i Hawaiki

Ka tu i te aponga mai i Hawaiki

I te whakatohuatanga mai i Hawaiki

Tena pukepuke ka tu,

Puke ka ranga,

Kai tu i te ata,

I te ata o tenei turakanga

I te ata o tenei whakarukunga

I te ata o Tu,

I te ata o Tama

I te ata o Tutawake

Aai!

Tena tokotoku ka tu,

Ka tu ki uta,

Ka tu ki tai,

Ka tu ki te hononu

Ka tu ki te parenga,

Ka tu ki te miri wai

Ooi.

Te Mokoputangaroametia,

Takiritia ra te tapu o Ruanuku,

He tapu ka kawea ki te wai,

Ka turakina, ka whakawaituhitia

Ooi.

Takiritia, takiritiara te tapu o te tama
nei,

He tapu kawea ki te wai,

Ka huhua, ke whakanoatia

Ooi,

Ka whakahekea

Ka whakamamatia

Ooi,

Takiritia i reira

Toro i reira toro he

Tona kinaki tona kinakai

Kia tu ko tane i te ata o Tu

I te ata o Tama,

Te marama i te ata taweke,

Te marama pokai tu,

Whanau au te marama,

Ko Tawake ko Tama,

Whanau au e te marama pokai tu,

Katahi, ka rua, ka torou, ka wha,

Pokai tu au e te marama,

Pokai e, pokai e,

Ka rima, ka ono, ka waru,

To au e te marama,

Pokai e, pokai e,

Kei te torutoru, kai te pekepeke,

Te karere na tama i tiki,

Ki runga te Rangihoaia,

E te rupe, rupe iho, rupe ake,

Kei tae heke iho, heke ake,

E rua e nau mai ki roto te whare

Ki tokotoko e Rupe

Naumai ki te moenga,

Ki te patu ki to taoroa

Ki to Honikura,

E Rupe,

Naumai e Rupe ki Maunganui,

Ki Maungaroa,

Ki Maungakariretoro,

Tenei to ara e Rupe,

Ko Mimira i te rangi e Rupe,

Raranga, raranga ra taku taka pau,

Ka pukea,

Heoi moenga mo maua ko aku rei tokorua,

Kotahi ka pukea, e te wai ka pukeato,

Ka pukea to he,

Ko Toto, ko Tama ko Manumea,

Ka pukea, ka pukea au e te wai,

Kapea, ko Tawake, ko Toi, ko Rauru,

Ka pukea, ka pukea,

Puke toro, puke toro he.

He Tua mo nga tamariki wahine. For female children. Karakia used by the Tohunga to banish tapu, repeated while standing in the water as one with Para-whenua, the personified form of water.

> Tena te pukepuke ka tu,
> Ka tu ki uta,
> Ka tu ki te tai
> Ka tu ki te hohonu
> Ka tu ki te parenga,
> Ka tu ki ahunga mai i Hawaiki,
> Ka tu ki te aponga mai i Hawaiki,
> Ka tu ki te whakatohuatanga mai i Hawaiki
> Tena tokotoko ka tu
> Ka tu i tenei ata
> I te ata o tenei turakanga
> I te ata o tenei waituhi
> I te ata o tenei whakarukutanga
> I te ata o Hine angiangi,
> I te ata o Hine-Korikori
> I te ata o wahine
> Tena te whakaruku ka kawe,
> Tena tokotoko ka tu,
> Ko te tokotoko o Hine,
> O Hine rauwharangi,

O Hine-i-te-iwaiwa,

Tena tokotoko ka tu

Ka tu ki uta

Ka tu ki tai

Ka tu ki te ahunga

Ka tu ki te aponga mai i Hawaiki

Whakahopu

Takahia ki tai,

Rukuruku,

Eaea,

Rukuruku,

Eaea,

Ooi.

Then a karakia is repeated to Io Matua, saying that the Tohunga is a properly trained and tapu person, who has a great knowledge in performing tapu rites, and that he is qualified to carry out this very tapu rite. The Tohunga then hands over the infant with karakia to the Atua and all the beings in the heavens.

The Tohunga next puts the karamu branch in the water for a moment, and turns round to take the infant from the mother, and with the child's head resting in the bend of his ringa matau (right arm), both turn to face the rising sun. He now repeats the karakia which follows, saying that the child is now under the care of the gods and all the beings in the heavens.

Ko te Tua mo te Tane, for a male child.

Tohi ki te wai no Tu; Whano koe. Tangaengae.

Etc.

Also the one for a female child, Ko te Tua mo te Wahine.

These two have been included in the chapter on children.

See Sir George Grey, *Ko nga Moteata, me nga Hakirara O nga Maori*, Wellington 1853, pp. 353, 361.

EDITORIAL NOTE

ON THE NIGHT before her death in 1930, I promised Makereti to dedicate her book for her as I have done, and to remove certain karakia, which also I have done. She asked me to communicate with the Arawa people to make certain that all that was written was true, and that nothing forbidden should be published. This I did, sending the manuscript to New Zealand by her son, who undertook to place it before the Arawa, and let me know if there were any error or objection. I have just received the manuscript, corrected by members of the Council, but especially by Te Aonui and Bella Wiari, Makereti's son and sister. I alone am to blame if there is any error in describing the plates, for she died suddenly, just before the time she had set to write full descriptions.

Her mother's name was originally Pia te Rihi. But I have used the name Pia te Ngarotu, which she took after her uncle's death, to signify that he "passed standing".

I am grateful to Professor Henry Balfour and also Dr. Raymond Firth for advice on doubtful points while reading the proofs.

FULL DESCRIPTION OF PHOTOGRAPHS

All the objects illustrated were Makereti's

I. MAKERETI ABOUT 1893. In her hair a feather of the huia bird, black with white tip, worn only by chiefs. Round her neck a greenstone *TIKI* whose name is Te Uoro. It has been buried with ancestors and dug up after a lapse of thirty years at five different times, and is over five hundred years old. The shoulder mat or cloak is of golden-brown kiwi feathers, worn only by chiefs, with a border of white pigeon feathers. I do not remember seeing this cloak among the regalia which she brought to England.

II. MAKERETI ABOUT 1908. Wearing the chiffon headdress which she first wore and made generally popular, and a cloak which belonged to her mother Pia te Ngarotu, made of white pigeon and green parrot feathers, the pigeon feathers being spotted with red parrot feathers. The *WHARIKI* or floor-mats are of woven flax-fibre, the pattern in black. At her feet are a calabash for water, a carved box for holding feathers used in making cloaks, and a *HINAKI*, or eel-pot. She is resting against the centre post of her home, Tuhoromatakaka (the name of an ancestor). This post is known as *POU-TOKO-MANAWA*, the post which supports the heart. At its foot is a *KOROWAI* cloak, of flax-fibre, with streamers of *KIEKIE* (Freycinetia banksii) fibre. Taken at Whakarewarewa.

III. MAKERETI ABOUT 1922. Wearing a cloak with strips of kiwi feathers and white wool with black wool streamers alternating, the greenstone *TIKI*, and greenstone ear-pendants. Holding a greenstone club, *PATU POUNAMU*. The wool and kiwi cloak is thus described in her notes: "Whakahekeheke. Kiwi and kuka huka mat; 49 × 46 inches. This is made in strips of kiwi and wool; worn by me at King George's Coronation."

IV. MAKERETI WEAVING. About 1926. Taken at Oddington or Oxford. Wearing a korowai cloak of flax-fibre with black *KIEKIE* streamers, and a fillet of *TANIKO* work of dyed flax-fibre. *TANIKO* borders are seen on chief's cloaks only. Above, an unfinished wool and kiwi cloak. She is at work on a *KOROWAI* cloak of flax and kiekie. Her note on this cloak is: "Korowai unfinished shoulder mat 49 inches across, depth 37 inches; unfinished part about 30 inches. In weaving a korowai mat, it is woven from the bottom, and finishes at the top." The *WHARIKI* or floor-mats are of flax-fibre, and there is a heap of white flax and black-dyed *KIEKIE* on the floor. On the box, an unfinished cloak, showing feathers tied in as the weaving proceeds. In the right foreground, *RAHOKUIA*, a very rare type of cloak of flax-fibre with short, curly, black tassels, illustrated in Plate IX.

V. THE CHIEF, MITA TAUPOPOKI. Wearing over all the kiwi feather cloak and the *PARE*, a flax cap with feathers interwoven, worn by chiefs only. His belt and the borders of the under cloaks are woven in dyed flax fibre. This *TANIKO* work is also worn only by chiefs. In his hands he carries the *TAIAHA*, whose positions are described on.

VI. MAKERETI WITH MEMBERS of her *KAINGA* at Whakarewarewa. Houses are named after ancestors.

VII. FEATHER CLOAKS. *Above*, A cloak belonging to her mother Pia te Ngarotu, made of flax, with white pigeon feathers and green parrot feathers interwoven, the white pigeon triangles being flecked with red parrot feathers. *Middle*, "Kahu Kura 52 × 38, a beautiful feather shoulder mat made in squares from the kaka (parrot), pigeon, tui (Parson bird), and weka (Woodhen) feathers, with kiwi down each side. This mat was given me by Captain Gilbert Mair." *Below*, "Feather mat 51 × 38 inches made from the pigeon, tui, and some peacock feathers, arranged in diamond shapes over a groundwork of white feathers."

VIII. CLOAKS AND CARVED BOXES. *Above*, the top cloak is "Kahu kiwi, 39 × 32 inches, with taniko border, given to me by Te Heuheu Tukino, Chief of Ngati Tuwharetoa tribe

(Taupo), and worn by him as a skirt at the Maori reception on the Race Course at Rotorua for the King and Queen." *Next, KAHU KIWI*, 38 × 42. *Under*, "Kaitaka or Paepaeroa 60 × 57 with taniko border. Only worn by a great chief." *Below*, Boxes of carved wood inlaid with haliotis shell, for holding feathers.

IX. *KORIRANGI* OR *KINIKINI* CLOAK, 53 × 49 inches, covered with thrums of flax. *RAHOKUIA*, flax, with short curly black tassels, "very rare".

X. *KOROWAI* CLOAK, 67 × 55 of flax with black *KIEKIE* streamers. *PAKE* or *PORA*, Rain-cloak, made of shreds of flax leaves interwoven with flax fibre, black and yellow dyed.

XI. *PIUPIU*. Skirts of flax, dyed black and yellow, and other material. These twist and untwist as a dancer moves. *POI* balls waved in various patterns by dancers.

XII. *TIKI* AND OTHER ORNAMENTS. In Makereti's notes, it appears that a *TIKI* takes a long time to complete, is the memorial of an ancestor and conveys his mana to the possessor and is valued for the mana conveyed (see description Plate I and index) and shows that possessor is descended from men of rank. Is worn round neck with plaited fibre and fastened at back with bone button, human or albatross; worn night and day; sometimes very tapu and not to be seen by others; averts witchcraft and accident.

XIII. *URUKEHU*. Father and child have very fair skin and reddish coloured hair.

XIV. THE TOHUNGA, TUTANEKAI. Taken at Whakarewarewa by Makereti.

XV. OLD CARVED *PATAKA* or Store House. Front and back carved, 56 in. wide. 2 sides, 9 ft. by 2 ft. 2 in. high, carved. *PAEPAE* (threshold board), carved. 2 *MAIHI* (verge-boards), carved. 2 *AMO* (supporting verge-boards) carved. 4 legs, carved. *TEKOTEKO* (figurehead at top).

XVI. OLD CARVED *PATAKA*, back and front.

XVII. OLD CARVED *PATAKA*, verge-boards, sides, tekoteko.

XVIII. BASKETS FOR FOOD. Two of the upper ones with loops and strings are used for cooking potatoes in the boiling-holes or hot springs. See index.

XIX. HUIA BIRDS, male and female, two views.

XX. TUHOROMATAKAKA, Makereti's House, Exterior.

XXI. MAKING PLAT-WORK PANELS for the interior of a house.

XXII. TWO-HANDED WEAPONS. 1. *POUWHENUA* (described on. 2–5, *TAIAHA*. 6, *TEWHATEWHA* (described on.

XXIII. TE RANGI WITH *TAIAHA*. 1, *POPOTAHI*. 2, *WHAKAREHU*. 3, *HUANUI*.

XXIV. *PATU*. 1, *WAHAIKA*. 2, 4, 6. *PATU POUNAMU*. 3, *PATU PARAOA*. 5, *KOTIATE*.

FIGURES IN TEXT1

PRINCIPAL GENEALOGIES

For the several shorter ones, see the Index, s.v. Genealogies

[1] Sketches as left by Makereti.

CPSIA information can be obtained
at www.ICGtesting.com
Printed in the USA
FSHW021520030920
73543FS